Transgenderism and Intersexuality in Childhood and Adolescence

Developmental Clinical Psychology and Psychiatry Series

Series Editor: Alan E. Kazdin, Yale University

Recent volumes in this series...

8: LIFE EVENTS AS STRESSORS IN CHILDHOOD AND ADOLESCENCE *by James H. Johnson*
9: CONDUCT DISORDERS IN CHILDHOOD AND ADOLESCENCE, 2nd Ed. *by Alan E. Kazdin*
10: CHILD ABUSE, 2nd Ed. *by David A. Wolfe*
11: PREVENTING MALADJUSTMENT FROM INFANCY THROUGH ADOLESCENCE *by Annette U. Rickel and LaRue Allen*
12: TEMPERAMENT AND CHILD PSYCHOPATHOLOGY *by William T. Garrison and Felton J. Earls*
13: EMPIRICALLY BASED ASSESSMENT OF CHILD AND ADOLESCENT PSYCHOPATHOLOGY, 2nd Ed. *by Thomas M. Achenbach and Stephanie H. McConaughy*
14: MARRIAGE, DIVORCE, AND CHILDREN'S ADJUSTMENT, 2nd Ed. *by Robert E. Emery*
15: AUTISM *by Laura Schreibman*
18: DELINQUENCY IN ADOLESCENCE *by Scott W. Henggeler*
19: CHRONIC ILLNESS DURING CHILDHOOD AND ADOLESCENCE *by William T. Garrison and Susan McQuiston*
20: ANXIETY DISORDERS IN CHILDREN *by Rachel G. Klein and Cynthia G. Last*
21: CHILDREN OF BATTERED WOMEN *by Peter G. Jaffe, David A. Wolfe, and Susan Kaye Wilson*
22: SUBSTANCE ABUSE IN CHILDREN AND ADOLESCENTS *by Steven P. Schinke, Gilbert J. Botvin, and Mario A. Orlandi*
23: CHILD PSYCHIATRIC EPIDEMIOLOGY *by Frank C. Verhulst and Hans M. Koot*
24: EATING AND GROWTH DISORDERS IN INFANTS AND CHILDREN *by Joseph L. Woolston*
25: NEUROLOGICAL BASIS OF CHILDHOOD PSYCHOPATHOLOGY *by George W. Hynd and Stephen R. Hooper*
26: ADOLESCENT SEXUAL BEHAVIOR AND CHILDBEARING *by Laurie Schwab Zabin and Sarah C. Hayward*
27: EFFECTS OF PSYCHOTHERAPY WITH CHILDREN AND ADOLESCENTS *by John R. Weisz and Bahr Weiss*
28: BEHAVIOR AND DEVELOPMENT IN FRAGILE X SYNDROME *by Elisabeth M. Dykens, Robert M. Hodapp, and James F. Leckman*
29: ATTENTION DEFICITS AND HYPERACTIVITY IN CHILDREN *by Stephen P. Hinshaw*
30: LEARNING DISABILITIES *by Byron P. Rourke and Jerel E. Del Dotto*
31: PEDIATRIC TRAUMATIC BRAIN INJURY *by Jeffrey H. Snow and Stephen R. Hooper*
32: FAMILIES, CHILDREN, AND THE DEVELOPMENT OF DYSFUNCTION *by Mark R. Dadds*
33: ADOLESCENTS AND THE MEDIA *by Victor C. Strasburger*
34: SCHOOL-BASED PREVENTION PROGRAMS FOR CHILDREN AND ADOLESCENTS *by Joseph A. Durlak*
35: CHILDHOOD OBSESSIVE COMPULSIVE DISORDER *by Greta Francis and Rod A. Gragg*
36: TREATING CHILDREN AND ADOLESCENTS IN RESIDENTIAL AND INPATIENT SETTINGS *by Robert D. Lyman and Nancy R. Campbell*
37: THE IMPACT OF FAMILY VIOLENCE ON CHILDREN AND ADOLESCENTS by *Javad H. Kashani and Wesley D. Allan*
38: CHILDREN'S ADJUSTMENT TO ADOPTION *by David M. Brodzinsky, Daniel W. Smith, and Anne B. Brodzinsky*
39: MOTOR COORDINATION DISORDERS IN CHILDREN *by David A. Sugden and Helen Wright*
40: CHILDHOOD SEXUAL ABUSE *by David M. Fergusson and Paul E. Mullen*
41: POVERTY AND CHILDREN'S ADJUSTMENT *by Suniya S. Luthar*
42: ALCOHOL USE AMONG ADOLESCENTS *by Michael Windle*
43: CREATING HEALTH BEHAVIOR CHANGE *by Cheryl L. Perry*
44: PSYCHOTIC DISORDERS IN CHILDREN AND ADOLESCENTS *by Robert L. Findling, S. Charles Schulz, Javad H. Kashani, and Elena Harlan*
45: LANGUAGE IMPAIRMENT AND PSYCHOPATHOLOGY IN INFANTS, CHILDREN, AND ADOLESCENTS *by Nancy J. Cohen*
46: TRANSGENDERISM AND INTERSEXUALITY IN CHILDHOOD AND ADOLESCENCE *by Peggy T. Cohen-Kettenis and Friedemann Pfäfflin*

Transgenderism and Intersexuality in Childhood and Adolescence

Making Choices

Peggy T. Cohen-Kettenis
Vrije Universiteit Medical Center, Amsterdam, The Netherlands

Friedemann Pfäfflin
Ulm University Clinic, Germany

Volume 46
Developmental Clinical Psychology and Psychiatry

For information:

Sage Publications, Inc.
2455 Teller Road
Thousand Oaks, California 91320
E-mail: order@sagepub.com

Sage Publications Ltd.
6 Bonhill Street
London EC2A 4PU
United Kingdom

Sage Publications India Pvt. Ltd.
B-42 Panchsheel Enclave
Post Box 4109
New Delhi 110 017 India

Printed in the United States of America

Library of Congress Cataloging-in-Publication Data

Cohen-Kettenis, Peggy Tine, 1948-
Transgenderism and intersexuality in childhood and adolescence: Making choices/Peggy T. Cohen-Kettenis, Friedemann Pfäfflin.
p.cm. – (Developmental clinical psychology and psychiatry series; 46)
Includes bibliographical references and index.
ISBN 07-619-1710-1 (Cloth)
ISBN 0-7619-1711-X (Paper)
1. Gender identity. 2. Sex. 3. Sex role. 4. Transsexuals—Identity. I. Pfäfflin, Friedemann. II. Title. III. Series: Developmental clinical psychology and psychiatry; v. 46. HQ1075. C654 2003
305.3—dc21

2002154520

This book is printed on acid-free paper.

03 04 05 06 10 9 8 7 6 5 4 3 2 1

Acquisitions Editor: Jim Brace-Thompson
Editorial Assistant: Karen Ehrmann
Production Editors: Olivia Weber
Denise Santoyo
Typesetter: C&M Digitals (P) Ltd.
Indexer: Kathy Paparchontis

CONTENTS

Series Editor's Introduction **vii**
Alan E. Kazdin

Preface **ix**

Acknowledgments **xiii**

List of Abbreviations **xv**

1. Typical Sexual and Psychosexual Differentiation **1**
General Terminology 1
Sexual Differentiation 2
Development of Gender Identity and Gender Role 4
Summary 15

2. Gender Identity Disorder in Childhood and Adolescence: A Cultural Blank Space **17**
Benefit of Historical and Cross-Cultural Data for Clinical Practice 18
Cross-Cultural and Historical References (Adults) 18
Cross Cultural and Historical References (Children and Adolescents) 21
Summary 21

3. Atypical Sexual Differentiation **23**
Introduction 23
Chromosomal/Gonadal Conditions 26
Female Pseudohermaphroditism 40
Male Pseudohermaphroditism 43
Other Conditions 48
Summary 48

4. Atypical Development of Gender Identity and Gender Role **51**
Specific Terminology 51
Clinical Picture 52
Correspondence Between Childhood Gender Identity Disorder and Transsexualism 62
Prevalence and Sex Ratio of Gender Identity Disorder 64
Theories About Atypical Gender Development 67
Summary 83

5. Clinical Management of Intersex Conditions **85**
Importance of Parent Counseling 85
Importance of Child Counseling 86
Neonatal Approach 87
Information and Support 88
Criticism of Clinical Policy 95
Summary 102

6. Clinical Management of Gender Problems in Children **105**
Introduction 105
Diagnosis 106
Interventions 120
Summary 128

7. Clinical Management of Gender Problems in Adolescents **131**
Diagnosis 131
Interventions 138
Effects of Sex Reassigment 148
Summary 151

8. Legal Issues of Intersexuality and Transsexualism **155**
Legal Sex Assignment of Intersexes 155
Legal Implications of Transsexualism in Adults 157
Legal Issues of Gender Identity Disorder in Childhood and Adolescence 168
Summary 177

References **181**

Name Index **210**

Subject Index **222**

About the Authors **231**

SERIES EDITOR'S INTRODUCTION

Interest in child development and adjustment is by no means new. Yet, only recently has the study of children benefited from advances in both clinical and scientific research. Advances in the social and neurobiological sciences; the emergence of disciplines and subdisciplines that focus exclusively on childhood and adolescence; and greater appreciation of the impact of such influences as the family, peers, and school have helped accelerate research on developmental psychopathology. Apart from interest in the study of child development and adjustment for its own sake, the need to address clinical problems of adulthood naturally draws one to investigate precursors in childhood and adolescence.

Within a few decades, the study of psychopathology among children and adolescents has proliferated considerably. Several different professional journals, annual book series, and handbooks devoted entirely to the study of children and adolescents and their adjustment document the proliferation of work in the field. Nevertheless, there is a paucity of resource materials that present information in an authoritative, systematic, and disseminable fashion. There is a need within the field to convey the latest developments and to represent different disciplines, approaches, and conceptual views to the topics of childhood and adolescent adjustment and maladjustment.

The *Sage Series on Developmental Clinical Psychology and Psychiatry* is designed to serve uniquely several needs of the field. The *Series* encompasses individual monographs prepared by experts in the fields of clinical child psychology, child psychiatry, child development, and related disciplines. The primary focus is on developmental psychopathology, which refers broadly here to the diagnosis, assessment, treatment, and prevention of problems that arise in the period from infancy through adolescence. A working assumption of the *Series* is that understanding, identifying, and treating problems of youth must draw on multiple disciplines and diverse views within a given discipline.

The task for individual contributors is to present the latest theory and research on various topics, including specific types of dysfunction, diagnostic and treatment approaches, and special problem areas that affect adjustment. Core topics within clinical work are addressed by the *Series.* Authors are asked to bridge potential theory, research, and clinical practice and to outline the current status and future directions. The goals of the *Series* and the tasks presented to individual contributors are demanding. We have been extremely fortunate in recruiting leaders in the fields who have been able to translate their recognized scholarship and expertise into highly readable works on contemporary topics.

In this book, Drs. Peggy Cohen-Kettenis and Friedemann Pfäfflin examine *Transgenderism and Intersexuality in Childhood and Adolescence.* The book is broad in its scope, delineating the range of the issues of sexual development, identity, and roles. Biological underpinnings and features of sexual differentiation; cultural and contextual issues; and ethical, legal, and policy issues are carefully described and integrated. Gender identity raises issues for the individual but also for society at large. For example, the book considers whether, for whom, and how to intervene and the many treatment options available over the course of infancy through adulthood. There are major dilemmas for clinical practice and society at large on which this book elaborates. Whether atypical forms of gender identity qualify or ought to be considered as a disorder and strong views of the public about gender identity reflect key contextual issues in which both research and clinical work are conducted. It is rare that a book elaborates a set of developmental paths or disorders and places these in the broader context of society at large. We are very fortunate to have such an enlightened, engaging, and authoritative statement on the topic.

— Alan E. Kazdin, Ph.D.
Yale University School of Medicine

PREFACE

Most adults do not question the fact that they are male or female. However, a very small minority face a discrepancy between their subjective experience of being a man or a woman and their biological sex. They are individuals with gender identity problems. In others, discrepancies exist between their genetic, gonadal, hormonal, or genital sex. These individuals suffer from so-called intersex conditions. Many have great difficulties in classifying members of these groups as males or females. Others do not even want to classify at all and insist on allowing for more than two sexes. They argue that the mere existence of only two social categories, men and women, creates intolerance.

Western cultures tend to reject certain deviations from the gender norm, making life hard for those who physically and/or psychologically have not differentiated completely in the male or female direction. If certain deviations from the gender norm are substantial enough they are regarded as psychiatric disorders (as defined in the *Diagnostic and Statistic Manual of Mental Disorders (DSM-IV),* American Psychiatric Association, 1994). A significant amount of research and clinical attention have been given to children who belong to this group. Though many enigmas remain, the study of these children has increased our understanding of their situation. But studying these children as if they have a psychiatric disorder has also met with resistance. Some claim that the "Gender Identity Disorders" are not disorders at all, only behaviors that are not tolerated by our homophobic society. In their view, these behaviors have been called "disorders" to achieve gender conformity at all costs or even to "prevent" homosexuality. The suffering of the child is not seen as suffering from a condition, but from a stigmatizing society.

When cross-gendered children enter puberty, new dilemmas emerge: Boys begin to grow beards and their voices become deeper, whereas girls develop breasts. When they come to gender clinics they have often already lived in the opposite gender role for an extended period of time. They very much want to take hormones to delay their puberty or even to start the development of physical characteristics of the opposite sex (e.g., breasts in boys and a beard in girls). To the despair of these youngsters, most clinicians are reluctant to prescribe hormones for this purpose to adolescents. Should one wait until adulthood before prescribing hormones when it is clear that they have a gender identity disorder and will never live in the role of their sex of birth?

In the field of sexual differentiation disorders, an intense dispute is taking place along similar lines. However, in this field doctors are often accused of intervening all too readily. If a child is born with genitals that are not clearly male or female, surgeons tend to "adjust" the child to the sex of assignment as early as possible. Since the early 1990s, adults with intersex conditions have heavily criticized this policy. Many of these adults are very unhappy with the result of their own treatment. They insist on letting children make their own decisions regarding the type and timing of their genital surgery in due time.

There are clinicians who do (e.g., "adjusting" babies with intersex conditions) and do not want (e.g., prescribing sex hormones to adolescents with gender identity disorders) to intervene medically. Though they seem to behave in opposite ways, they may act out of a similar motive: the fear of bringing or leaving children in a situation between that of "male" and "female." This, in their view, is not in the best interest of the child.

Another question concerns to which sex a child with ambiguous sex characteristics should be assigned. We do not yet know much about the factors determining gender identity development in children with intersex conditions. To make a perfect prediction in any individual case, whether the child will be happier as a girl or as a boy, is impossible. Some argue that one should refrain altogether from assigning children to one of the sexes. By doing so we would force society to accept and get used to more gender variance. This would ultimately make life easier for gender variant individuals. Whether children in our society will actually be happier when growing up as a member of a "third sex" is, however, questionable.

Whichever side one takes in these debates, all discussants agree that large numbers of children with gender problems and with an atypical sexual differentiation suffer psychologically and existentially. These children are seen in clinics on a daily basis. Clinicians cannot sit and wait until more research has been done or consensus is reached. They are continuously faced with dilemmas and have to make choices even without a substantial empirical knowledge base. The choices they make have far-reaching consequences for their patients. The discussion on gender problems in adults touches sensitive strings. When it comes to children and adolescents the issues are sometimes beyond a rational discussion.

In this volume, we give an overview of the research, clinical insights, and ethical dilemmas for those confronted with these patients.

ACKNOWLEDGMENTS

We gratefully acknowledge the contributions of the many children and their parents who came to us for help and support. In doing so they helped us in better understanding nonstandard gender development. They shared their distress, but also their problem-solving capacities and their creativity. It has always been a challenge and at the same time inspiring and pleasurable to work with these youngsters and their families.

We also thank the members of the Gender Team at the Child and Adolescent Psychiatry Department of the University Medical Center Utrecht (UMCU): Karin Tobias-Dillen, Jan Duyx, Tineke Mooibroek, Ciska van der Laan, Winkie Sandberg, and Dr. Hanna Swaab-Barneveld; and the members of the Sexual Differentiation Disorders team of the Wilhelmina Kinder Ziekenhuis/UMCU: Dr. Monique de Vroede, Dr. Maarten Jansen, Dr. Tom de Jong, Pieter Dik, Aart Klijn, Dr. Jacques Giltay, and Ineke van Seumeren. The many patient discussions enormously increased my (P. C.-K.) knowledge and understanding of atypical sexual differentiation and gender development. Maarten Jansen and Tom de Jong were so kind as to allow us to use photographs of their patients.

We thank Professor Dr. jur. Michael R. Will and Professor Dr. jur. Heinz-Peter Mansel for their juridical advice; Dr. Luk Gijs and Professor Dr. Louis Gooren for their valuable comments on earlier drafts; Margreet van Eck, Irene de Jonge, and Elke Kunert for lots of help in finding references; Russell Deighton and Liesbeth Klein for polishing our nonnative English; and Margreet van Eck, Joke van Katwijk, and Eleonore Cohen for their administrative assistance and Max Cohen for his technical assistance when preparing the book.

LIST OF ABBREVIATIONS

17ß-HSD	17ß-hydroxysteroid dehydrogenase deficiency
5α-RD	5α-reductase deficiency
AIS	androgen insensitivity syndrome
BSTc	central part of the bed nucleus of the stria teminalis
CAH	congenital adrenal hyperplasia
CBCL	child behavior checklist (a parent questionnaire listing emotional and behavioral problems of the child)
CVAH	congenital virilizing adrenal hyperplasia
DES	diethylstilbestrol
DHT	dehydrotestosterone
DSM	*Diagnostic and Statistic Manual* (of mental disorders)
FM	female-to-male transsexual
GID	gender identity disorder
HBIGDA	Harry Benjamin International Gender Dysphoria Association
ICD	International Classification of Diseases
KS	Klinefelter Syndrome
LH	lutinizing hormone
MF	male-to-female transsexual
MIS	Müller Inhibiting Substance
MMPI	Minnesota Multiphasic Personality Inventory
PAIS	partial androgen insensitivity syndrome
PIQ	performance IQ
SOC	Standards of Care
SR	sex reassignment
SRS	sex reassignment surgery
SRY	a gene located on the Y chromosome
TRF	teacher report form (of the CBCL)
VIQ	verbal IQ
WISC-R	Wechsler Intelligence Scale for Children—Revised
WAIS	Wechsler Adult Intelligence Scale

To our children
Eleonore and Max Cohen
Vincent and Tycho Pfäfflin

1

TYPICAL SEXUAL AND PSYCHOSEXUAL DIFFERENTIATION

GENERAL TERMINOLOGY

Terminology in the field of typical and atypical psychosexual differentiation is confusing and in some areas controversial. Similar terms are used for different concepts, whereas different terms sometimes refer to one single concept.

Sex and *gender* are often used interchangeably, but some authors insist on making a distinction between the two. They argue that, in referring to behavior, the term *sex* (as in "sex differences") implies that there is a biological basis for the behavior (e.g., Deaux, 1993). For clinicians there is yet another reason to make a distinction between these terms. Whereas in most people every next (psycho-)sexual differentiation phase is in line with the previous one, in many conditions that are discussed in this book, this is not the case. In order to avoid confusion, we use the term *gender* when discussing one's personal and social status as a male or female. We use the term *sex* to refer to biological maleness or femaleness. An exception is made in Chapter 8, as, in the legal world, the terminology differs somewhat from that of the medical and psychological worlds. Terms such as *legal sex change* are used in Chapter 8.

Over the years the concepts *gender identity* and *gender role* have also been used quite differently. In the 1950s one of the founding fathers of modern sexology, John Money (1994), proposed the two-sided concept gender identity/role. Here, gender identity is the private manifestation of gender role, and gender role is the public manifestation of gender identity. In his view, gender identity disorders (see below) stem from an incongruity between the assigned sex and the two-sided concept gender identity/role. However, in persons with a gender identity disorder, the gender role, which, according to Money, is the public expression of one's gender identity, is, at least for some period, seriously blocked. Their gender identity, but not their gender role, may thus be opposite to their assigned sex. For this reason and because in research the concepts are usually dealt with separately, we prefer to use the term *gender role* as separate from gender identity. In the current literature gender role is defined as behaviors, attitudes, and personality traits which, within a given society and historical period, are typically attributed to, expected from, or preferred by persons of one gender or the other (Golombok & Fivush, 1994). A more neutral term with regard to etiology is *sex-typed behavior.* We use the term interchangeably with *gender role behavior*.

Developmental psychologists have largely focused on cognitive components of gender identity (Fagot & Leinbach, 1985; Kohlberg, 1966; Ruble & Martin, 1998). For instance, Kohlberg (1966) defined gender identity as the "cognitive self-categorization as boy or girl" (p. 88) and Fagot and Leinbach (1985) consider gender identity to be "the concept of the self as male or female" (p. 685). Much of the extensive research in this field concentrates on the implications of achieving more or less sophisticated levels of understanding of being a boy or a girl. Recently, however, there seems to be more interest in more affective components, such as feeling of contentment with one's gender (Egan & Perry, 2001). In their formulations of the concept, clinicians have always put more emphasis than developmental psychologists on the affective aspects of gender identity. In his definition of *core gender identity,* Stoller (1985) speaks of an "inner conviction that the sex of assignment was right" (p. 11). Hoenig (1985) refers to the "subjective awareness of maleness or femaleness" (p. 14). The distinction between the two aspects is also clearly made in the Gender Identity Interview, an instrument to assess gender identity confusion in young children (Zucker et al., 1993). This instrument contains two factors: cognitive gender confusion and affective gender confusion.

SEXUAL DIFFERENTIATION

Sexual differentiation is a stepwise process starting with the difference of the sex chromosomes: Females have two X chromosomes, and males have an X and a Y chromosome (Figure 1.1). The sex chromosome provided by the maternal ovum is always an X chromosome; the sex chromosome coming from the sperm may be either an X or a Y chromosome. If the father's sperm contains an X chromosome, the child will genetically be a girl with an XX chromosome pair. When a Y chromosome comes from the father's sperm,

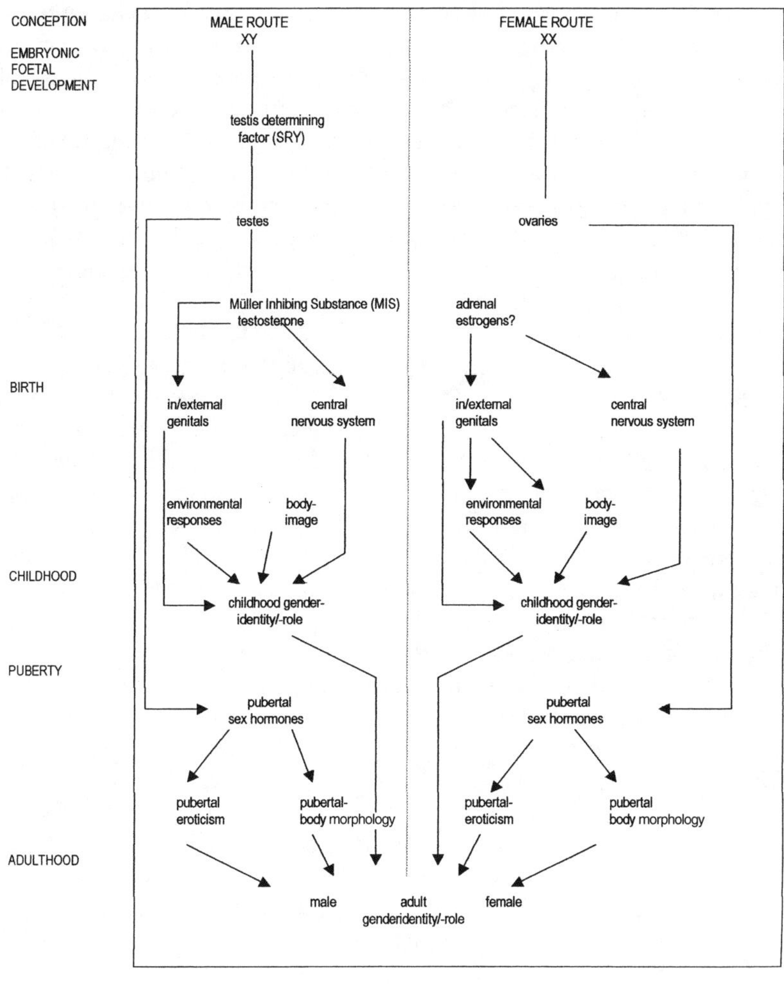

Figure 1.1 A Modification and Expansion of Money's Model of the Differentiation of Gender Identity/Role

SOURCE: Money (1994).

the child will have an XY chromosome configuration and will genetically be a boy. In the first weeks after conception, the anatomical structures destined to become the internal and external genitals are still undifferentiated and identical in female and male embryos (gonadal ridges, internal ducts, and external genitals). When a Y chromosome is present, a gene located on the Y chromosome (SRY) induces the undifferentiated gonadal ridge to become a testis. In the absence of a Y chromosome, the embryonic gonadal ridge will develop into ovaries provided two X chromosomes are present.

Around 7 weeks postconception, the testes will start to produce testosterone and anti-Müllerian hormone or Müller Inhibiting Substance (MIS). Until then the embryo has two pairs of rudimentary reproductive structures, the Müllerian ducts and the Wolffian ducts (Figure 1.2). The inherent property of the organism is to develop along female lines. The hormones of the testes direct a male development.

The Wolffian ducts develop into male internal reproductive organs. In the presence of high levels of testosterone, produced by the Leydig cells of the testis, Wolffian sexual structures will differentiate into the epididymis, seminal vesicles, prostate, vas deferens, and urethra. The MIS, produced by the Sertoli cells of the developing testes, causes the Müllerian ducts to regress. In the absence of testes and therefore androgens, the Wolffian ducts will regress. In the absence of functional testicular tissue, the Müllerian ducts will develop into the uterus, fallopian tubes, and the superior part of the vagina. This is the normal situation in the female fetus.

The external genitals also develop from identical structures (the genital tubercle, the genital folds, the urethral folds, and the urethral opening) (Figure 1.3). After 3 months of pregnancy, in males, testosterone and its derivative dihydrotestosterone (DHT) direct the genital tubercle to become the penis and the genital swellings fuse to form a scrotum, whereas in females, in the absence of testosterone, these structures become a clitoris and labia. Shortly before birth, testicles descend into the scrotum.

In mammals, gonadal hormones appear to influence the development and programming of the central nervous system (Fitch & Denenberg, 1998; Gorski, 2000). In lower mammals, future sexual and nonsexual behavior is preprogrammed in the brain to match the sex-specific gonadal and genital development.

DEVELOPMENT OF GENDER IDENTITY AND GENDER ROLE

Introduction

The current major theories in the field of gender development are cognitive developmental theory, gender schema theories, and social learning theories. In the original *cognitive developmental theory* of Kohlberg (1966),

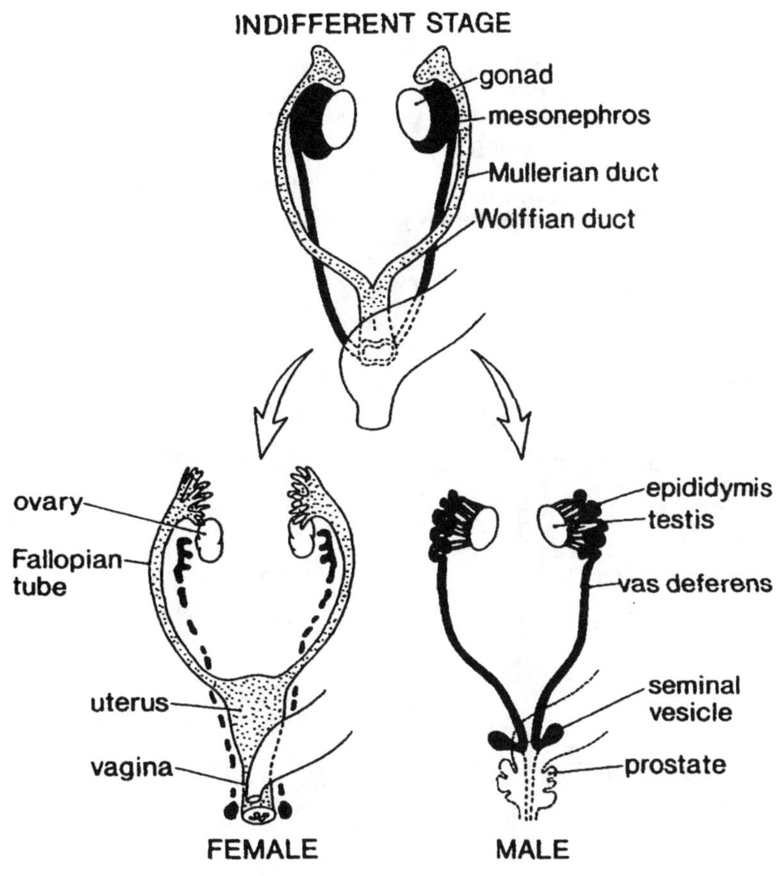

Figure 1.2 Development of the Wolffian and Müllerian Duct Systems
SOURCE: George and Wilson (1988). Reprinted from Knobil, Neill, Greenwald, Markert, & Pfaff (Eds.). (1994). *The Physiology of Reproduction* (2nd Ed.). © 1994. Used with permission from Lippincott, Williams & Wilkins.

the ability of a child to understand gender was viewed as essential for gender role development. He theorized that children seek out and adopt sex-typed behaviors only after completely understanding the irreversibility of their own sex. According to him, it is this understanding that motivates the adoption of sex-typed behaviors. Research in this field has largely focused on the relationship between various levels of understanding and the development of sex-typed behaviors (Ruble & Martin, 1998). *Gender*

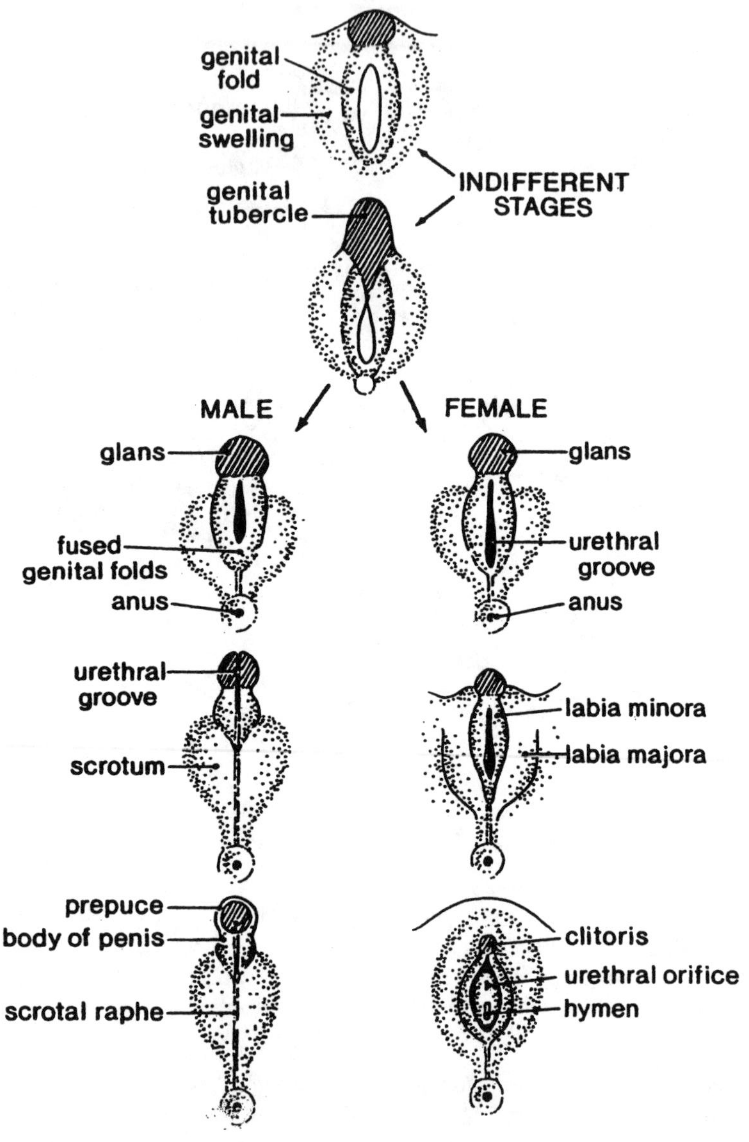

Figure 1.3 Development of the External Genitals

SOURCE: George and Wilson (1988). Reprinted from Knobil, Neill, Greenwald, Markert, & Pfaff (Eds.). (1994). *The Physiology of Reproduction* (2nd Ed.). © 1994. Used with permission from Lippincott, Williams & Wilkins.

schema theorists proposed that gender schemas, which are cognitive networks of gender-related information, influence the individual's perception and behavior (Bem, 1981; Martin & Halverson, 1981). It is assumed that the growth of gender knowledge motivates children to actively try to match their attitudes and behavior to their own-gender schema and to avoid attitudes and behaviors belonging to the other-gender schema. Research in this field has concentrated on the development of schemas and the consequences of gender schematic processing. According to *social learning theorists* (Bandura, 1977; Mischel, 1966) sex-typed behavior develops by rewards for gender-appropriate play and behavior and punishment for gender-inappropriate play and behavior and by observational learning (imitating the behavior of important same-sex adults, especially parents). In later versions, social learning theorists, now called *social cognitive theorists*, included cognitive factors. Expectancies, as mediating the relation between past reward and punishment experiences and behaviors (Bandura, 1986; Bussey & Bandura, 1999; Mischel, 1979), were used to explain the development of sex-typed behavior. Internalization of these reinforcement contingencies is assumed to motivate children to engage in gender self-socialization.

Gender Development: Cognitive Aspects

Much of what is now known about the very first beginnings of gender development comes from cognitive developmental studies. It has become clear that learning about being a boy or a girl starts in infancy. Habituation studies have shown that 9-month-old babies are able to visually discriminate between the sexes. In these studies, babies are repeatedly shown different faces from one category (familiar category), for example, pictures of females. After a while they lose interest. When a picture of a male face (contrast category) was presented, the fixation times were longer than when a picture of a new female face was shown (Fagot & Leinbach, 1993). Around 2 months earlier babies can discriminate between male and female voices (Miller, Younger, & Morse, 1982). However, at that age they are not yet able to label the sexes. Fagot and Leinbach (1989) developed a gender-labeling task and found that children are able to perform these tasks at approximately 28 months. The labeling of adults happens somewhat earlier than the labeling of children. As toddlers are often hardly aware of genital differences, they use hairstyle and clothing as a criterion for classification (Fagot & Leinbach, 1993; Intons-Peterson, 1988a), although Bem (1989) found that some preschoolers recognize genital differences when pictures instead of drawings are used.

Whether children need complete constancy in order to learn gender concepts and behavior is still an unsettled question. According to Kohlberg (1966) complete knowledge (gender constancy) that category membership is irreversible is a prerequisite. Gender constancy develops in stages (Slaby & Frey, 1975). First, children learn to identify their own and others' sex (called *gender labeling* or *gender identity*). Next, children learn that gender is stable over time (*gender stability*). Finally, they learn that gender is permanent and that it is not dependent on appearance or activities (a boy does not become a girl overnight if he puts on a wig or plays with Barbie dolls) (*gender consistency*). The opinions differ as to the age at which children reach the gender consistency stage. Differences in definition of the concept, and in methods of measurement, underlie differences in outcome. Some have found that children of 3 or 4 years of age are able to complete gender constancy tasks (Bem, 1989; Slaby & Frey, 1975), whereas others find that not even 7-year-olds fulfill these tasks (Emmerich, Goldman, Kirsh, & Sharabany, 1977). However, in most studies it was found that only children between the ages of 5 and 7 years will make consistent and systematic use of genital information as a criterion of classification (Lutz & Ruble, 1995). Long before that age, children appear to have knowledge about gender stereotypes. For instance, 3-year-old children who saw videotaped infants labeled male rated these infants as "big," "mad," "fast," "strong," "loud," "smart," and "hard." When labeled female they were rated as "small," "scared," "slow," "weak," "quiet," "dumb," and "soft" (Haugh, Hoffman, & Cowan, 1980). Three-year-olds also believe that "boys hit people" (Kuhn, Nash, & Brucken, 1978). Gender stereotype knowledge increases rapidly after 3 years of age (Picariello, Greenberg, & Pillemer, 1990; Serbin, Powlishta, & Gulko, 1993; Signorella, Bigler, & Liben, 1993) and appears to develop throughout childhood (Martin, Wood, & Little, 1990). In their thinking about sex-typed traits and behaviors, young children are fairly rigid. Only after age 7 do they become more flexible (Signorella et al., 1993). Interestingly, in Signorella et al.'s meta-analysis, it was found that girls have more stereotype knowledge than boys, but in preschool children no differences were found in flexibility. By mid-childhood, however, girls have more flexible stereotypes than boys (Canter & Ageton, 1984). Once established, gender stereotypes (which are conceptually close to gender schemata) influence the way new information is processed. Children remember gender schema-consistent information better than inconsistent information and even distort gender schema-inconsistent information (Carter & Levy, 1988; Cordua, McGraw, & Drabman, 1979; Martin & Halverson, 1983; Signorella & Liben, 1984).

According to some cognitively oriented theorists (including schema theorists), children also need only basic information rather than extensive knowledge about gender to develop sex-typed behavior (Fagot, 1995). Support for this idea was found in a study among children between 20 and 30 months of age. Children who passed labeling tasks spent about 80% of their time in same-sex groups, whereas children who did not spent only 50% of their time in same-sex groups (Fagot, 1985). Also, girls, but not boys, who labeled pictures of girls and boys correctly behaved significantly less aggressively than girls who did not pass the labeling task (Fagot, Leinbach, & Hagan, 1986). Furthermore, children prefer same-sex toys (Carter & Levy, 1988), imitate same-sex models (Bussey & Bandura, 1999), and reward peers for gender-appropriate behavior (Lamb & Roopnarine, 1979) before they reach complete gender constancy. So a full understanding of gender is perhaps not important in the very early stages of gender development. Lutz and Ruble (1995) argue, however, that somewhat later it may be associated with increased motivation to regulate behavior according to gender norms.

The relative emphasis thus far on cognitive factors and processes may give the false impression that gender development is a process devoid of emotion and affect, but this is far from true. Children learn that gender is not neutral. Many affective meanings are associated with gender (Shields, 1995), and from the research on sex stereotype knowledge we know that children are aware of the different values placed on the sexes. Children over 10 years of age are conscious of the lower value of female roles (Intons-Peterson, 1988b). As soon as they identify with one of the sexes, these values will affect their self-perception and self-concept. For instance, they are more positive about their own sex than about the other sex (e.g., Yee & Brown, 1994), but this positive bias declines with age, more so for girls than for boys.

Gender Segregation

At very early ages children become interested in same-sex playmates. Even before entering nursery school, they show same-sex affiliative behaviors (La Freniere, Strayer, & Gauthier, 1984). They like same-sex peers better than other-sex peers and spend a fair amount of time in the company of same-sex children (e.g., Fagot, 1985; Serbin, Powlishta, & Gulko, 1993). Changing same-sex peer preference appears to be difficult (Serbin, Tonick, & Sternglanz, 1977). Cross-sex play increases when children are reinforced to do so, but without reinforcement old levels of same-sex play soon reccur.

Various factors may explain this phenomenon (Maccoby, 1998; Maccoby & Jacklin, 1987); knowledge of group membership seems to be very important. This knowledge engenders group processes that bind members of each group together (adopting in-group/out-group beliefs and behaviors, enhancing the distinctiveness and positive evaluation of the own group, etc.) and fosters the formation of same-sex groups. Compatibility of play styles may also have an impact on gender segregation. For instance, boys' rough-and-tumble play may draw boys together and keep girls from playing with boys. Another possibility is that girls are less interested in playing with boys because boys use different techniques to wield influence (using physical force instead of verbal persuasion) and boys are more dominant in mixed-sex interactions or boys find girls boring because, under conditions of intense stimulation, they become excited faster than girls. A last possibility is that, until adolescence, any signs of romantic interest in the opposite sex are strongly avoided.

Children thus spend an important part of their time in all-male or all-female groups. Summarizing characteristics of these male and female subcultures, Maccoby and Jacklin (1987) note that boys play in larger groups, play in more public places and with less proximity to adults, play rougher and with more body contact, and fight more and their social interaction is oriented more toward issues of dominance. Girls' groups are less hierarchically organized and their friendships are more intense. They refer (pp. 249-250) to a study of Maltz and Borker (1982) showing that boys and girls use speech differently. In girls it appears to be used to create and maintain relationships, to criticize others in acceptable ways, and to interpret accurately the speech of other girls. In boys speech is used to attract and maintain an audience, to assert one's position of dominance, and to assert oneself when others have the floor. So gender segregation has far-reaching consequences for children's social development and friendships. Girls more often have a best friend and they talk more intimately with their friends; boys less often have a best friend, and they more often play in larger groups, where group status is an important theme. However, in the course of adolescence most boys and girls focus on and spend more time with the other sex (e.g., Leaper & Anderson, 1997).

The Role of Environment

Social learning theorists have indicated how children learn about gender by observation of role models and by differential treatment. This differential treatment may be more or less direct (e.g., offering boys and girls certain toys) or be more subtle or indirect (e.g., decorating boys' and girls' rooms in blue and pink respectively or choosing certain types of clothing). An immense body of literature supports the notion that parents, other adults, teachers, peers, and the media are gender-socializing agents (e.g., Bussey & Bandura, 1999). For instance, even though the actual sex of an infant is unknown (in the so-called baby-X paradigm), adults interact differently with children labeled as boys than with children labeled as girls (Stern & Karraker, 1989). Parents, fathers in particular, encourage sex-typed activities and they tend to do so when children are still young and when the sex of the child is not yet obvious to outsiders (Lytton & Romney, 1991; Siegal, 1987). Mothers talk more to daughters than to sons and use more supportive and directive speech with daughters than with sons (Leaper, Anderson, & Sanders, 1998). Teachers praise and criticize boys more than girls, talk more and give more feedback to boys than to girls, and praise boys for certain types of behaviors (giving the right answer) and girls for others (obedience and compliance) (Cherry, 1975; Simpson & Erikson, 1983; Stockard, 1980). Peers reinforce same-sex and punish cross-sex behavior (Carter, 1987). The types of reactions may be different within girls' and boys' groups. In 3- to 5-year-olds it was found that girls choosing boys' toys are more ignored by other girls than if they choose girls' toys. Boys choosing girls' toys are ridiculed and even beaten.

Adults and children are not just influencing gender development by their reinforcement of behaviors. As role models, parents and peers also shape children's gender attitudes and behaviors (e.g., Blair, 1992; Shell & Eisenberg, 1990; Turner & Gervai, 1995). Furthermore, gender development seems to be strongly influenced by the media. This was nicely illustrated by a study among children living in a Canadian town unable to receive television. Before television was introduced, they were less traditional than a control group. Two years later their attitudes had changed dramatically in the more traditional direction (Kimball, 1986).

The Role of Sex Hormones

Animal and human studies have convincingly shown that sexual differentiation concerns not only the genitals but also the brain (Breedlove, 1994). Most studies regarding biological influences on gender development investigated the relationship between (sex) hormones and behavior. It has been found that both androgens and estrogens play a significant role in the development of sex-typed behavior and characteristics (for reviews see Collaer & Hines, 1995; Fitch & Denenberg, 1998; McEwen, 1992). They do so at various times in development, sometimes through permanent and early changes in the brain (so-called organizing effects) or through ongoing changes in the nervous system throughout life (so-called activating effects). Although the distinction is still often used, the two processes are less dichotomous than was long assumed (Arnold & Breedlove, 1985). Because gender identity starts to develop very early in life and is fixed around puberty, activating effects seem to play a minor role in this process (but see the discussion below on guevedoces). The literature reviewed in this chapter focuses primarily on organizing effects.

Most of our current knowledge concerning organizing hormone/behavior relationships in humans comes from "experiments by nature." These cases concern individuals whose brains were prenatally exposed to atypical hormonal levels, due to various innate chromosomal or hormonal conditions (see Chapter 3), or individuals whose mothers took medication that altered the prenatal hormonal milieu of their children. However, increasing numbers of studies involving nonclinical populations support and complement many findings in clinical groups.

From the clinical studies we know that girls exposed prenatally to unusually high levels of androgens have more masculine and less feminine interests regarding toys, clothing and makeup, infant care, sports, and playmates. They score higher on spatial ability tasks, are more likely to be left-handed, and show more tomboyish behavior and aggressive tendencies than controls. In this group the chances of the development of gender identity disorder and a homosexual orientation are relatively high (Berenbaum, 2000; Collaer & Hines, 1995; Meyer-Bahlburg et al., 1996).

Daughters of mothers who took androgen-based progesterone during pregnancy are more tomboyish, prefer male-typical toys and male playmates, and have higher levels of reported aggression. They are also more independent and self-sufficient as compared to controls. Daughters of mothers who took diethylstilbestrol (DES), a synthetic estrogen that masculinizes and defeminizes brains and behavior in female rodents, showed a malelike pattern of language lateralization and higher rates of homosexual imagery or homosexuality than controls. Effects of exogenous hormones on male behavior and interests are less clear and often conflicting (see Collaer & Hines, 1995; Reinisch, Ziemba-Davis, & Sanders, 1991.

Of particular interest with regard to gender identity development is an early study by Money, Hampson, and Hampson (1957). They assessed the gender identity of 105 adults with intersex conditions, at that time called hermaphrodites. These individuals had ambiguous genitals at birth, so a decision had to be made as to their sex assignment. Only 5 of the 105 developed a gender identity and role that was inconsistent with their sex assignment and gender of rearing. Money et al. (1957) therefore concluded that the sex assignment and gender of rearing was a better predictor of gender identity and role than any other sex characteristic (e.g., chromosomal, gonadal, or hormonal). For many years, this study was used to endorse the view that rearing, more than prenatal hormones, determines gender identity and role. Contradicting the findings of Money et al. is the work of Imperato-McGinley, Peterson, Gautier, and Sturla (1979). They described a group of intersexes in the Dominican Republic. These XY individuals with testes have an enzyme defect (5α-reductase deficiency) which prenatally blocks the conversion of testosterone into dihydrotestosterone. As a result, they are born with feminine-looking external genitals. They were usually raised as girls and seemed to have a female gender identity. However, at puberty, these girls developed male sex characteristics: growth of their "clitoris" and scrotum, lowering of the voice, masculine muscle development, and masculine body fat distribution. After puberty, many youngsters adopted a male gender identity and gender role and developed a sexual attraction toward females with no problem (Imperato-McGinley et al., 1979). Based on their observations, the authors concluded that socialization is less important than brain exposure to androgens, as far as gender identity is concerned. Critics have put forward that the children might have had an ambiguous upbringing, as they were called *guevedoces* (which means "penis at twelve") or that the adoption of the male role was more a matter of adjustment to a higher social status than a real change of gender identity (Fausto-Sterling, 1992; Herdt & Davidson, 1988). Furthermore, a study among people with the same condition in New Guinea, by Herdt and Davidson (1988), casts doubt on the smoothness of the gender role reversal. In their view the reversal is the consequence of social trauma rather than a long-term effect of exposure to androgens *in utero*.

The nature/nurture discussion on gender development was recently renewed when a follow-up of a famous case of male identical twins was published (see also Chapter 5). One of the boys lost his penis due to a circumcision accident. The parents were advised to reassign the child to the female gender and raise him as a girl. Early reports showed that, in contrast to the twin brother, the reassigned child seemed to develop as a "real girl," despite the fact that she had many tomboyish traits (Money, 1975a). Later the boy appeared to become increasingly unhappy as a girl, and as an adolescent he reassumed the male role. He married and became the stepfather of children (Diamond & Sigmundson, 1997). The easily drawn conclusion from this case, that prenatal hormones determine gender identity, seems to be premature. A genetic male who underwent a similar accident, but was reassigned at a younger age than the twin, was reported to have masculine behavior and interests and to be attracted to women. However, as an adult she had no gender identity problems (Bradley, Oliver, Chernick, & Zucker, 1998).

Extrapolating the above findings on atypical gender role development to normal development has obvious limitations. In many children with intersex conditions, there is much parental concern about their being a boy or a girl from the outset. Some parents are, for some time, uninformed about the sex of their child. Many children are ill at birth and need medical interventions. Moreover, the conditions that have been studied are highly heterogeneous. Timing, duration, and level of prenatal hormone exposure vary between conditions or between individuals with similar conditions and are usually unknown. So if converging evidence came from studies in which normal variations in prenatal hormone levels are related to postnatal behavior and cognition, it would significantly strengthen the clinical findings. There are a few studies that seem to support a prenatal hormone effect on certain aspects of gender role behavior. In a study of 351 women, Udry (1994) found that androgens in the second trimester of pregnancy, combined with and in interaction with adult androgens, were related to a broad composite measure of gender role behavior and characteristics in adult women. Among young boys, progesterone and testosterone levels in umbilical cord blood predicted timidity (Jacklin, Maccoby, & Doering, 1983). Among girls, testosterone levels in umbilical cord blood were related to visual/spatial ability at 6 years of age (Jacklin, Thompson-Wilcox, & Maccoby, 1988). Testosterone in amniotic fluid was, at various ages, related to sex-related cognitive performance in girls but not or less so in boys (Finegan, Niccols, & Sitarenios, 1992; Grimshaw, Sitarenios, & Finegan, 1995). At 10, relationships were found in both sexes between prenatal testosterone and cerebral lateralization (Grimshaw, Bryden, & Finegan, 1995).

Another research paradigm comes from the study of opposite- versus same-sex twin pairs. It is assumed that fetal androgens may be transferred from the male to the female fetus through amniotic diffusion (Resnick, Gottesman, & McGue, 1993) and the female fetus is thus androgenized. Indeed it has been found that females with a male twin performed better with regard to spatial ability (Cole-Harding, Morstad, & Wilson, 1988), showed more cerebral functional asymmetry (Cohen, van Goozen, Cohen-Kettenis, & Buitelaar, 2001), were higher in sensation seeking (Resnick et al., 1993), were reported to be more willing to break or bend rules

(Loehlin & Martin, 2000), and held more masculine attitudes than females with a female twin (Miller & Martin, 1995).

The data coming from both clinical and nonclinical groups are thus suggestive of a hormonal influence on a limited number of gender role behaviors. Whether prenatal hormones directly influence gender identity is less clear. This does not mean that gender role behaviors, even those that are most likely influenced by hormones, are entirely determined by biological forces. Environmental forces exert their influence, despite the fact that for some behaviors limits are set.

SUMMARY

Sex, gender identity, and gender role usually develop in accordance with each other. The cornerstone of this development is the sex-dimorphic constitution established at the very beginning of human life when egg and sperm fuse. In addition to the 46 chromosomes, which are not sex-dimorphic, an individual will have either two X chromosomes and thus be female or one X and one Y chromosome each and thus be male. In the first weeks after conception, the internal and external genitals are still undifferentiated and identical in female and male embryos. Under the influence of a gene located on the Y chromosome internal and external genitals transform into male structures or, when this gene is absent, follow the route to female structures. Gonadal hormones influence the development and programming of the central nervous system.

The newborn does not yet have self-awareness of his or her sex and gender. Such self-awareness evolves gradually during infant life. A number of different theories have tried to explain this evolution, emphasizing the influences of cognitive and affective learning in the interaction with parents, peers, and environment. Gender labeling, gender stability, and gender consistency develop gradually. Long before children make consistent and systematic use of genital information as a criterion for sex classification they have knowledge about gender stereotypes and display either female or male gender role behavior. Toy and game preferences as well as preferences for same-sex peers are expressed much earlier than gender consistency is reached.

Nature as well as nurture, anlage (bodily outfit, hormones), and environmental influences play important parts in the shaping of gender role behavior and gender identity. Adults and children influence gender development directly by reinforcing or discouraging sex-typed behaviors and indirectly by offering role models.

In animal and human research, it has been found that sex hormones play a significant role in the development of sex-typed behavior and characteristics. They do so at various times in development. In early stages, they have organizing effects and in later stages, activating effects. Knowledge about organizing effects is derived from "experiments by nature," which are described in more detail in Chapter 3. Extrapolating findings on atypical gender role and gender identity development to normal development has, however, obvious limitations. Such atypical conditions are highly heterogeneous. Timing, duration, and level of prenatal hormone exposure vary widely in such conditions, as do medical interventions and psychosocial reactions by parents and peers. Findings in nonclinical groups and in comparison groups of opposite- versus same-sex twins suggest that levels of sex hormones in certain developmental phases may exert an influence on a limited number of gender role behaviors, which still allows for a great variety of such behaviors due to other environmental influences.

2

GENDER IDENTITY DISORDER IN CHILDHOOD AND ADOLESCENCE

A Cultural Blank Space

In the process of gender identity formation during childhood and adolescence many challenges have to be overcome and many conflicts mastered. Societies and cultures offer a wide range of patterns to help stabilize growing youngsters, including various rituals for gender role rehearsals. Some societies encourage opposite gender role rehearsals at least in certain developmental periods; others discourage such behavior. Respective examples from Sumatra, New Guinea, Melanesia, among the Pilagá of Argentina, and among the Yolngu of Arnhem Land (Australia) were described by Money and Ehrhardt (1972).

The majority of individuals develop their gender identity in accordance with their bodily outfit. Even though adult transgenderism and transsexualism (see Chapter 4 for definitions) have precursors in childhood and adolescence, it is still an extremely rare case that these cross the clinical threshold. During our professional lives, we have been consulted by approximately 350 cross-gendered children and adolescents and their families and more than a thousand adult transsexuals. Including the figures from other specialized centers in the United States, Canada, and the United Kingdom and individual case reports from the literature, the number of clinical descriptions of child and adolescent gender identity disorder (GID) patients amounts to less than a thousand, most of whom are Caucasian and some of whom are of Indian, black, Southeast Asian (Suriname, Indonesia, China, and adopted children from Ceylon), South American, or mixed origin. In a group psychotherapy study on female-to-male transsexuals (FMs) in Turkey (Yüksel, Kulaksizoglu, Türksoy, & Sahin, 2000) 11 of the 40 participants were between 16 and 20 years old. Most probably, this selection bias of clinical samples is due to the prolonged periods of youth and adolescence in Western cultures. As they are not only sex-dimorphically but also gender-dimorphically accentuated, gender nonconformities attract special attention. In addition, Western health care systems allow consultation with a psychologist or a medical doctor, whereas in other cultures such facilities are either nonexistent or not available for the majority of the population.

BENEFIT OF HISTORICAL AND CROSS-CULTURAL DATA FOR CLINICAL PRACTICE

Apart from curiosity as a motivating force for historical and cultural studies there is a second important motive for knowing more about life in earlier epochs and in other parts of the world. It allows us to mirror and reflect our own attitudes and behaviors. Knowledge derived from historical and cultural sources may be used to justify our own decisions. The demonstration of "transsexual" phenomena throughout history and cross-culturally may be used as an argument for their legitimacy as a "natural" phenomenon. The inclusion of Green's (1966) chapter in Benjamin's (1966) first monograph on transsexualism obviously served such purposes. Observing a wide variety of gender roles in other cultures may encourage tolerance for alternative lifestyles in a polarized dichotomous male/female culture. In such a broad sense, historical and cross-cultural studies are useful.

For all practical purposes, in the clinical management of individual children and adolescents with GID and their families, however, the use of comparative and historical studies is limited. Even detailed reports about how, for instance, 18th-century tribes in Samoa handled the wish of a 15-year-old girl to live as a man would help little in solving the respective wish of a teenage girl in a Catholic boarding school in Paris, Texas, whose parents are divorced, the father supporting the girl's wish, the mother being strongly opposed. In such a case the Standards of Care of the Harry Benjamin International Gender Dysphoria Association, a professional organization in the field of GID (Meyer et al., 2001), would provide better advice than any other scientific or anecdotal data.

CROSS-CULTURAL AND HISTORICAL REFERENCES (ADULTS)

Historical References

Individual clinical cases and clinical samples give little if any and only indirect information about the cultural significance of the phenomena described. It is, however, remarkable that clinicians as well as other scientists from the very beginning of the surfacing of the clinical concepts of transvestitism, transsexualism, and, later, transgenderism, referred to historical and anthropological precursors and parallels. The first monograph on transsexualism (Benjamin, 1966) contained such a chapter, authored by Green (1966) and covering mythology and demonology, classical history, the time from the renaissance period to the end of the 19th century as well as cross-cultural data from American Indians and other people from all over the world. This chapter was later expanded in Green and Money (1969) and Green (1974).

Gender issues in Byzantium have been investigated by Ringrose (1994). Dekker and van de Pol (1989) evaluated old Dutch sources and described a number of breathtaking histories of female transvestites. Based on hitherto inaccessible historical sources, a German diplomat (Steinkühler, 1992) reexplored the touching story of the great French diplomat Chevalier d'Eon, who spent half of his long life as a man and the other half as a woman while serving as a French diplomat at the court of Czarina Catherine the Great in St. Petersburg, Russia, and whose history was the source of much of the story in Mozart's opera *Figaros Hochzeit* ("The Marriage of Figaro"). Trumbach (1994), van der Meer (1994), Hekma (1994), and Grémaux (1994) added historical sketches from more recent settings and places.

Historical research usually is not undertaken to just reconstruct the past but to use past events and figures to shed light on today's situation (Bolin, 1994). A number of groundbreaking monographs and edited books bridge the gap between historical findings and present issues of transgenderism (Bullough & Bullough, 1993; Bullough, Bullough, & Elias, 1997; Ekins & King, 1996, 2001; Herdt, 1994a; Hirschauer, 1993; Lang, 1998).

Cross-Cultural References

Meanwhile, there is abundant anthropological, sociological, and psychological literature on cross-dressing, transsexualism, transgenderism, and corresponding phenomena in many countries of the world or in smaller ethnic groups. It is beyond the scope of this clinically oriented book to summarize this rich literature or even to give a full bibliography; only references of exemplary research are mentioned.

The literature on changing gender in native American (Indian) cultures would fill a whole library. A short introduction is found in Greens' (2000) encyclopedic contribution. Lang (1998) gives an excellent review of the history of classifications and interpretations of the former *berdache* phenomenon, now usually described as the *two-spirit* or *two-spirited* phenomenon, which differed widely within 133 North American Indian cultures and over time. Lang discusses earlier seminal work by Callender and Kochems (1983) and Williams (1986), as well as Gay American Indians and Roscoe (1988) and many other authors. She distinguishes four different patterns of alternative gender roles, at the same time emphasizing the great tradition of gender variance among native Americans: (1) crossing out of the gender role, giving up either one's own gender role or gender status; (2) gender role mixing, including many more than just the two dichotomous and polarized male and female genders that are known in other cultures; (3) gender role change; and (4) gender role splitting.

A variant of the forth type was described by Rösing (1999, 2001) for the Amarete culture in the Andes mountains in Bolivia. There, a gender role proliferation is found, and a person may have up to 10 different gender roles, some of which are permanent while others are dependent on the land one owns or the office one holds or what one does. They are not combined with transvestism.

Other authors focused on other parts of the world. Ako (2001) described the first sex reassignment surgery (SRS) in Japan, a sensation considering the predominance of collective and corporate identities as compared to individual (gender) identity and as it is usually experienced in Western cultures in traditional as well as in modern Japan. Besnier (1994) investigated Polynesian gender liminality; Coleman, Colgan, and Gooren (1992) male cross-gender behavior in Myanmar, Burma; Gooren (1992) the *khusra* in Pakistan; Herdt (1994b) the "third sex" in New Guinea; Heiman and Lé (1975) transsexualism in Vietnam; Matzner (in press) the *kahtoey* in Thailand; Nanda (1994) the alternative sex and gender role of the *hijras* in India; and Teh (2001) the *mak nyahs* in Malaysia.

The third issue of the journal *Sexualities* was a special issue dedicated to transgender in Latin America, with contributions from Kulick (1998a, 1998b), Lancaster (1998), Levi (1998), Prieur (1998), Braiterman (1998), Klein (1998), Murray (1998), and Butler (1998). Similar to Garber's (1992) work and some of the books mentioned earlier (Bullough & Bullough, 1993; Bullough et al., 1997; Ekins & King, 1996, 2001; Herdt, 1994a; Hirschauer, 1993; Lang, 1998) these contributions connect sociological, historical, and cultural studies. Ethnological and comparative cultural studies mirror each other. They serve to provide a fresh view of one's own culture. What seems familiar unveils itself as alien, and what seems alien turns out to be familiar. The projective exportation of Western views that characterized 19th-century ethnological research has been transformed to a much more open attitude accepting that Western attitudes are as native as tribal cultures are cultured.

CROSS-CULTURAL AND HISTORICAL REFERENCES (CHILDREN AND ADOLESCENTS)

In contrast to the plentitude of historical and cultural research on adult transgender experience, there is a total lack of such data as regards GID in childhood and adolescence. This generalization holds true even if there are scattered bits of information and anecdotal material about the early determination of adult destinies and behaviors of persons who see themselves and/or are seen by others as what now may be subsumed under the umbrella term of transgenderism. This is remarkable and calls for an explanation.

There seem to be a number of major reasons for this lack of data. First, in many cultures maturity is reached much earlier than in Western cultures, at least in certain spheres of life, for example, hunting, fishing, "working," and pair bonding. In these cultures what we call adolescence does not exist or is much shorter. Second, juveniles are granted more behavioral freedom than adults as regards role conformity. Nonconformity to role expectations is tolerated much more than in adults and usually evaluated as a transient state which does not have to be taken all too seriously. Third, juveniles usually were not the primary interlocutors for anthropologists. Due to cultural as well as language boundaries, communication was difficult enough with adults; qualified interpreters were lacking. As is known from the work of Margaret Mead (1928, 1930, 1935), large proportions of the data she collected were second-hand information. Fourth, as GID in childhood and adolescence are rather recent phenomena even in Western cultures, anthropologists were not prepared to look for them elsewhere. It may well be that these phenomena have existed even in earlier epochs. This, however, is just hypothetical. They were certainly not diagnosed as GID, perhaps not even recognized, and thus neither acknowledged nor reported.

SUMMARY

Even though adult transgenderism and transsexualism have precursors in childhood and adolescence, it is still rare that these conditions cross the clinical threshold in this early stage in life. The number of such cases described in the international clinical literature amounts to far less than a thousand. The fact that most of them are described by Western authors may be attributed to the prolonged periods of youth and adolescence in Western cultures and the availability of clinical services.

There are a large number of articles and chapters on transgenderism, transsexualism, and corresponding phenomena in adults, covering different epochs and cultures from various continents. Early ethnology and historiography was mainly inspired by curiosity and the aim of demonstrating the superiority of the researcher's own culture as compared to the times and circumstances he was describing. In addition, such research also served to justify sex reassignment in Western cultures by demonstrating that cross-gender behavior was widespread geographically and culturally and had been reported on since ancient times. Thus, it could be concluded that the desire for sex change is "natural."

It had been only since the early 1990s that researches have tried to bridge the gap between historical and cross-cultural findings on the one hand and present issues of transgenderism and corresponding issues on the other hand. However, in cross-cultural and historical knowledge about gender identity disorders in youths and adolescents, there is still a blank space and a large field for further research.

3

ATYPICAL SEXUAL DIFFERENTIATION

INTRODUCTION

Under ordinary circumstances each step in the sexual differentiation process is contingent upon and consistent with the former. In intersex conditions, there are incongruities between one or more steps in sexual differentiation (chromosomal, gonadal, hormonal, or genital). At a certain point the development deviates from the normal male or female route (Table 3.1). Prevalence figures for intersex conditions are not known. Depending on the

TABLE 3.1 Chromosomes, Gonads, Sex Hormones, and Genital Structures in Men, Women, and Some Intersex Conditions

	SChr.	*Gonads*	*T*	*DHT*	*WD*	*MD*	*Extern. Gen.*
46,XY men	**XY**	**testes**	**+**	**+**	**+**	**–**	**male**
KS	XXY	testes	+, low	+	+	–	male, small
XYY	XYY	testes	+	+	+	–	male
46,XX women	**XX**	**ovaries**	**–**	**–**	**–**	**+**	**female**
TS	XO	streak	–	–	–	+	female
CAH	XX	ovaries	+[a]	±[a]	–	+	ambiguous
CAIS	XY	testes	+[b]	+[b]	–	–	female
PAIS	XY	testes	+[b]	+[b]	±	–	ambiguous
5α-RD	XY	testes	+	–	+	–	fem/amb
17β-HSD	XY	testes	+	–	+	–	fem/amb

Note: KS = Klinefelter Syndrome; TS = Turner Syndrome; CAH = congenital adrenal hyperplasia; CAIS = complete androgen insensitivity syndrome; PAIS = partial androgen insensitivity syndrome; SChr. = sex chromosomes; T = testosterone; DHT = dehydrotestosterone; WD = Wolffian ducts (male internal genitals); MD = Müllerian ducts (female internal genitals); Extern. Gen. = external genitals.

a. High levels of androgens come from the adrenal glands

b. Despite high androgen levels, the body is not or not sufficiently responsive definition of intersex, population estimates range from 0.1 to 2% (Blackless et al., 2000).

At fertilization, when chromosomal sex is established, an unusual chromosome configuration may develop. Examples of such configurations are karyotypes of 47,XXY (Klinefelter Syndrome, KS) or 45,XO (Turner Syndrome). Sometimes different karyotypes are present in one person (e.g., 45,XO/46,XX). This is referred to as mosaicism.

With regard to the gonads, interference with normal development occurs when the SRY gene is absent and a fetus does not develop testes despite a 46,XY chromosomal configuration. Male differentiation may also be hampered when the testes do not secrete enough androgens for sufficient masculinization of the genitals (e.g., because of defective testosterone production of the Leydig cells or lesions of the testes). In the ovaries, germ cell disappearance may be so accelerated that babies possess streak gonads at the time of birth, which is the case in Turner Syndrome.

Müllerian or Wolffian duct development requires a normal hormonal milieu; if this is not the case, the internal genital structures develop atypically. For instance, 46,XY fetuses without anti-Müllerian hormone may have both male and female internal structures. This condition is sometimes discovered accidentally when, during surgery on a boy, a uterus is found.

Intersex children may be born with ambiguous genitals (Figure 3.1). Ambiguous genitals are present in 46,XX children who were prenatally exposed to unusually high levels of androgens or in 46,XY children who prenatally were insufficiently exposed to androgens or had a genetic defect causing cells to be non- (or only partially) responsive to androgens. The degree of ambiguity varies considerably between conditions and between individuals with the same condition. Children with a 46,XX karyotype may have a somewhat enlarged clitoris, or a clitoris the size of a penis, and labia that are partially or completely fused, thus looking like an empty scrotum. Likewise, following deficient androgen exposure, 46,XY children may have a small penis, or a penis that is not much larger than a clitoris, and a partially fused or even split scrotum. The urethral opening often is not at the tip of the penis, but located at lower parts of the penis or even at the perineum. This unusual positioning is called hypospadias.

When there is no manifest ambiguity at birth and the child has no health problems, discrepancies between genital sex and gonadal, hormonal, or chromosomal sex are often discovered only at later ages. The deviations from the typical route may thus occur in any phase of sexual differentiation, may become manifest at any age, may be complete or incomplete, and may have an impact on one or more physical sex characteristics.

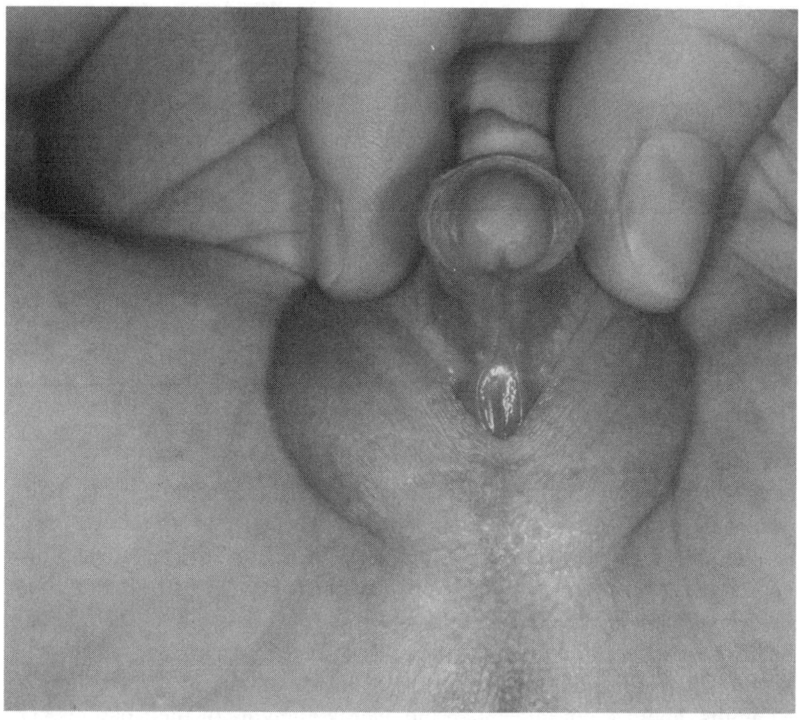

Figure 3.1 Ambiguous Genitals Due to Congenital Adrenal Hyperplasia
Note: With thanks to Dr. T. De Jong, Wilhelmina Kinderziekenhuis/UMC Utrecht.

Sexual differentiation disorders can be classified in various ways. Traditionally, genetic sex or gonadal histology is used as an organizing principle. Female and male pseudohermaphroditism, true hermaphroditism, and gonadal differentiation disorders are then the resulting categories. In true hermaphroditism both testicular and ovarian tissue are present. Female or male pseudohermaphroditism indicates that respectively only ovarian or testicular tissue is present. In incomplete or complete gonadal dysgenesis one or both gonads are streak gonads. Some of these conditions co-occur with sex chromosome anomalies, while others do not, but the two phenomena are frequently associated (Grumbach & Conte, 1998).

Relevant topics in the clinical approach to children with intersex conditions differ somewhat between conditions. We now describe the major chromosomal/gonadal conditions and female and male pseudohermaphroditism. For each condition we present data, when available, on physical aspects, cognitive functioning, school performance, personality characteristics, psychopathology, and (psycho-)sexual development and functioning. It appears to be very useful to have such information when counseling these children and their parents. A separate chapter focuses on the clinical management.

CHROMOSOMAL/GONADAL CONDITIONS

Klinefelter Syndrome (47,XXY)

General Aspects of Klinefelter Syndrome

Individuals with Klinefelter Syndrome have an extra X chromosome. At birth, there is no genital ambiguity. They are assigned and raised as males. They may have small testes and a small penis and may develop gynecomastia during puberty (Figures 3.2 and 3.3). Sometimes other genital anomalies are present, such as hypospadias or cryptorchism. Puberty may be delayed or pubertal development may stop before the last pubertal phase has been reached. In a longitudinal study a dramatic growth spurt has been found between 5 and 8 years. Primarily because of their long legs, they are, as adults, about 8 cm taller than the average heights of their parents. The average height is at the 75th percentile (Stewart, Bailey, Netley, & Park, 1990). In contrast, the head circumference may be around the 10th percentile (Ratcliffe, Masera, Pan, & McKie, 1994). This height-to-head circumference ratio could be useful in the recognition of KS in children. The majority of men with KS have the typical 47,XXY chromosome configuration, but mosaicism (e.g., 46,XY/47,XXY or variants such as 48,XXYY or 48,XXXY) also occurs. The incidence of KS is about 1 per 600 live-born boys (Nielsen & Wohlert, 1991).

In KS, Verbal IQ is usually lower than Performance IQ (e.g., Robinson, Bender, & Linden, 1991; Walzer, Bashir, & Silbert, 1991, Ratcliffe, 1999; see Rovet, Netley, Keenan, Bailey, & Stewart, 1996, for a review), though the Full-Scale IQ (FSIQ) on the Wechsler Intelligence Scale for Children—Revised (WISC-R) is usually in the normal range. After age 15, there appears to be fall-off in FSIQ (Rovet et al., 1996). Verbal and/or speech development are often delayed and expressive language is more impaired than receptive language (Walzer et al., 1991). Defects in auditory information processing and auditory memory seem to underlie the expressive language problems. A delayed motor development may interfere with writing skills and competitive sports (Salbenblatt, Meyers, Bender, Linden, &

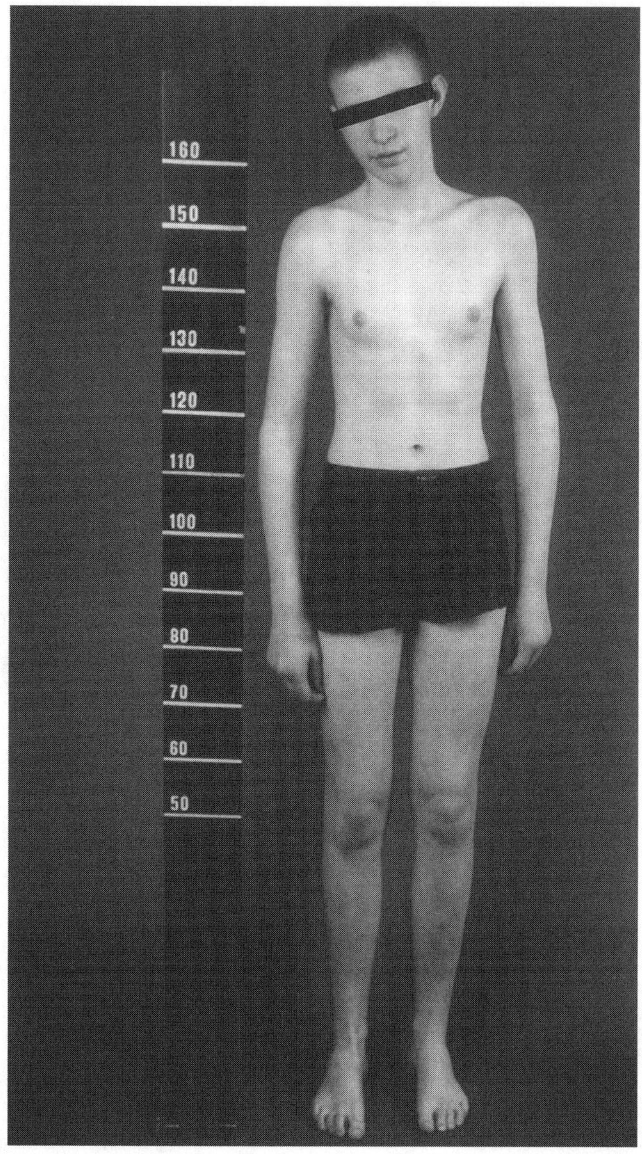

Figure 3.2 Sixteen-Year-Old Boy With Klinefelter Syndrome. Note the tall stature with the relatively long arms and legs and the marked gynecomastia.

Note: With thanks to Dr. M. Jansen. Wilhelmina Kinderziekenhuis/UMC Utrecht.

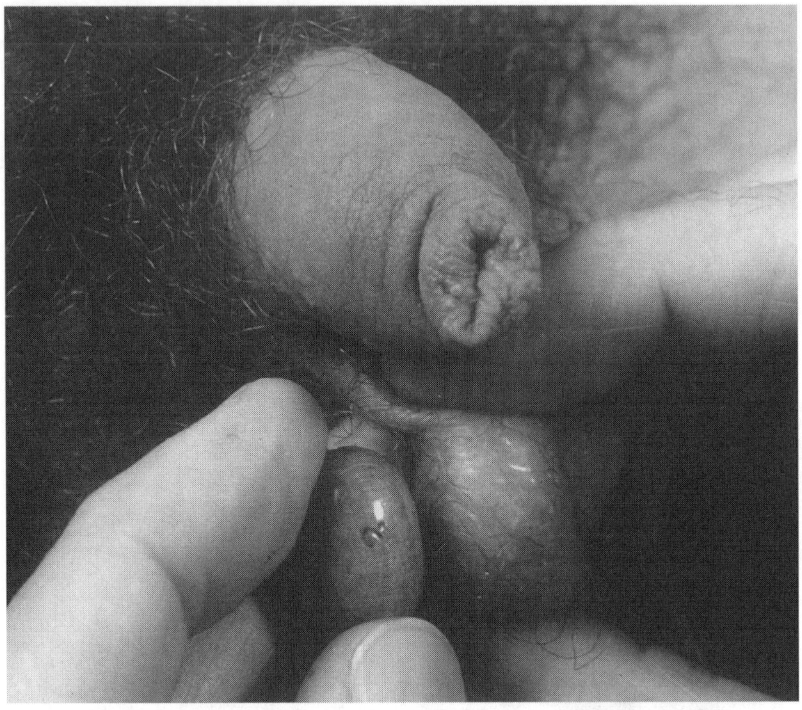

Figure 3.3 Same Boy as Shown in Figure 3.2. Note the small testicles (3 ml) in relation to advanced pubic hair development and penile growth.

Note: With thanks to Dr. M. Jansen. Wilhelmina Kinderziekenhuis/UMC Utrecht.

Robinson, 1987). At school, children with KS not only have problems with reading and spelling, but, with increasing age, there is also a steady decline in math achievement. These problems are related to deficits in recall, working memory, and comprehension. As a result of the learning disabilities, the majority of the children need special education. Without support, school performance is often poor (e.g., Graham, Bashir, Stark, Silbert, & Walzer, 1988; Pennington, Bender, Puck, Salbenblatt, & Robinson, 1982; Ratcliffe, Murray, & Teaque, 1986; for a review see Jenssen Hagerman, 1999).

Boys with KS may have problems in relationships with peers and sibs from the age of 3 years on. Personality characteristics such as quietness, unassertiveness, timidity, passivity, and inadequacy have been observed and they are often hypoactive (Mandoki & Summer, 1991; Nielsen,

Christensen, Friedrich, Zeuthen, & Ostergaard, 1973; Stewart et al., 1982; Ratcliffe, 1999). Boys with KS seem to be more insecure, dependent, nervous, and less assertive in adolescence than controls (Bancroft, Axworthy, & Ratcliffe, 1982; Theilgaard, 1984). Probably as a result of the physical characteristics (tall, immature, gynecomastia, small genitals) and the verbal difficulties, relationship problems may get worse in adolescence. Especially in unfavorable family circumstances, conflicts (with parents) due to frustration and problems with aggression regulation are common (Bender, Linden, & Robinson, 1987). There can also be inertia, lack of initiative, and tiredness. In one longitudinal population-based study 54% of the patients received a psychiatric diagnosis (Bender, Harmon, Linden, & Robinson, 1995) compared with 14% of the controls. In another study, the rate of psychiatric referrals was 26% as compared to 9%. Most of the problems in the referred group were of an internalizing nature; that is, these patients exhibited anxiety and depression (Ratcliffe, 1999).

Treatment with testosterone at the beginning of or shortly after puberty is often necessary for complete masculinization, muscle development, and prevention of osteoporosis. It can also have a favorable effect on concentration, school performance, and tiredness (Nielsen, Pelsen, & Sørensen, 1988), which, in turn, may influence self-esteem and interpersonal relations.

Gender Identity and Gender Role

Men with KS often feel less masculine and are rated by others as less masculine than other men, but their masculine and feminine interests and activities have not been found to differ from those of controls. They have been reported to have less pleasure in gymnastics and boys' games (Bancroft et al., 1982; Theilgaard, 1984; Schiavi, Theilgaard, Owen, & White, 1988), but generally they have no cross-gender interests or behavior. From this it appears that the large majority of men with KS, despite their lessened masculinity in behavior and interests, have masculine gender identities. However, in some, it is probably the combination of their vulnerabilities that led to gender identity problems or even transsexualism (Cryan & O'Donoghue, 1992; Davidson, 1966; Hoaken, Clarke, & Breslin, 1964; Miller & Caplan, 1965; Miller, 1972; Seifert & Windgassen, 1995) (see also the vignette on "Oliver").

Sexual Activity, Sexual Orientation, and Fertility

While adolescents with KS masturbate less, adults are less interested in females and in sexuality, start to be sexually active at later ages, are sexually less active, and have more limited sexual experience than controls (Ratcliffe, Bancroft, Axworthy, & McClaren, 1982; Schiavi et al., 1988; Sørensen, 1992). The men in Schiavi et al.'s study, however, reported no less sexual satisfaction than other men. In a 20-year follow-up, 59% of a group of 34 men with KS were married or had a long-standing heterosexual relationship (Nielsen & Pelsen, 1987). In Schiavi et al.'s study more of the men with KS than controls said they had engaged in homosexual activities. Nonmosaic men with KS are usually reported to be infertile, but at least one case exists of proved fertility in a nonmosaic KS man (Laron, Dickerman, Zamir, & Galatzer, 1982).

VIGNETTE: Oliver, 6 years old

Oliver's parents knew their child had KS before his birth. They came to our clinic when he was 4 years old, because they wanted to be better informed about the condition. They hoped that this would help them prevent future problems. At the time they had no complaints about his behavior or development.

Oliver's mother had experienced a normal pregnancy and delivery and had not used medication during pregnancy. Oliver had not developed any physical illnesses. His language and motor development had been somewhat delayed. He also seemed emotionally young for his age. Unlike many boys with KS, Oliver was relatively short. Other children, mostly older girls, liked to play with him and tended to treat him as a baby. He had some trouble playing with children of his own age.

After a year his mother returned to our clinic. She thought he was behaving in a rather feminine way and wanted to know whether this was typical for boys with KS. As she had a very "feminine" brother and uncle she wondered whether this behavior runs in families.

From the assessment it appeared that Oliver was still emotionally young. He was living in a fairytale world and it was difficult for him to remain attentive during the testing session. He focused very much on his own needs and had trouble following orders. It was not always clear whether he did not understand the questions or whether he was just not interested in giving adequate answers. Despite all this, his parents reported no behavior problems on the Child Behavior Checklist.

With regard to gender development, it appeared that Oliver was able to identify the sexes correctly. However, he did not yet completely understand the various aspects of gender. For instance, he thought that he would later, as an adult, become a mommy instead of a daddy and that boys who wear dresses become girls. He said he liked to be a girl and wanted to become a mommy, but he also said he liked to be a boy, because "boys can play with girls' dresses." In his dreams he was Snow White or Sleeping Beauty. If a fairy would cast a spell on him he would like to become Snow White. He had a complete preference for girls on a peer preference task and a strong preference for girls' toys on a toy preference task. At the Draw-a-Person test, his first drawing was a girl, the second one a boy. The only difference between the two drawings was that the girl had longer hair than the boy. Oliver was not ashamed of his interests and behavior. At the time his parents were not interested in any form of therapy or further counseling.

When Oliver was 6 years old, he and his parents returned again. Because of his immaturity he had remained in the second kindergarten grade for another year. At school, his teachers had concerns about his reading progress and his social behavior. On the Teacher Report Form he scored in the clinical range on social and thought problems. His teacher found him to be a very friendly and gentle boy, but no match for the other boys in his class because of his unassertiveness.

Oliver's earlier feminine interests had remained. His parents reported that he still liked to cross-dress and to play with girls and he occasionally said he wanted to be a girl. This time his gender knowledge was adequate. Play observation revealed that he played longer with girls' toys than with boys' and only with feminine dress-up apparel. He preferred girls as playmates. His answers to a gender identity interview were more mixed. Despite average intelligence (Wechsler VIQ = 92 and PIQ = 108), he seemed to answer somewhat randomly.

47,XYY

General Aspects of 47,XYY

Boys with a 47,XYY karyotype are assigned and raised as males. They have no ambiguous genitals at birth. Also, there are no other typical physical characteristics. The characteristics that have been described are usually unremarkable, such as tallness or various skeletal deformities. Subnormal genital development and hypogonadism may also occur (Fryns, Kleczkowska, Kubien, & Van den Berghe, 1995). Puberty may be mildly delayed. The frequency of 47,XYY karyotype is about 1 per 900 live-born boys (Nielsen & Wohlert, 1991).

The IQ of 47,XYY boys is somewhat lower than that of siblings and other controls, but in the normal range. As in KS, boys with 47,XYY seem to have language and speech deficits, although perhaps less severe than boys with KS (e.g., Nielsen, Sørensen, & Sørensen, 1982; Ratcliffe, 1999; Robinson et al., 1991; Walzer et al., 1991). In boys with 47,XYY more neuromotor dysfunction has been found (Salbenblatt et al., 1987). They also show more motor activity and distractibility when compared to 46,XY and 47,XXY boys (Walzer et al., 1991). Their distractibility usually begins between 2 and 3 years, whereas in 47,XXY it seems to be a consequence of the learning problems. School problems and learning disabilities partly seem to be the result of impaired teachability (Walzer et al., 1991; see also Jenssen Hagerman, 1999).

In the 1960s and 1970s publications indicated that boys identified with 47,XYY had an increased risk of criminality (Price & Whatmore, 1967), but in later studies this was not always replicated (Nielsen & Wohlert, 1991; Theilgaard, 1983). From more recent work it appeared that, in an unselected sample of adolescents and adults, 47,XYY males had higher frequencies of antisocial behavior (mostly property offences) and more criminal convictions than controls. This was mainly mediated through lowered intelligence (Gotz, Johnstone, & Ratcliffe, 1999). It may also be that 47,XYY boys get into trouble because they have difficulties delaying gratification of their needs rather than that they engage in violent crime (Money, 1993). Testosterone levels did not correlate with aggression on psychological testing (Schiavi, Theilgaard, Owen, & White, 1984). Long-term outcome of 19 boys between 16 and 27 revealed that in 46% psychiatric referrals were made as compared to 9% of a control group (Ratcliffe, 1999). The complaints were difficult and defiant behavior, temper tantrums since early childhood, stealing, and school-related enuresis (see also the vignette on "Adrian"). Most had a diagnosis of conduct disorder, but also depressive reactions to environmental stress.

Testosterone treatment is rarely necessary, as the testosterone levels are usually in the normal range (e.g., Ratcliffe, Butler, & Jones, 1990) or even higher than those in controls (Schiavi et al., 1984).

Gender Identity and Gender Role

In general gender identity does not seem to be problematic, but a few reports exist on gender identity problems and even transsexualism in men with 47,XYY (Buhrich, Barr, & Lam-Po-Tang, 1978; Haberman, Hollingsworth, Falek, & Michael, 1975; Snaith, Penhale, & Horsfield, 1991; Taneja, Ammini, Mohapatra, Saxena, & Kucheria, 1992; Wagner, 1974). When men with 47,XYY were compared with men with KS and controls, they showed no more atypical gender role behavior in childhood than controls. With regard to adult gender role, interviewers have rated them as less masculine. They also manifested less self-acceptance and there were problems with masculine identification (Schiavi et al., 1988; Zeuthen, Hansen, Christensen, & Nielsen, 1975).

Sexual Activity, Sexual Orientation, and Fertility

In the sexual life of 47,XYY men their impulsiveness may create problems (Baker, Jelfer, Richardson, & Clark, 1970; Daly, 1969; Money, Gaskin, & Hull, 1970; Money, 1975b). In Schiavi et al.'s study (1988) 47,XYY men were less often married, but had more sexual partners and reported more masturbatory behavior than controls. They were less sexually satisfied, expressed less guilt about masturbation, and reported having engaged in and fantasized more about unconventional sexual activities than controls. Fertility seems to be reduced (Martini et al., 1996).

VIGNETTE: Adrian, 15 years old

Adrian came to the clinic when he was 15 years old because he had been caught shoplifting and because he had temper outbursts that were difficult to handle by his parents. They wondered whether this behavior was related to his condition. For years his parents had not known what was wrong with their son. He had attended a special school because of his language and learning problems, he had no friends, and was emotionally very flat. The combination of his tallness (he was 2.03 m) and the other characteristics made his mother suspect that he might have a genetic deficit. Her request for a test was granted by the pediatrician and resulted in the finding of a 47,XYY chromosome configuration.

When Adrian was conceived, his mother was 39. She already had two daughters. Her pregnancy and delivery were normal. She had not used medication during pregnancy. Adrian was a healthy child. As a baby he had been extremely quiet. His language and motor development were somewhat delayed. From early on there had been many problems with other children, despite his very friendly nature. For instance, as a young child he often tried to get other children's toys in a physical manner or pushed them when they stood in his way, because he was unable to attain his goals in a verbal way. His tall appearance made other children afraid to tease him, but because he was very naive, they easily took advantage of him. Although he was emotionally and verbally immature, children and adults tended to overestimate him because of his tallness. Adults often punished him for his impulsiveness, which he found difficult to control. He spent most of his time at his parents' farm, playing alone or with his older sisters.

After he entered puberty, his problems increased. His mother discovered that he took money from her and he also took little objects or candy from shops. Because they lived in a small village, the shopkeepers knew his mother. The thefts had not yet resulted in serious consequences because the shopkeepers knew about Adrian's situation and understood that his stealing was typically impulsive, not planned. His mother often found the money on a table in his room or still in his pocket, as if he had forgotten why he had taken it. At his neighbors' house, he once crushed an expensive small antique sculpture he had picked up to admire. When this neighbor unexpectedly entered the room he had put it under his jacket.

Testing revealed that Adrian had an IQ of 75. He was functioning 4 years below his age level on the Beery, a psychomotor test. His attention and memory were weak, but in line with his cognitive profile. It also appeared that he had problems monitoring and regulating his behavior and that he did not adequately use feedback.

His poor cognitive and social functioning combined with his weak impulse control made it likely that he would remain dependent on his parents or institutions for the rest of his life. An example of the kind of trouble he encountered was that he was once fired from a temporary job, because he had been masturbating in a corner of his working place (a storage room), unaware of the fact that this could be seen through a security video camera.

Turner Syndrome (45,XO) or Gonadal Dysgenesis

General Aspects of Turner Syndrome

Individuals with Turner Syndrome have only one sex chromosome (X). They are assigned and raised as females. Turner Syndrome girls typically have a short stature and underdeveloped and endocrine inactive ovaries (streak gonads). They may also have a broad variety of other physical characteristics, such as a webbed neck, low posterior hairline, low-set ears, small jaws, pigmented naevi, nail dysplasia, a high arched palate, a shield thorax, an increased carrying of the elbow, middle ear problems, congenital heart defects, and urinary tract anomalies (Figures 3.4 and 3.5) (for an overview, see Jensen Hagerman, 1999, p. 210). The second X chromosome may be completely or partially deleted, or there may be a ring chromosome. Approximately 1 of 2,500 newborn females has Turner Syndrome (Hook & Warburton, 1983).

As a group, individuals with Turner Syndrome have an IQ in the average range. However, they have lower IQs than controls and show specific deficits in various cognitive functions, such as visual–spatial/perceptual abilities, nonverbal memory function, motor function, executive function, and attentional abilities (Ross, Zinn, & McCauley, 2000; see also Jenssen Hagerman, 1999). Performance IQ is about 1 *SD* lower than verbal IQ (Rovet, 1993, 1995). Mental retardation is encountered in a subgroup of individuals with Turner Syndrome. This may be related to additional chromosomal abnormalities. Girls with Turner Syndrome often have a nonverbal learning disability (Rovet, 1993, 1995) and may have problems with math. These problems may be related to their visual–spatial deficits. Girls with Turner Syndrome may also be somewhat hyperactive (McCauley, Feuillan, Kushner, & Ross, 2001; Rovet, 1993). Whether all cognitive problems are genetically determined or partly result from estrogen deficiency remains to be investigated (Ross et al., 2000).

Psychologically individuals with Turner Syndrome may function nonoptimally. In a large study comparing 274 girls with Turner Syndrome and girls with short stature, it was found that the girls with Turner Syndrome had more emotional and behavior problems than the short stature group. In the Turner Syndrome group 23% had scores equivalent to clinical cases, whereas only 4% of the girls with short stature scored in the clinical range (Skuse, Percy, & Stevenson, 1994). Behavior and emotional problems differ in severity, depending on the parental origin of the normal X chromosome. Girls with a maternal X chromosome were doing less well than girls with a paternal X chromosome. Turner girls also appear to be emotionally immature and socially less competent than other girls with or without short stature. They have fewer and less satisfying social relationships and lower self-esteem (e.g., McCauley, Feuillan, Kushner, & Ross, 2001; McCauley, Ross, Kushner, & Cutler, 1995; Siegel, Clopper, & Stabler, 1998; Skuse, Elgar, & Morris, 1999).

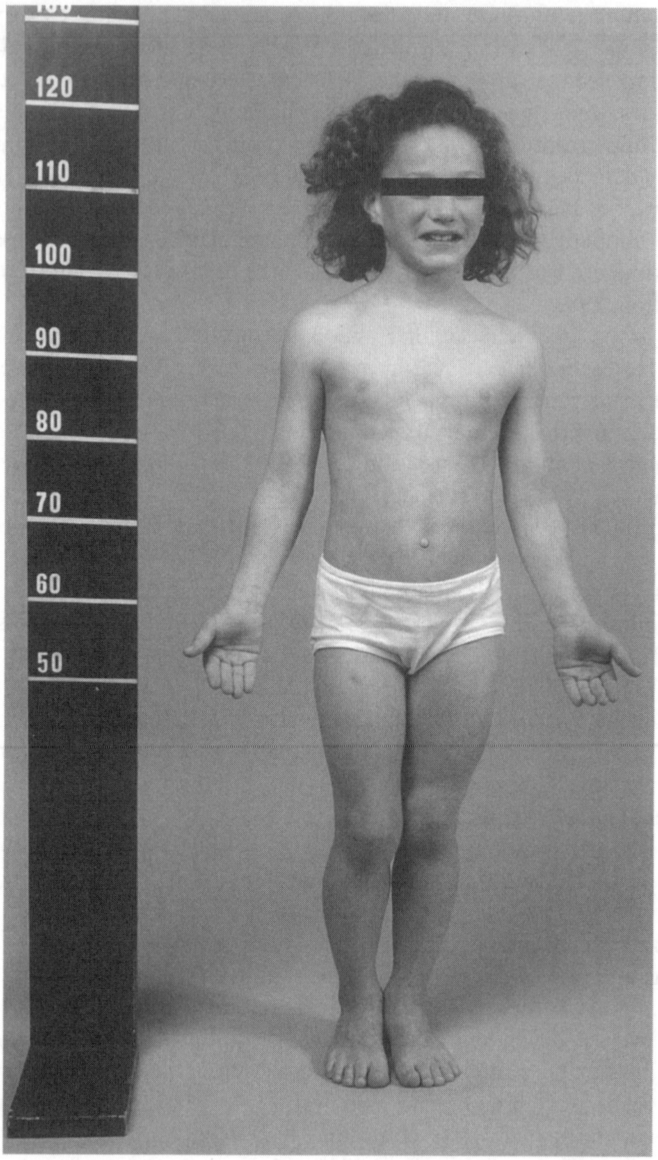

Figure 3.4 Nine-Year-Old Girl With Turner Syndrome. Note small stature, broad thorax with widely spaced nipples (shield thorax), slight webbing of neck and increased carrying angle at elbows.

Note: With thanks to Dr. M. Jansen, Wilhelmina Kinderziekenhuis/UMC Utrecht.

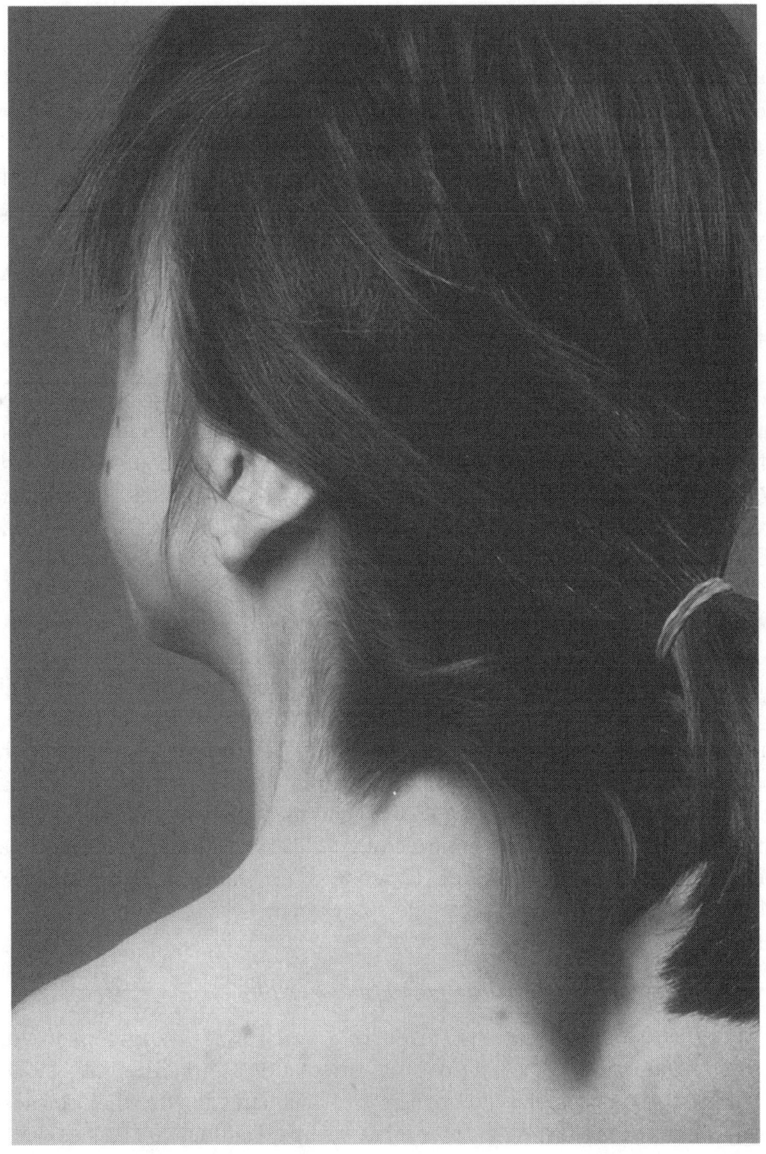

Figure 3.5 Sixteen-Year-Old Girl With Turner Syndrome. Marked webbing of neck and low posterior hairline. Note also low-set ears and multiple pigmented naevi in the face.

Note: With thanks to Dr. M. Jansen, Wilhelmina Kinderziekenhuis/UMC Utrecht.

Case reports exist of women with various psychiatric disorders, such as schizophrenia, bipolar affective disorder, anorexia nervosa, and depression (e.g., Darby, Garfinkel, Vale, Kirwan, & Brown, 1981; Nicholls & Stanhope, 1998), but psychopathology findings among adult women with Turner Syndrome are somewhat contradictory. In a thorough psychiatric evaluation of 15 individuals with Turner Syndrome none had a psychiatric diagnosis (Bender, Harmon, Linden, & Robinson, 1995). It has even been suggested that women with Turner Syndrome may have a decreased rather than increased risk of psychopathology (Bamrah & MacCay, 1989; see El Abd, Turk, & Hill, 1995, for a review). As in mental retardation, severe psychiatric problems may be associated with karyotype (e.g., mosaicism versus 45,X0; Skuse, Perey, & Stevenson, 1994).

Girls with Turner Syndrome will need estrogen treatment to induce pubertal development and to prevent osteoporosis. Treatment is usually started around the age of 12 years. Growth hormone therapy is often given because of short stature. Depending on their congenital physical abnormalities girls with Turner Syndrome may need a variety of other treatments. Guidelines exist for appropriate treatment of individuals with Turner Syndrome (Committee on Genetics/American Academy of Pediatrics, 1995).

Gender Identity and Gender Role

Individuals with Turner Syndrome have a female gender identity. At all ages they show as many, or even more, feminine interests and activities than controls (see also the vignette on "Mary"). They are less tomboyish, less involved in sports, and less aggressive. They report more parental rehearsal, are more interested in jewelry and makeup, and prefer girls' toys and girls' games more than controls (e.g., Downey, Ehrhardt, Morishima, Bell, & Gruen, 1987; Ehrhardt, Greenberg, & Money, 1970; Money & Mittenthal, 1970; Pavlidis, McCauley, & Sybert, 1995).

Sexual Activity, Sexual Orientation, and Fertility

With occasional exceptions (Fishbain & Vilaruso, 1980), women with Turner Syndrome have a heterosexual orientation (Ehrhardt et al., 1970). Their first sexual experience appears to occur later in life, they are less likely to have long-lasting partner relationships, and they are less sexually active than controls (Downey, Ehrhardt, Gruen, Bell, & Morishima, 1989; Holl, Kunze, Etzrodt, Teler, & Heinze, 1994; Pavlidis et al., 1995; Raboch, Kobilkova, Horejsi, Starka, & Raboch, 1987). In one study women with Turner Syndrome had a more negative body image than a normative sample. Despite a lower frequency of sexual intercourse compared to a normative sample, they reported moderate to high levels of sexual satisfaction (Pavlidis et al., 1995).

Because women with Turner Syndrome have streak gonads they are usually infertile. In countries where in vitro fertilization is available, infertility may become less of a problem (Vockrodt & Williams, 1994). Successful natural pregnancies of women with Turner Syndrome may occur in women with mosaicism (Saenger, 1996).

VIGNETTE: Mary, 14 years old

Mary came to our clinic when she was 13. Her parents were concerned because they felt she had been somewhat depressed since she began taking estrogens. Her condition was discovered in infancy, when she appeared to have heart problems. Mary had been an easy baby. Her language development was normal, her motor development somewhat slow. The most important childhood events were the many doctor and hospital visits. The relationship between Mary and her mother was close. Both parents had a job, but her mother had always been at home after school hours. Her mother found it difficult, both for herself and for Mary, that her daughter would not be able to have children of her own. Mary attended a regular high school (to prepare her for an administrative career), where she was a somewhat below-average student. Other children had never teased her, but she did not have many friends. Her few friends were always younger than she was. She lived a sheltered life.

Her mother had told her step by step about her condition. From early on Mary knew that her heart problems and short stature were related to "wrong cells in her body." She also knew she would never menstruate and would need to take hormones to develop breasts as a result of her syndromes. Her mother had explained that she would not be able to have children of her own. Mary was a very feminine-looking child. She loved Barbie dolls and stereotypical girls' clothing, jewelry, and long hair. As an adolescent she remained extremely stereotypically feminine in appearance and interests. The only difference between her and her friends was that, at 14, she was not very interested in boys.

Psychological assessment revealed that she had an IQ of 93 (verbal 96; performance 89). She appeared to be an insecure child who felt very dependent on others, such as her friends and her mother in particular. Since she was in high school she increasingly realized that she was different from her friends because she had hormone treatment, did not menstruate, was infertile, and had a short stature. The fact that other girls still treated her like a child made her feel like an outsider. This was what bothered her most. She did not yet want to think much about marriage, partly because she wondered whether she would ever find a partner (and was not yet interested in finding one) and partly because the thought of leaving her parents' house was threatening to her. There was no serious psychopathology.

FEMALE PSEUDOHERMAPHRODITISM

Virilized genitals in girls may have various causes. The mothers may have had a virilizing tumor during pregnancy or may have used virilizing medication (e.g., progestins). However, the most common cause of female pseudohermaphroditism is congenital (virilizing) adrenal hyperplasia (CVAH or CAH).

Congenital Adrenal Hyperplasia or Adrenogenital Syndrome

General Aspects of Congenital Adrenal Hyperplasia

Congenital adrenal hyperplasia (CAH) is caused by an autosomal recessive defect. Due to an adrenal enzyme deficit (most commonly 21-hydroxylase), adrenal cortisol and aldosterone production is deficient and the bulk of hormone production is shifted to prenatal overproduction of adrenal androgens, beginning in the third month after conception. In girls, this may lead to genital virilization with or without salt loss (salt-wasting or simple virilizing form). An impaired synthesis of the adrenal androgen aldosterone results in salt loss (salt-wasting form). Virilization may range from minor clitoral enlargement to external genitals that look like a penis and an empty scrotum.

The estimated incidence of CAH is 1:5,000 or 15,000 live births (New, 1995). Men may also suffer from the condition. Unlike affected women, they have no genital ambiguity at birth. Congenital adrenal hyperplasia women have IQs equivalent to those of well-matched controls (Collaer & Hines, 1995), but probably differ in sex-related cognitive abilities from nonaffected siblings or other controls. They show more malelike visual-spatial abilities (e.g., Hampson, Rovet, & Altman, 1998; Resnick, Berenbaum, Gottesman, & Bouchard , 1986). This also applies to certain verbal abilities (Helleday, Bartfai, Ritzén, & Forsman, 1994; Plante, Boliek, Binkiewicz, & Erly, 1996).

Cortisone therapy restores the hormonal balance after birth. Dexamethasone treatment in utero suppresses the fetal adrenal hyperandrogenism and prevents virilization of the external genitals in affected girls. The suppression of adrenal overproduction of androgens may be less than optimal. Concerns exist, however, about the long-term effects of this kind of treatment (Miller, 1999). The virilized genitals are often surgically feminized shortly after birth (for a criticism of early genital surgery see Chapter 5).

Gender Identity and Gender Role

As a consequence of the genital virilization, 46,XX infants are not always recognized as girls at birth. In these cases, the male sex is assigned to the infants and they are raised as boys (Chan-Cua, Freidenberg, & Jones, 1989; Hochberg, Gardos, & Benderly, 1987; Kandemir & Yordam, 1997; Money & Daléry, 1976).

Women with CAH mostly have feminine gender identities, but gender dysphoria or less strong feminine identification have been reported several times (Hochberg et al., 1987; Hurtig & Rosenthal, 1987; Meyer-Bahlburg et al., 1996; Slijper, 1984; Slijper et al., 1992; Zucker et al., 1996). In childhood and adolescence, masculine gender role behavior is common. Many girls with CAH have more masculine and less feminine interests regarding toys, clothing and makeup, infant care, sports, and playmates (e.g., Berenbaum, 1999; Berenbaum, Duck, & Bryk, 2000; Dittmann et al., 1990; Ehrhardt, Evers, & Money, 1968; Slijper, 1984; for a review see Zucker, 1999) (see also the vignette on "Alexandra"). Female adolescents and adults (but not children) with CAH had higher scores on aggression scales than sibling and cousin controls (Berenbaum & Resnick, 1997). Most of the findings suggestive of an effect of prenatal brain exposure to androgens have been found to be stronger in the more seriously affected salt-wasting than in the simple virilizing group.

Sexual Activity, Sexual Orientation, and Fertility

In women with CAH, heterosexuality is the rule but the incidence of homosexuality as compared to population norms or other control groups is increased (Dittmann, Kappes, & Kappes, 1992; Ehrhardt et al., 1968; Money & Schwartz, 1977; Money, Schwartz, & Lewis, 1984; Zucker et al., 1996). In general, their sexual lives differ from control groups in terms of timing of psychosexual milestones (delayed), sexual experience (less), sexual activity and imagery (less), sexual motivation (less), partnership and marriage (less), and sexual self-image (less favorable) (Kuhnle, Bullinger, & Schwarz, 1995; Mulaikal, Migeon, & Rock, 1987; Slijper et al., 1992; Zucker et al., 1996). Fertility seems to be lower than in nonaffected women. This may be caused by nonoptimal hormonal treatment, low interest in the maternal role, or reduced heterosexual activity. This last factor could be due to elevated bi- or homosexuality; low sexual motivation; decreased functionality of the vagina and/or sensitivity of the clitoris; body image problems; or concurrent atypical hormone levels, which influence libido (Meyer-Bahlburg, 1999).

VIGNETTE: Alexandra, 5 years old

Alexandra was 5 years old when she came to our clinic. She was born in Curaçao. Her father was unknown. Her mother used alcohol and drugs. Without much success, her mother had tried to take care of her daughter until Alexandra was 3 years old. Because Alexandra's genitals were somewhat virilized at birth, the doctors wanted to further investigate her as a baby but her mother left the hospital and did not show up at appointments. When Alexandra was 3 years old, an aunt of her mother, who was a social worker, became her legal custodian. The mother agreed that her aunt would raise the child. It was only then that the aunt became aware of Alexandra's condition. Because the local doctors were unable to treat her properly she started an application procedure to allow Alexandra to be treated in the Netherlands.

Medical assessment revealed that Alexandra had entered puberty precociously. At 5 she already had some pubic and axillary hair, acne, and her clitoris had grown to a length of 5 cm. She had always been extremely tomboyish in toy preference, play activities, clothing preference, and peer preference, although she lived in a culture where behaving like a typical girl was very important. Alexandra preferred to be called Alex. There were many behavior problems.

Alexandra had a full-scale IQ of 81. Psychological assessment revealed that she was not confused regarding her gender. She knew that she was a girl, that she had been a baby girl, and that she would later become a mommy. She said that she wanted to be a girl, but her observed and reported interests were primarily masculine. When playing with dress-up apparel, she used primarily military uniforms, but she was interested in jewelry too. During the play observation she showed much aggressive play with guns and a plastic knife. Aggressive themes were also apparent in her stories. When drawing a person the first person she drew was a male Dracula. As an adult she wanted to become a policewoman and marry. Alexandra had a diagnosis of Attention Deficit Hyperactivity Disorder.

MALE PSEUDOHERMAPHRODITISM

Undervirilization of 46,XY children may be the result of defects in the biosynthesis of testosterone or of defects in androgen receptors in androgen-dependent tissues. Defects in the production or responsiveness to MIS may lead to uterine strictures. These conditions are rare. As a consequence only small numbers of such individuals have been studied. A little more is known about the psychological outcome of undervirilization of the androgen insensitivity syndromes and certain enzyme defects [5α-reductase deficiency (5α-RD) and 17β-hydroxysteroid dehydrogenase deficiency (17β-HSD)].

Androgen Insensitivity Syndrome (Testicular Feminization)

General Aspects of Androgen Insensitivity Syndrome

Androgen receptors of 46,XY individuals may be completely or partially insensitive to androgens. At birth, 46,XY children with partial androgen insensitivity syndrome (PAIS) have almost normal female or ambiguous external genitals. They have functional testes that produce androgens but, because the body cells are insensitive to the biological effects of androgens, the male external genitals do not develop normally. Anti-Müllerian hormone is produced normally, so the Müllerian ducts regress. However, the external genitals show a wide range of ambiguity. Depending on the degree of masculinization of the genitals and the estimated possibilities to function adequately as adult males or females, these children are assigned to the male or female sex (Meyer-Bahlburg, 1999).

Children with the complete form of androgen insensitivity (CAIS) have undeveloped Wolffian ducts and female-appearing external genitals.

Therefore the diagnosis is often made at later ages, for instance, when inguinal hernias appear to contain testicles that have failed to descend into the scrotum or at puberty when menstruation does not occur. These infants are always raised as females. Their appearance is completely feminine. The pubic, facial, and axillary hair are sparse or absent, as this is androgen-dependent. The incidence of androgen insensitivity is about 1:20,400 (Bangsboll, Qvist, Lebech, & Lewinsky, 1992).

For children with PAIS who are raised as boys, surgery may be needed to more completely masculinize the genitals (for criticism of early genital surgery see Chapter 5). Their penile length, though, often remains relatively short. When raised as girls, their external genitals are surgically feminized shortly after birth. In adolescent girls with CAIS, vaginal dilation surgery may be performed to deepen the vagina to allow sexual intercourse. At puberty, female breast development and body shape result from conversion of testicular testosterone to estrogen secretion (MacDonald, Madden, Brenner, Wilson, & Siiteri, 1979). The gonads are often removed, because of a risk of cancer at a later age. When they have been removed before puberty, estrogens are given at puberty and thereafter to induce and maintain secondary sex characteristics.

Gender Identity and Gender Role

It is not certain that individuals with PAIS raised as girls will always develop an uncomplicated female gender identity. For instance, two case studies report a (potential) gender identity conflict. In one study, a patient brought up as a girl and supposedly having a female gender identity became psychotic after the testicles, and thereby signs of physical virilization, were removed in adulthood (Quattrin, Aronica, & Mazur, 1990). Another study describes a patient assigned to the male sex at birth, but reassigned several days later. This very masculine patient was sexually attracted to women and requested sex reassignment at age 30 (Gooren & Cohen-Kettenis, 1991). In a study of Money and Ogunro (1974), including two individuals raised as girls (one after reassignment at 2 years old and one as a "hermaphroditic" girl) and eight as boys, gender identity developed according to gender of rearing. In a study by Slijper, Drop, Molenaar, and de Muinck Keizer-Schrama (1998), one in seven individuals raised as girls developed a gender identity disorder. In a small group of individuals with PAIS who were raised as males, reduced preferences for male playmates and lower scores on childhood masculinity were found. As an adult, one of the four men with PAIS decided to live as a woman, despite assignment and rearing as a male (Hines, Ahmed, & Hughes, 2000).

Individuals with CAIS, consistently raised as girls, have a female gender identity. They are usually described as feminine in their gender role behavior, but there may be more variability than has long been assumed (see the vignette on "Betty"). In a recent comparison between women with CAIS recruited through the United Kingdom Database of Ambiguous Genitalia and Intersex Disorder and an Androgen Insensitivity Support Group, it appeared that the first group recalled more masculine-typical toy, activity, and playmate preferences as children and overall ratings of childhood masculinity than the support group (Hines et al., 2000).

Sexual Activity, Sexual Orientation, and Fertility

Women with CAIS are typically heterosexual in behavior and imagery (Lewis & Money, 1983; Masica, Ehrhardt, & Money, 1971; Money, Ehrhardt, & Masica, 1968; Money & Ogunro, 1974). In the above English study, comparing women with CAIS recruited through the United Kingdom Database and the Support Group, it appeared that the Database group was more strongly heterosexual (Hines et al., 2000).

Women with CAIS do not differ from other women in marriage and relationship patterns (Hines et al., 2000). Women with PAIS and CAIS are infertile because they are born with male gonads, which are usually removed later in life.

VIGNETTE: Betty, 2 years old

Betty was seen at our clinic when she was 2 years old. At 9 months she had undergone surgery for an inguinal hernia. During the operation it appeared that Betty had bilateral testes and it was discovered that she had CAIS. Because her external genitals were not ambiguous the surgeons did not expect any gender development problems and advised the parents not to reassign her to the male sex.

When she was 3 years old, her parents became worried, because she had such a clear interest in boys' toys and activities. Upon testing, various aspects of her gender role behavior indeed appeared to be very masculine, but she did not seem to suffer from GID. The parents had counseling for a while to help them deal with their anxieties and feelings of guilt about a possible "wrong" decision.

Subsequently, they were advised on an irregular basis when they had questions regarding the rearing of their daughter.

When Betty was 5 years old, she was again seen at our clinic. Testing revealed that she had an average IQ (105) and that there were no serious behavioral or emotional problems. However, she repeatedly stated she wanted to be a boy and wanted to have a penis. Later she wanted to become a truck driver. She did not want to marry or have children. Her behavior was even more masculine than before. She never played with girls. Betty insisted on having a male haircut and wearing boys' clothes. This time Betty fulfilled the *DSM-IV* criteria for GID.

Enzyme Deficiencies: 5α-Reductase Deficiency and 17β-Hydroxysteroid Dehydrogenase Deficiency

General Aspects of Enzyme Deficiencies

Enzyme deficiencies may affect the biosynthesis of testosterone or the conversion of testosterone into dihydrotestosterone. Dihydrotestosterone is a more biopotent androgen than testosterone and necessary for the formation of the male external genitals. Both enzyme defects affect the development of the external genitals, because DHT is lacking.

Children with 5α-RD are born with ambiguous or female-appearing external genitals. Their testes can be abdominal, inguinal, or labial. Children with 17β-HSD have either mildly ambiguous or female-appearing external genitals. The internal genitals develop normally and the Müllerian ducts regress. Many are raised as females (Imperato-McGinley, Peterson, Gautier, & Sturla, 1979; Imperato-McGinley, Peterson, Stoller, & Goodwin, 1979; Rösler & Kohn, 1983). In that case, testes have to be removed before puberty, because the associated high androgen levels would induce masculinization and, at puberty, estrogen treatment is necessary to feminize the body. If the children are raised as boys, genital surgery can make the appearance of the external genitals more masculine. Whether this type of surgery in infancy is desirable has become a controversial topic (see Chapter 5). The cognitive or general psychological development of affected children has hardly been studied.

Gender Identity and Gender Role

Children with 5α-RD and 17β-HSD who are raised as boys have a male identity and behave like boys. When they are assigned and raised as girls, the outcome is more varied. Imperato-McGinley, Peterson, Gautier, and Sturla (1979) were the first to describe a gender identity change around or after a masculinizing puberty in 17 of 18 5α-RD individuals who were "unambiguously" raised as females. Similar reports appeared on the 17β-HSD group (e.g., Imperato-McGinley, Peterson, Stoller, & Goodwin, 1979; Rösler & Kohn, 1983). They confirmed the earlier findings on the 5α-RD group (e.g., Al-Attia, 1996; Mendez et al., 1995; Mendonca et al., 1996). This change, however, did not happen in all affected individuals, even when they were living in societies that highly value the male role (see also the vignette for "Tineke"). It must be noted that many of the reports do not or only roughly describe their rearing, psychosexual development, and final outcome. So it remains unclear whether the gender identity change was induced by prenatal hormonal programming of the brain, cultural advantages associated with the male role, or a combination of the hormonal and environmental forces. The last possibility was put forward by Zucker (1999), who stated that the gender identity change could be a homophobic reaction in individuals with a hormonally induced sexual attraction to women in a society that strongly disapproves of homosexuality.

Sexual Activity, Sexual Orientation, and Fertility

As noted above, only very little is known about the psychosexual development and outcome of both groups. Regarding the persons who were raised as girls, there are occasional referrals to marriage and sexual intercourse, heterosexual attraction, and relationships with men (e.g., Mendonca et al., 1996), but systematic studies are lacking. When individuals with 5α-RD and 17β-HSD are raised and live as women, infertility results from removal of the testes. When they live as men, fertility may be impaired.

VIGNETTE: Tineke, 10 years old

Tineke came to our clinic when she was 10 years old. A cousin of hers had just been born with slightly atypical genitals. An attentive physician had referred the baby for further investigation. She was diagnosed with 17β-HSD. When Tineke's parents heard about the diagnosis, they wondered whether Tineke might have the same condition. At birth she too had slightly atypical genitals. Because none of the physicians who saw her for checkups seemed to worry about it, they thought that it was probably within normal variations.

Growing up, Tineke appeared to be an overactive child. Her somewhat conservative parents were unhappy about her unladylike behavior. She liked sports, casual clothes, and skating. At school there were no learning problems. There were problems between Tineke and other people, and she had received treatment for this. First she had individual psychotherapy; later, when she was diagnosed with ADHD, she received medication.

When she came to our clinic upon discovery of her condition she was a cute, skinny 10-year-old girl with long hair. She appeared to have an IQ of 113, but there was a large discrepancy between her verbal IQ (95) and performance IQ (132). Her feelings about how she felt as a girl and her gender role were explored, but there was no indication that she was unhappy about being a girl. When she was 13 she came to our clinic again, because there were great problems between her and her parents. Part of the problem was that she started to have boyfriends of whom her parents did not approve.

OTHER CONDITIONS

Various other conditions, such as cloacal exstrophy, idiopathic micropenis, congenital penile agenesis, true hermaphroditism, mixed gonadal dysgenesis, Leydig cell hypoplasia, and vanishing testis syndrome, are associated with ambiguity or malformation of the external genitals. They are not discussed here as the issues are largely the same as in the other groups with genital ambiguity and even less systematic studies have been done among these groups than among the groups discussed earlier. Gender identity differentiation in individuals with genital ambiguity, rare conditions included, is extensively discussed by Zucker (1999).

SUMMARY

In intersex conditions, there are incongruities between one or more steps in the process of sexual differentiation. They may occur in any phase of this process, become manifest at any age, be complete or incomplete, and have an impact on one or more physical sex characteristics as well as on the psychosexual development.

Atypical chromosomal developments occur at the time of fertilization and include a missing sex chromosome (Turner Syndrome), an additional

X chromosome (Klinefelter Syndrome), an additional Y chromosome (XYY individuals), or various forms of mosaicism (coexisting different karyotypes in one individual).

During fetal (intrauterine) development, atypical gonadal structures and functioning may result in an insufficiency or absence of sex hormone secretion. As a result, 46,XY children may have no or not enough testosterone to develop male external genitals. Absence of anti-Müllerian hormone may result in a boy with both male and female gonadal structures.

Intersex children may or may not be born with ambiguous external genitals. The degree of the ambiguity varies widely. Ambiguous genitals are present in some 46,XX children who were exposed prenatally to unusually high levels of androgens or in some 46,XY children with either insufficient exposure to androgens or a genetic defect causing their hormone receptors to be unresponsive to androgens. Enzyme deficiencies may also lead to genital ambiguity.

When, at birth, the external genitals are unambiguous and the child has no additional health problems that warrant closer clinical examination, discrepancies between genital sex, gonadal, hormonal, and chromosomal sex may remain undetected until puberty or even later.

There are several major groups of intersex conditions: (1) chromosomal intersex conditions, (2) female pseudohermaphroditism, (3) male pseudohermaphroditism, and (4) true hermaphroditism. All of them are rather rare, but they pose great challenges to the child, his or her parents, and the health professionals involved. For the first three groups of these conditions, the general aspects, mechanisms, and prevalence are described and the consequences for the development of gender role behavior and gender identity as well as for sexual activity, sexual orientation, and fertility are discussed.

4

ATYPICAL DEVELOPMENT OF GENDER IDENTITY AND GENDER ROLE

As a result of hundreds of developmental psychology studies, our understanding of the process of typical gender development has increased considerably over the past 3 decades. When it comes to deviations from the typical route, however, much remains enigmatic. Empirical work in this field is much more limited, due to the rarity of the various conditions and because, for ethical reasons, certain types of studies cannot be conducted.

Over the years, different terms have been used for individuals with gender problems. This reflects the many diverse views and theories about atypical gender development. We briefly review the most commonly used terms.

SPECIFIC TERMINOLOGY

The term *transsexual* emerged in the professional literature in the work of Hirschfeld in 1923. In his work he did not yet make a distinction between transvestism, effeminate homosexuality, and transsexualism. Only in the late 1940s did the term come to be used in its modern sense: to denote individuals who desired to live (or actually lived) permanently in the social role of the opposite gender and who wanted to undergo sex reassignment (Cauldwell, 1949). This desire for sex reassignment (SR) originates from an experienced discrepancy between one's assigned sex, on the one hand, and one's basic sense of self as a male or female, on the other. In 1973, Fisk proposed the term *gender dysphoria syndrome*. This term encompassed transsexualism as well as other gender identity disorders. *Gender dysphoria* indicates the distress resulting from conflicting gender identity and assigned sex.

In the widely used psychiatric classification system *Diagnostic and Statistic Manual of Mental Disorders III* (*DSM-III*), transsexualism first appeared as a separate diagnosis in 1980 (American Psychiatric Association, 1980). For children, a separate diagnosis, *gender identity disorder of childhood,* was introduced. In addition, there was a diagnosis of *gender identity disorder of adolescence or adulthood, nontranssexual type* for cross-gender-identified individuals who did not pursue SR. The diagnosis *gender identity disorder not otherwise specified* was used for those who did not fulfill criteria for the specific gender identity disorders. In the current *DSM* version, *DSM-IV* (American Psychiatric Association, 1994), only one specific diagnosis, *gender identity disorder*, is included (see Table 4.1). Here, gender identity disorder is viewed as basically one disorder that can develop along different routes and can have various levels of intensity (Bradley et al., 1991). As a consequence, a diagnosis of gender identity disorder no longer implies a specific treatment. This is less the case in the *International Classification of Diseases-10* (*ICD-10*; World Health Organization, 1992). For disorders in the field of gender identity, *ICD-10* provides five diagnoses (see Table 4.2), which makes it easier to base treatment decisions (e.g., whether SR is indicated) on the specific diagnosis (e.g., transsexualism). The larger number of gender identity disorder diagnoses that can be given in the *ICD-10* system also does more justice to the variety of individuals with cross-gender identities that mental health professionals encounter clinically. A disadvantage of the *ICD-10* is that, as in earlier *DSM* versions, it still has different criteria for boys and girls in the diagnosis of gender identity disorder in childhood.

Between the publications of *DSM-III* and *DSM-IV*, the terms *transgenderism* and *transgenderist* have been increasingly used. The terms were proposed by individuals taking a gender identity, gender role, and/or sexual orientation position in between those of sex-typical heterosexual men and women. Now they are also used by transsexuals. In the term, no mention is made of distress or disorder to avoid stigmatization and medicalization of the condition.

CLINICAL PICTURE

Children

In children, first signs of GID may be visible as early as 2 years. Young children may actually state that they are or will later become members of the opposite sex. Recently, a study was published that suggests that children

TABLE 4.1 DSM-IV Diagnostic Criteria for Gender Identity Disorder (American Psychiatric Association, 1994)

A. A strong and persistent cross-gender identification (not merely a desire for any perceived cultural advantages of being the other sex).

In children, the disturbance is manifested by four (or more) of the following:

1. Repeatedly stated desire to be, or insistence that he or she is, the other sex
2. In boys, preference for cross-dressing or simulating female attire; in girls, insistence on wearing only stereotypical masculine clothing
3. Strong and persistent preferences for cross-sex roles in make-believe play or persistent fantasies of being the other sex
4. Intense desire to participate in the stereotypical games and pastimes of the other sex
5. Strong preference for playmates of the other sex

In adolescents and adults, the disturbance is manifested by symptoms such as a stated desire to be the other sex, frequent passing as the other sex, desire to live or be treated as the other sex, or the conviction that he or she has the typical feelings and reactions of the other sex.

B. Persistent discomfort with his or her sex or sense of inappropriateness in the gender role of that sex.

In children, the disturbance is manifested by any of the following:

1. In boys, assertion that his penis or testes are disgusting or will disappear or assertion that it would be better not to have a penis or aversion toward rough-and-tumble play and rejection of male stereotypical toys, games, and activities;
2. In girls, rejection of urinating in a sitting position, assertion that she has or will grow a penis, assertion that she does not want to grow breasts or menstruate, or marked aversion toward normative feminine clothing.

In adolescents and adults, the disturbance is manifested by symptoms such as preoccupation with getting rid of primary and secondary sex characteristics (e.g., request for hormones, surgery, or other procedures to physically alter sexual characteristics to simulate the other sex) or belief that he or she was born the wrong sex.

C. The disturbance is not concurrent with a physical intersex condition.

D. The disturbance causes clinically significant distress or impairment in social, occupational, or other important areas of functioning.

Code based on current age:

302.6 Gender Identity Disorder in Children
302.85 Gender Identity Disorder in Adolescents or Adults

Specify if (for sexually mature individuals):

Sexually Attracted to Males
Sexually Attracted to Females
Sexually Attracted to Both
Sexually Attracted to Neither
302.6 Gender Identity Disorder Not Otherwise Specified

(Continued)

TABLE 4.1 Continued

This category is included for coding disorders in gender identity that are not classifiable as a specific Gender Identity Disorder. Examples include

1. Intersex conditions (e.g., androgen insensitivity syndrome or congenital adrenal hyperplasia) and accompanying gender dysphoria
2. Transient, stress-related cross-dressing behavior
3. Persistent preoccupation with castration or penectomy without a desire to acquire the sex characteristics of the other sex

with GID have a developmental lag with regard to certain aspects of gender learning (Zucker et al., 1999). Young children with GID appeared to be less likely than children without GID to label the sexes correctly. They also made more mistakes when answering questions regarding the stability of gender in time and across situations. So it may be that, at younger ages, children with GID are, more often than other children, cognitively confused about gender. It may also be that these "cognitive errors"' are actually distortions of reality, motivated by a strong wish to be of the opposite sex. Normally intelligent children with GID who are 6 years or older are usually able to identify their own sex, but regularly express a desire to belong to the opposite sex. When children have had negative experiences in reaction to their cross-gender behavior and desires, it is not uncommon for them to cease to talk about their wish to belong to the opposite sex. This does not mean that their feelings about the subject have changed. The continuity of their wish to change sex becomes evident when, after puberty, they actually start pursuing SR.

Parents of boys with GID often report that, from the moment their sons could talk, they insisted on wearing their mothers' clothes and shoes. Cross-dressing typically continues to exist in childhood. In older children it may become less manifest, especially in families that do not allow the boy to wear girls' clothes. However, mothers report that they often find girls' clothes hidden in closets or under beds, though their sons deny that they still use them.

Boys With Gender Identity Disorder

Boys with GID are usually primarily interested in playing with girls' toys, such as Barbie dolls, and they find girls' games and activities (e.g., jumping rope) far more amusing than boys' games and activities (e.g., soccer). Though they may be as interested as other children in active play they dislike rough-and-tumble play. In contrast to boys without GID, they seem to like to quietly play in relatively small groups that consist of girls. When

TABLE 4.2 *ICD-10* Diagnoses for Gender Identity Disorders (F64) (World Health Organization, 1992)

Transsexualism (F64.0) has three criteria:

1. The desire to live and be accepted as a member of the opposite sex, usually accompanied by the wish to make his or her body as congruent as possible with the preferred sex through surgery and hormone treatments
2. The transsexual identity has been present persistently for at least 2 years
3. The disorder is not a symptom of another mental disorder or a genetic, intersex, or chromosomal abnormality

Dual-Role Transvestism (F 64.1) has three criteria:

1. The individual wears clothes of the opposite sex in order to experience temporary membership in the opposite sex
2. There is no sexual motivation for the cross-dressing
3. The individual has no desire for a permanent change to the opposite sex

Gender Identity Disorder of Childhood (F64.2) has separate criteria for girls and for boys.
For girls

1. The individual shows persistent and intense distress about being a girl and has a stated desire to be a boy (not merely a desire for any perceived cultural advantages of being a boy) or insists that she is a boy
2. Either of the following must be present:
   - a. Persistent marked aversion to normative feminine clothing and insistence on wearing stereotypical masculine clothing
   - b. Persistent repudiation of female anatomical structures, as evidenced by at least one of the following:
     - i. An assertion that she has, or will grow, a penis
     - ii. Rejection of urination in a sitting position
     - iii. Assertion that she does not want to grow breasts or menstruate
     - iv. The girl has not yet reached puberty
     - v. The disorder must have been present for at least 6 months

For boys

- i. The individual shows persistent and intense distress about being a boy and has a desire to be a girl or, more rarely, insists that he is a girl
- ii. Either of the following must be present:
  - a. Preoccupation with stereotypic female activities, as shown by a preference for either cross-dressing or simulating female attire or by an intense desire to participate in the games and pastimes of girls and rejection of stereotypical male toys, games, and activities.
  - b. Persistent repudiation of male anatomical structures, as evidenced by at least one of the following repeated assertions:
    - i. That he will grow up to become a woman (not merely in the role)
    - ii. That his penis or testes are disgusting or will disappear
    - iii. That it would be better not to have a penis or testes
    - iv. The boy has not yet reached puberty
    - v. The disorder must have been present for at least 6 months

Other Gender Identity Disorders (F64.8) has no specific criteria
Gender Identity Disorder, Unspecified (F64.9) has no specific criteria

Either of the previous two diagnoses could be used for those with an intersexed condition playing "mother and father" they choose to be the mother if the girls allow them to do so. Their second choice is to be "child" but they avoid playing the father. In fantasy play, they like to take the role of princess or fairy.

Almost all boys with GID have a strong preference for girls as playmates. Especially at younger ages most of them develop real friendships with girls, though some are rejected as a playmate by both boys and girls. When growing up their girlfriends sometimes find it difficult to maintain their friendship with a boy. As femininity in boys is hardly accepted, other boys tend to tease and even bully boys with GID. For these boys being teased increases with age. In our sample of 86 boys with GID under 12, we found a correlation of .38 ($p < .001$) between an item "being teased a lot" on the Child Behavior Checklist, a widely used parent report questionnaire of emotional and behavioral problems of children and age (CBCL; Achenbach & Edelbrock, 1983; Dutch version by Verhulst, Van der Ende, & Koot, 1996). Clearly, effeminate boys run the risk of becoming loners as they grow up. Sometimes cross-gendered boys show feminine body motor behavior or speak with high-pitched voices (Rekers & Morey, 1989). This increases the risk of being teased by other children even when the child tries to conceal his feminine interests.

Boys with GID often express distress about being a boy and having a male body. Some boys actually seem to dislike their genitals. When showering they hide their genitals and pretend to have girls' genitals. More often than not they sit down when urinating, despite their father's urging them to urinate in a standing position. Some boys actually state that they want to cut off their penis or ask parents to bring them to a doctor who will remove their penis. Young boys sometimes believe that their penis will automatically fall off when they grow up and that they will grow breasts like their mothers. Mothers may report feeling uneasy about their sons' interest in their breasts.

We have observed in boys as young as 5 years a "sexual" interest in other boys. One of our patients said he was in love with a boy in his class and wanted to marry him. His mother told us that this boy once came to their home to play. On that occasion, her son had tried to kiss the object of his desire. The boy never came again.

Girls With Gender Identity Disorder

Girls with GID are equally early as boys in behaving in a typical cross-gendered way, but their cross-dressing is less conspicuous and rarely becomes noticeable before they enter school. Instead, parents report that their daughters, from early on, like to wear comfortable clothes and dislike typically feminine clothing and jewelry. When they become older they often insist on having dark-colored "cool" clothes, wear boys' underwear, and refuse to wear anything that could be considered cute. Girls with GID typically wear their hair very short and are regularly mistaken for boys.

Cross-gendered girls are interested in playing with boys' toys such as moving objects (cars and trains) or construction play (e.g., Legos). They love sports, ball games in particular, and rough-and-tumble play. They are often active children who prefer to play outside. When role playing they like to have heroic male roles, such as Batman or Superman. For older elementary school "catching girls" (by boys) is a popular game. Girls with GID invariably choose the side of the boys and catch girls. Boys are the preferred playmates of girls with GID. As in boys without GID, the friendships of girls with GID seem to be more focused on common activities and interests than on sharing of intimacy. When they are good in sports and have pleasant personalities, the girls may actually be quite popular among boys. Cross-gender behavior is more accepted in girls than in boys. As a result girls with GID are less ostracized and teased than boys with GID. We found significant differences between parents of boys and parents of girls in answers that were given in response to the CBCL item "being teased a lot" (Verhulst et al., 1996) ($\chi^2 = 9.86$, $df = 2$, $p < .007$, $N = 112$). Similar differences were also found on a teacher questionnaire, the teacher version of the CBCL (teacher report form or TRF; Verhulst, Van der Ende, & Koot, 1997; $\chi^2 = 7.20$, $df = 2$, $p < .027$, $N = 63$ (N is lower than for the CBCL, as the TRF was introduced in our clinical routine at a later time). In girls, motor behavior is not always clearly masculine. However, some girls try to move in typically boyish ways. Other girls make an effort to speak with a low-pitched voice.

Girls with GID can be very distressed about being a girl and having a female body. Unlike boys, they do not so much dislike their own genitals, but they are preoccupied with having a penis. They often put handkerchiefs or other objects in their underpants to pretend they have a penis. One girl asked her parents: "If I cannot have a real one, buy me an iron one." Even older girls say that they know that they have a female body which cannot change by itself, yet they hope deep in their hearts that, by a miracle, they will grow a penis someday. Whereas boys sit when urinating, girls attempt to urinate in a standing position, for instance, against trees when playing outside in gardens or parks. One girl always sat back to front on the toilet seat, because facing the wall when urinating made her feel more like a "real" boy. The idea that they will have breasts and menstruate when they grow up is usually abhorrent to girls with GID.

VIGNETTE: Gerrit, 7 years old

Gerrit (IQ 110) was referred to our clinic by the family physician, because his parents were concerned about his angry outbursts. They wondered whether his cross-gender interests and behavior were influencing his moods. Gerrit had a brother, who was 3 years older, and a sister, 2 years younger, than he. His parents had a lower-middle-class background.

From the day he could label the sexes, Gerrit had said he was a girl. He loved to use his mother's purses and shoes and often tried (but was not allowed) to dress in his sister's clothes. Lacking a wig, he used towels, pretending they were his "long hair." From kindergarten age onward buying clothes was a source of much conflict between him and his mother. He insisted on having typical feminine clothing such as pink-colored shirts, girls' underwear, or lacquered shoes.

Gerrit always had two or three girlfriends and often played with his sister. With them he played with his numerous Barbie dolls and dress-up apparel and played girls' games (e.g., jumping rope), whereas his toy cars and trains remained untouched. He had an aversion to rough sports such as soccer. At school he was quite popular with the girls, but had no contact with the boys.

Gerrit's mother said that when the boys were bathing, Gerrit regularly pulled his penis between his legs saying that he was just like his sister. This made his brother feel embarrassed. Gerrit had never verbally expressed unhappiness about his genitals, but once "for fun" pretended that he was cutting off his penis with a pair of scissors. He always urinated in a sitting position.

VIGNETTE: Nina, 6 years old

Nina (IQ 87) came to our clinic because her parents wanted to have pedagogical advice. Nina used to tell everybody: "I am Nina and I am a boy." She looked very much like a boy. Her hair was cut very short and she looked and acted "tough." She deliberately spoke with a low voice. Like other girls with GID, she hated to wear dresses. She was very strong-willed and her parents had given up trying to make her look like a girl. They had even allowed her to wear boxer shorts with a fly.

At her first visit to the clinic, it appeared that, at school, when she had her first swimming lessons, some of the children had noticed her underwear and teased her. She subsequently refused to take swimming lessons or participate in school gymnastics. At her soccer club, she was allowed to shower separately as her team members were all boys.

Nina was very fond of her father. He was the coach of her soccer team, took her riding on his motorbike, and let her sometimes accompany him on his work trips as a truck driver. When asked about the future, she said she also wanted to become a truck driver or maybe a policeman. She never wanted to have breasts or babies, because "that's for girls."

Adolescents

Adolescents with extreme forms of GID who come to our gender clinic have usually been children with GID. After elementary school, they try to deal with their gender feelings in many different ways. Some do not make much change in their behavior or appearance and start high school as a clearly cross-gendered child. The parents of these children have witnessed their cross-gender behavior for years. Though they usually expected that their child would become gay or lesbian, the announcement of their child that they want SR does not come as a great surprise. Because of the extremeness and continuity of the cross-gender behavior, some of these parents allow their child to change their social role at very early ages. An increasing number of young adolescents already live completely in the opposite gender role when they enter our clinic. Upon entering high school, such families have made an arrangement with school that the child will have an opposite sex name and will be registered in the "new" sex. When they grow older, some fall in love and have sexual relationships with same-sex peers. There is a wide variability in how they handle such contacts. Sexualized behavior ranges from having crushes at a great distance from the person involved to actual dating and sexual activity. Sexually active youngsters invariably exclude involvement of their primary sex characteristics from their lovemaking.

A second GID group consists of children who try, in high school or even before entering puberty, to adjust to gender-typical norms. They wear gender-neutral or gender-typical clothing and a gender-typical hairstyle and behave as inconspicuously as possible. When it appears that their gender dysphoria does not change, or even increases, some continue to do so until the problem becomes evident in other ways. For instance, a parent may discover the child's gender dysphoria by reading his or her diary. Others then start to show their cross-gender feelings more openly. How fast they make changes in their appearance, how obviously cross- gendered they choose their outfit, and when they tell their parents or others about themselves largely depends on the attitudes of schoolmates, teachers, their family, and their own personalities. In adolescents who fear the consequences of whether their gender problem will become public, gender identity disorder is not always easily observable from behavior or appearance. For sharp observers, however, it will be clear that some preferences, such as opposite-sex friends, interests, and hobbies, are or remain cross-gendered. Parents of children who conceal their gender problem are naturally stunned when they hear about their children's SR wish.

Adolescents who do not fulfill all criteria for GID are a heterogeneous group. Some enter the clinic with an SR request but appear to be ambivalent about it during the diagnostic phase. Some have a strong SR wish during the intake phase, but change their minds when they understand that it might be the wrong solution to their problem (see the vignette for "Gwen"). Others attend the clinic without even having a wish for SR. Instead they are confused about their identity and seek professional advice. A number of them turn out to be ego-dystonic homosexuals. In others still the gender problem seems to be secondary to psychopathology such as pervasive developmental disorder. The adolescents with less extreme GID usually show a mixed pattern of current and past GID symptoms.

If adolescents are sent to a clinic by parents or other adults, they do not come to fulfill their own needs. In that case assessment is much more difficult than when they actually seek help themselves. If they come for themselves, there is less denial of and shame about the gender problem and it is usually not very hard to discuss their thoughts and feelings.

VIGNETTE: Johanna, 16 years old

Johanna applied for SR when she was still in high school. Her father was a computer programmer, her mother a housewife. Johanna had two sisters. The 2-years-older sister was a Dutch language university student; the 3-years-younger one was still in high school. Johanna has always been a quiet, "easy" child. As a child she was not particularly interested in typical girls' activities and objects, but this also applied to her sisters. Her parents therefore were not alarmed by her behavior. She was, however, in contrast to her sisters, fond of soccer and she had several very close male friends. When she went to high school, she became even more quiet than usual and started to make a sad impression on her parents. Her male friends went to other schools. Unlike her sisters, she never dated and became a loner. At school, her grades were still high and there were no obvious signs for her distress.

When, one day, her mother saw her daughter putting on a very tight T-shirt of her sister's to hide her breasts, Johanna's transsexualism became apparent. Although they were shocked, her parents immediately sought help. The family doctor referred her to the gender clinic. Johanna fulfilled all criteria for SR. At age 17 she started using a hormone treatment to stop her menses, and after 4 months testosterone was prescribed. One year later she had breast surgery, and her uterus and ovaries were removed. At 19, her birth certificate was changed. By then, Johanna/Jaap went to university. Three years later he came to the clinic again. He wanted to discuss having a metaidoioplasty (transformation of the hypertrophic clitoris into a micropenis) with a neoscrotum and implanted testicles. He'd had a girlfriend for more than 4 years and they had been living together for 3 years. Jaap wanted the metaidoioplasty to feel more complete as a man. Sexually he and his girlfriend had found noncoital ways to make love. After he had this operation, Jaap graduated from university.

Jaap was interviewed for a follow-up study when he was 26. He said he was satisfied with his life. He was still living with his girlfriend. Because it was difficult to find work as a psychologist he had started a small business.

VIGNETTE: Gwen, 15 years old

Gwen came to our clinic to apply for SR. She was the only child in a family of non-Dutch origin. There were regular contacts with the extended family. Gwen's grandparents frequently visited their daughter and her family and Gwen often slept over at her grandparents' home.

When Gwen was 12 years old, her mother noticed that she became nervous and quiet. At the time Gwen was also refusing to wear feminine clothes, whereas before she wore dresses when she attended church or family parties. According to her parents, she had always been somewhat tomboyish but not in an extreme way. She had had female friends, but had also enjoyed playing with boys. She had never been very preoccupied with boys' games, so it was unclear why she suddenly made a move toward masculinity. Her parents wondered why she seemed to have problems with her developing body.

It took a while before Gwen told her mother that her grandfather was sexually abusing her when he visited her parents' house on his own and her parents were at work. From that moment on her parents refused to let him into their house. However, Gwen's aversion toward her femininity remained. She hoped that living as a man would make her feel better, but psychological assessment revealed a picture of Gwen that was inconsistent with her wish to live as a man. She did not score very gender-dysphoric on a gender dysphoria scale (see Chapter 7) and she did not score high on a body dissatisfaction scale (see Chapter 7). In a series of interviews, she mentioned not having problems seeing herself naked in the mirror. She also thought she would be sexually attracted to heterosexual boys, but never had any sexual experience with boys of her own age. When it was explained to Gwen what SR entailed she became hesitant. An additional problem of Gwen's was her low verbal IQ of 76, which was significantly lower than her performance IQ of 100. This might explain why she remained so preoccupied with a concrete "solution" to her emotional problems and why she did not seem to be bothered with inconsistencies in her history and feelings regarding gender. To overcome her sexual abuse Gwen was referred to a local mental health agency for individual therapy.

CORRESPONDENCE BETWEEN CHILDHOOD GENDER IDENTITY DISORDER AND TRANSSEXUALISM

Not all children with GID turn out to be transsexuals after puberty. Prospective studies of boys with GID (Green, 1987; Money & Russo, 1979; Zucker & Bradley, 1995; Zuger, 1984) show that the first phenomenon is more strongly related to later homosexuality than to later transsexualism. These findings are in accordance with retrospective studies that have shown that male and female homosexuals recall more cross-gendered behavior in childhood than male and female heterosexuals (e.g., Bell, Weinberg, & Hammersmith, 1981; for a review see Bailey & Zucker, 1995).

Zucker and Bradley (1995) describe six North American follow-up studies of boys with GID. Of 99 boys included in these studies, 6% had a transsexual outcome. This is probably an underestimation of the true numbers. The clinicians involved had usually lost contact with their patients over the years. The questions that had to be asked are sensitive and in some studies there was reliance on mothers' reports only. In their own follow-up, Zucker and Bradley (1995) reported that 14% of 45 prepubertal children with GID seen at the Child and Adolescent Gender Clinic of the Clarke Institute of Psychiatry in Toronto later had a wish for SR in adolescence. Cohen-Kettenis (2001) reports on children who were seen at the Child and Adolescent Psychiatry Department of the University Medical Center Utrecht. Of the 129 children who were referred before the age of 12, 74 were over 12 and therefore potential applicants for SR. Of these 74, 17 intensely gender dysphoric adolescents (23%; 8 girls and 9 boys) applied for SR. Their mean age at assessment in childhood was 9 years (range 6–12). Reapplication occurred on average 3 years later (range 0–9 years; the 0 refers to 3 children who already had a strong wish for SR at the first assessment and were still in contact with the clinic when they turned 12). Of the 17 children, 3 adolescents had started cross-sex hormone treatment at the time of publication. Eight adolescents were eligible for using LHRH agonists to prevent further masculinization or feminization, of whom 6 had actually started taking the hormones. One girl delayed the diagnostic procedure after the sudden death of her father, and in 5, eligibility for hormone treatment was likely but not completely certain. Eight of the 17 were living full-time in the cross-gender role, 1 without having started hormone treatment. So the percentage of children with GID who came to the clinic as adolescents wanting SR (23%) appeared to be much higher than the reported percentages in the literature. Due to the fact that many of the 73 adolescents were still very young, it is possible that the final numbers in adulthood will be higher. As most of the follow-up investigations on children with GID do not go beyond young adulthood, we basically have no data yet.

The difference between percentages of SR applications among the Utrecht patients and percentages as mentioned in the literature may be due to the fact that this gender clinic is the only one in a small country. The relatively close distance to the clinic may lower the threshold for parents to seek help once they are convinced that their children's gender identity problem remains or has become more intense. Another difference with most gender clinics is that, in Utrecht, various treatment options are offered. Some adolescents would never have returned to the clinic if they had thought that at the University Medical Center Utrecht only psychotherapy would be offered. Instead they would have waited until they were old enough to apply for SR in an adult clinic.

Still it should be noted that most children with gender identity disorder do not become transsexuals. Various explanations have been given for this outcome. It may be because gender identity disorders are more mixed in childhood, with respect to severity, than in adulthood. In that case, only the extremely cross-gendered cases would become transsexuals, whereas the mild cases would become homo- or heterosexuals. It is also possible that children with GID who had been psychotherapeutically treated in childhood were less likely to develop a wish for SR. However, no treatment intervention studies with long-term follow-ups exist that support this explanation. A last explanation is that parents of future transsexuals do not seek professional help when their children are still young, so mental health professionals would mainly see the "nontranssexual" children with GID. If this is true, it is not clear why mostly parents of pretranssexuals avoid seeking help. Though we can imagine that parents feel uncomfortable about their child's behavior and deny it or hope that it will disappear by itself, it is unclear why this would primarily be the case in the pretranssexual group.

PREVALENCE AND SEX RATIO OF GENDER IDENTITY DISORDER

There are no epidemiological studies providing data on the prevalence of childhood GID, so estimations of this prevalence come from indirect sources. Because it has been found retrospectively (Bell et al., 1981; Bailey & Zucker, 1995) that a high number of homosexual men and women recall childhood cross-gender behavior, the prevalence of homosexuality may give an indication of GID prevalence in childhood. According to Sandfort (1998), this would be 2–6% for men and 2% for women. As the correlation between childhood GID and homosexuality is not 1, these estimations cannot be very precise.

Cross-gender behavior has been investigated in a few studies. In one study among nonclinical preschool children (Fagot, 1977), cross-gender behavior was found in 6.6% of 106 boys and 4.9% of 101 girls. These children obtained preference scores for opposite-sex activities that were at least 1 standard deviation above the mean of the opposite sex and preference scores for same-sex activities that were at least 1 standard deviation below the mean of their own sex. The CBCL includes two items referring to cross-gender behavior and identification (item 5: "behaves like opposite sex"; and item 110: "wishes to be of opposite sex"). In their standardization study in the United States, Achenbach and Edelbrock (1981) found that 6% of parents of 4- to 5-year-old nonreferred boys endorsed item 5, whereas 0.7% of parents of 12- to 13-year-old boys did. The percentages of the age groups between 5 and 12 years were in between 6 and 0.7%. For girls, the range was 11.8% in 4- to 5-year-olds to 12.9% in 12- to 13-year-olds. In a Dutch normative sample of girls and boys, ages 4–11 years, the percentages were 2.6% for the boys and 5.0% for the girls (Verhulst et al., 1996). The percentages for item 110 were much lower: In the U.S. sample, only 1.3% of the parents of 4- to 5-year-old boys reported that their son wished to be of the opposite sex. This percentage was 0% for the 12- to 13-year-old boys. For girls, the percentages were 5% in the 4- to 5-year-olds to 2.7% in the 12- to 13-year-olds. In the Dutch 4- to 11-year-olds the percentages were 1.4% for the boys and 2.0% for the girls. In another Dutch study among 648 mothers of 0- to 12-year-old children, 8% of the mothers reported that their daughters played with boys' toys and 3% of the mothers reported that their sons played with girls' toys. They also reported that 19% of the boys and 21% of the girls pretended to be members of the opposite sex at least occasionally while playing. Ten percent of the mothers of both boys and girls report that their children said at least occasionally that they wanted to be a member of the opposite sex (Cohen-Kettenis & Sandfort, 1996). So, although certain low percentages of cross-gender behavior are found in nonclinical samples, it is unlikely that all these children are fulfilling the criteria for GID. The answers that parents gave on CBCL item 110 are probably closer to actual prevalence of GID than their answers to CBCL item 5, but exact information on prevalence rates will only become available once proper epidemiological studies have been carried out.

Prevalence estimates of transsexualism among adolescents and adults (that is 15 years and above) are usually based on the number of transsexuals, treated at major centers, or on responses of registered psychiatrists to surveys concerning their number of transsexual patients within a particular country or region. The numbers vary widely across studies. In the first years of transsexual treatment, prevalences were reported in the 1:100,000 (males) and 1:400,000 (females) range (Pauly, 1968). Later studies indicate higher prevalences: in the Netherlands about 1:10,000 (males) and 1:30,000 (females) (Bakker, van Kesteren, Gooren, & Bezemer, 1993) and in Scotland about 1:12,000 (Wilson, Sharp, & Carr, 1999). The highest prevalence was reported in Singapore with about 1:3,000 in males and 1:8,000 in females (Tsoi, 1988). In both the Netherlands and Singapore, earlier studies also reported a lower prevalence (Eklund, Gooren, & Bezemer, 1988; Tsoi, Kok, & Long, 1977). The lower numbers in the early studies may reflect the relative inaccessibility of SR in the 1960s and 1970s or the social stigma of transsexuals preventing individuals from seeking SR, but they may also be explained by differences in methodology. For instance, in former West Germany, estimations were not based on numbers of patients who had undergone SR within the country, but on approved legal applications between 1981 and 1990 (Weitze & Osburg, 1998). Their actual numbers, about 1:40,000 for males and 1:100,000 for females, are in between very low and very high numbers that were based on patients seen in treatment centers and might be a better indication of the true numbers than the data from clinics.

In most studies, transsexualism is more common in men than in women. Usually a 3:1 ratio is reported (see Landèn, Wålinder, & Lundström, 1996, for a review). Landèn et al. (1996) attribute this to the fact that studies probably differ in the number of subtypes of MFs that are included in the various studies (for a discussion of subtypes see below). Exceptions to the 3:1 sex ratio in adults have been found in studies on transsexualism in Poland and former Czechoslovakia, before the downfall of communism. Here, sex ratios of 5 females to 1 male were reported (Brzek & Sipova, 1983; Godlewski, 1988). To establish whether cultural factors have influenced this ratio it would be interesting to know how the numbers have changed over the past decade. However, thus far such studies have not yet been conducted.

The majority of the prepubertal children attending gender clinics are boys. The boy-to-girl ratios are 5.75:1 in Canada ($N = 358$), 2.93:1 in the Netherlands ($N = 130$, Cohen-Kettenis, Owen, Bradley, Kaijser, & Zucker, in press), and 3.81:1 in the UK ($N = 53$, Di Ceglie, Freedman, McPherson, & Richardson, 2002). The sex ratio of adolescents at the three gender clinics, however, approaches a 1:1 relationship (boys to girls: 1.2:1, $N = 133$, clinical data of the Utrecht gender clinic; 1.4: 1, $N = 43$, Zucker & Bradley, 1995; 1.4: 1, $N = 69$, Di Ceglie et al., 2002). It might be that a small but equal number of the boys and girls with GID who were seen in childhood apply for SR relatively early in life. The fact that sex ratios again substantially depart from 1:1 in adulthood may be due to a higher number of boys than girls with GID applying for SR in adulthood.

THEORIES ABOUT ATYPICAL GENDER DEVELOPMENT

Subtypes of Gender Identity Disorders: Relevance for Theories on Atypical Gender Development

Gender identity disorder in adulthood is not a homogeneous phenomenon. As early as 1918, Hirschfeld distinguished five types of habitual or persistent cross-dressers. He estimated that 35% of cross-dressers are homosexual, 15% are bisexual, and 35% are heterosexual. [Although it is confusing and therefore unfortunate, in much of the scientific literature on transsexuals, the terms *homosexual* and *heterosexual* are applied to transsexuals exactly as they are to individuals *without gender dysphoria* – to refer to erotic attraction to members of the same or the opposite (chromosomal) sex, respectively.] Hirschfeld thought the remaining 15% included some asexual cases, but consisted mostly of *automonosexuals* (men who are erotically aroused by the thought or image of themselves as women). Later, several authors identified and classified different types of initially only male gender dysphorics and arrived at similar distinctions (Bentler, 1976; Buhrich & McConaghy, 1978; Freund, Steiner, & Chan, 1982; Hamburger, 1953; Leavitt & Berger, 1990; Money & Gaskin, 1970-1971; Person & Ovesey, 1974a, 1974b; Randell, 1959; Wålinder, 1967). Although these authors may have differed in the number of subtypes or in the percentages each of their subtypes consisted of, they identified and labeled a homosexual type more consistently than any other category of cross-gendered male.

Blanchard (1985, 1988, 1989) made a distinction between various subtypes of nonhomosexual transsexuals and homosexual transsexuals and actually investigated similarities and differences between the groups. He concluded that the nonhomosexual subtypes are more similar to each other than any of them are to the homosexual type. He suggested that the main types of nonhomosexual gender dysphoria are variant forms of a single underlying disturbance: *autogynephilia*. The characteristic feature of autogynephilia is the tendency to be sexually aroused by the thought of being a woman, often reported as erotic arousal in association with cross-dressing.

Homosexual and (all subtypes of) nonhomosexual male transsexuals appeared to differ in their reports of erotic arousal while being cross-dressed. Only a minority of the homosexuals reported a history of such erotic arousal, whereas a majority of the nonhomosexual groups acknowledged such a history. Furthermore, the homosexual groups were younger at initial presentation, reported more feminine identification, and were less likely to report sexual stimulation by cross-gender fantasy (the thought or image of themselves as women) than the nonhomosexual group (Blanchard, 1985, 1988, 1989). Leavitt and Berger (1990) found another difference between their probably comparable subtypes of male transsexuals. Their two sexually active groups (one whose members did and another whose members did not use their penis during sexual activity) displayed more masculinity in their development and more evidence of emotional disturbance than a group that was abstinent from sexual activity (called the "nuclear" group). With respect to outcome of SR homosexuals were less likely to regret SR than nonhomosexuals (Blanchard, Steiner, Clemmensen, & Dickey, 1989). There were also differences between the groups in height and weight. The homosexual MFs were shorter, lighter, and lighter in proportion to their height than nonhomosexual MFs and also shorter than men in the general population, which might be related to differences in timing of puberty between the groups (Blanchard, Dickey, & Jones, 1995). In only one study were homosexual and nonhomosexual FMs compared on a number of variables (Chivers & Bailey, 2000). Compared to nonhomosexual FMs, homosexual FMs reported greater childhood gender nonconformity, preferred more feminine partners, experienced greater sexual rather than emotional jealousy, were more sexually assertive, had more sexual partners, had a greater desire for phalloplasty, and had more interest in visual sexual stimuli. In a recent study, most of these findings were confirmed and extended in a large sample ($N = 187$) of both MFs and FMs (Smith, 2002). Homosexual transsexuals reported more childhood gender nonconformity and were younger when applying for SR. A lower percentage of homosexual than of nonhomosexual transsexuals reported being or having been married and (a history of) sexual arousal while cross-dressing. Moreover, they had an appearance that was already more compatible with the desired sex and they functioned better psychologically than nonhomosexual transsexuals. However, at follow-up, many of the pretest differences in psychological functioning had disappeared.

These findings indeed seem to indicate that there are at least two subtypes of transsexuals who follow different developmental routes. One group has been extremely cross-gendered from early in life, never had any sexual interest in cross-dressing, is attracted to same-sex partners, and pursues SR relatively early in life. The other group has been more stereotypical with regard to gender role behaviors as a child, is (or used to be) sexually aroused when cross-dressing, and is attracted to the opposite sex. This group applies for SR after having tried to live much longer in the social role of their biological sex, for instance, by marrying. Psychologically they are significantly less stable than the first group, perhaps as a consequence of their living in this role or perhaps because of other factors.

In the Smith (2002) study, the patterns of differences between homosexual and nonhomosexual transsexuals were not entirely similar for male-to-females (MFs) and female-to-males (FMs). Sex differences were also observed in earlier studies. Most of the differences indicated a more favorable development in FMs. For instance, they more often had close ties to their parents and siblings, established stable partnerships more frequently solely with the same biological sex, and were more satisfied with their lives. When they first consulted a physician about sex change, they were already more integrated socially and sexually (Fleming, MacGowan, & Costos, 1985; Kockott & Fahrner, 1988; Steiner & Bernstein, 1981). Female-to-males were younger when applying for SR than MFs and less often had a history of marriage and children than their MF counterparts (Landèn, Wålinder, & Lundström, 1998; Smith, 2002). Female-to-males also had less sexual experience with opposite sex partners and more frequently exhibited cross-gender behavior in childhood than did MF transsexuals. Finally, FMs seemed to function better psychologically not only before but also after treatment (Pfäfflin & Junge, 1992, 1998; but see Bodlund, Kullgren, Sundblom, & Höjerback, 1993). As in most studies, no distinction has been made between homosexual and nonhomosexual FMs, it is as yet hard to tell whether these differences point to different etiologies or are a reflection of the fact that most FMs belong to the homosexual group (Coleman, Bockting, & Gooren, 1993; Kuiper, 1991).

Like adults, children also vary in type and intensity of cross-genderedness (see also Chapter 6). Most children with GID do not become transsexual, but a substantial minority do. So one would expect that children with GID could be classified into at least two subgroups: prehomosexual and pretranssexual children with GID. The problem is that it is not yet possible to predict which children will and which will not become transsexuals. It is even less clear which children with GID will develop gender problems other than transsexualism. And to complicate things further, from the above it might be clear that not all adult transsexuals (e.g., heterosexual transsexuals) have been children with a full-blown GID (see Table 4.3).

The available theories and supporting evidence thus refer to subgroups who developed a variety of gender identity disorders. From our discussion of this literature, it will be evident that theorists and researchers usually have experience with one age group. The work we discuss on children

TABLE 4.3 Subtypes of Gender Identity Disorders

1a. Child with GID	→	2a. Homosexual adult
1b. Child with GID	→	**2b. Homosexual transssexual (GID) adult**
1c. Child with GID	→	2c. Transgendered, but not transsexual adult
1d. Child with GID	→	2d. Heterosexual adult
1e. Child without (complete) GID	→	**2e. Nonhomosexual transsexual (GID) adult**
1f. Child without (complete) GID	→	2f. Transgendered, but not transsexual adult

will probably largely refer to groups 1a and 1b in Table 4.3, as most of the children with GID will belong to groups 2a and 2b in adulthood (although very little is as yet known about groups 2c and 2d). When we discuss the work on adults we largely refer to groups 2b and 2e.

The factors that have been put forward to explain atypical gender development have not always been embedded in a broader theoretical framework. In some cases, one single factor was seen as the primary cause of cross-gender development; in other cases multiple factors are included.

Psychological Theories

In the older literature on transsexualism in (mostly male) adults, the phenomenon has been described as a perversion (Volkan & Berent, 1976), a condition closely related to paranoid schizophrenia (Siomopoulos, 1974), a defense against homosexuality (Socarides, 1970), an extreme conflict-free closeness to the mother ("blissful symbiosis"; Stoller, 1968), a narcissistic disorder (Chiland, 1988), a defense against separation anxiety (Person & Ovesey, 1974a, 1974b), and so on. Most of these notions were based on single case studies or reports on extremely small groups and have never been empirically tested.

In the (clinical) literature on children (boys) with GID, certain parental characteristics, such as a maternal wish for a daughter or paternal absence, have been considered to be the primary or even the single factor in GID development (e.g., Charatan & Galef, 1965). Such parental characteristics would give the children insufficient possibilities to identify with the same-sex parent and/or expose them to cross-gender reinforcement patterns. Some of these hypotheses have been tested, but either no support for the hypotheses was found or the interpretation of the outcome was problematic. For instance, the wish for a daughter was found in only 26% of 52 mothers of feminine boys. This was not statistically different from the 19% of mothers of a control group (Roberts, Green, Williams, & Goodman, 1987).

In a sample of 103 boys with gender identity disorder, a much higher percentage was found (43%), but unfortunately for this group no comparison group was available. Such a wish appeared to be associated more with characteristics of the sibship (daughters were hoped for by mothers who had only or mostly elder sons) than with boyhood femininity per se (Zucker et al., 1994). Paternal (emotional) distance from their cross-gendered sons, as measured by recalled shared father/son time, was found by Green (1987). However, this characteristic could be a cause as well as a consequence of the feminine development of the boy. The idea that cross-gender reinforcement patterns will direct gender identity and gender role in atypical ways seemed to be supported by the findings of Roberts et al. (1987) showing that parents' recalled reactions to their son's initial feminine behaviors ranged from neutral to positive. But Zucker and Green (1992) rightly emphasize that in the normal population parents will rarely be confronted with extreme cross-gender behavior. It is therefore hard to know whether they would react differently from parents of children with GID.

Green's theory (1974) combined several parental and child-related factors. He expected that the mothers' strong wish for a daughter was a possible motivating force behind their reinforcement patterns (Green, 1987). He considered their reinforcement and lack of discouragement of their sons' feminine behaviors as both causing and perpetuating the gender problem. The appearance of the children may also trigger feelings and behavior in parents that that affect the child's gender development. The clinical observation that boys with GID are very attractive (Stoller, 1968) was supported in clinical and experimental studies among boys (Green, 1987; Zucker, Wild, Bradley, & Lowry, 1993), whereas the opposite was found for girls with GID (Fridell, Zucker, Bradley, & Maing, 1996). College students who were blind to the clinical condition of pictured children rated boys with gender identity disorder as more "attractive," "beautiful," "handsome," and "pretty" than control boys. They were also judged as "less all-boy," "masculine," and "rugged," whereas girls with GID were judged to look "more handsome," "masculine," "rugged," and "tomboyish" than control girls (McDermid, Zucker, Bradley, & Maing. 1998). Although the preferences of children with GID for certain hairstyles and clothing may have been responsible for this finding, morphological features of the face may also have accounted for the findings. Green (1987) found that mothers retrospectively described their GID sons as more beautiful and feminine than mothers of control boys. So it is conceivable that the children's physical (facial) traits, from early on, have contributed to atypical gender role reinforcement patterns on the part of their parents. However, it remains very unlikely that even the factors that have been found to differ between children with and without GID will by themselves be sufficient to induce a GID. Therefore, some theories have been developed proposing that a combination of these with other factors results in a cross-gender identity in children.

Biopsychological Theories

Since the early 1990s, two fairly comprehensive theories have been formulated that have given a new impetus toward etiological research in the field (Coates, 1990; Zucker & Bradley, 1995). Coates's theory (1990) about cross-gender development includes multiple cumulative risk factors. She states that various factors must converge during a critical period of development. Some children are vulnerable to developing GID because of their temperament. She describes six temperamental factors that occur frequently in her clinical sample of boys. These are (Coates, 1990, pp. 427-428)

- A sense of body fragility that expresses itself in avoidance of rough-and-tumble play
- Anxiety that expresses itself as timidity and fearfulness
- A vulnerability to separation and loss
- An unusual capacity for positive emotional connection to others
- An unusual ability to imitate
- Sensory sensitivities to sound, color, texture, odor, temperature, and pain

Coates states that this temperament is further shaped by the fact that the boys, for various reasons, primarily play with girls in their preschool years. As a result they have little or no experience with other boys, which interferes with their development of masculine play skills, such as throwing a ball or rough-and-tumble play. According to Coates (1990), many GID mothers have experienced a situation of chronic family dysfunction or a traumatic experience in the first 3 years of life of the child (e.g., death or severe illness in the family). Mothers' resulting *state* psychopathology (e.g., affect disorders), their *trait* psychopathology (borderline, narcissistic, or dependent personality disorders), or both predispose the child to chronic separation anxiety and depression. Boys will develop cross-gender symptoms as a defense against their separation anxiety. They try to overcome the feared loss of mother by having reparative fantasies of self-fusion with their mothers and think that "having Mommy" is similar to "being Mommy."

Coates indeed found, in two consecutive samples of boys with gender identity disorder, high rates of trauma (e.g., family violence) experienced by the mothers during the child's first 3 years of life (45 and 78% respectively) (Coates, 1985; Coates, Friedman, & Wolfe, 1991). According to the mothers, these traumata usually coincided with the first intense cross-gender behaviors in the child. This firmly supported her idea that trauma induces maternal emotional absence, thus creating separation anxiety, the primary predisposing condition of GID in the boys. One should bear in mind, however, that such high percentages of trauma are thus far only reported in clinical populations from one center, located in a primarily low socioeconomic neighborhood. It is likely that the high percentages of disrupted family situations were a reflection of the numbers in this area and were not necessarily linked to the children's gender problems. Coates's findings certainly require corroboration from other centers.

Zucker and Bradley (1995) have integrated several aspects of the above ideas into a broader theory. In their view, the "anxiety about self-value or self-worth" is a core component of GID development. Because of this anxiety, cross-gender identification stands for an identification of being the opposite sex as more secure, safe, or valued. Cross-gender identification does not necessarily mean identification with the opposite-sex parent, as is stated in Coates's theory. According to Zucker and Bradley (1995), two conditions have to be fulfilled to develop the feeling that being the other sex is more secure or safe. First, children need to be in so much emotional distress that they must seek a solution to survive. This distress may be produced by general factors related to the child's temperament, parental characteristics, or both. Next, during a sensitive developmental period (i.e., when the child is developing a coherent sense of self), specific factors create a situation in which the resulting anxiety induces cross-gender behavior.

One general predisposing factor is a constitutional vulnerability to high arousal in stressful situations. According to Zucker and Bradley (1995) these children have more difficulties with affect regulation, especially within the context of an insecure mother/child relationship. Another general factor is parental difficulty with affect regulation, which may also be constitutionally based. These difficulties may interfere with a secure attachment of the child, effective problem-solving between parents, and parental limit-setting. Poor setting of limits leads to a lack of discouragement of cross-gender behaviors and an increase in oppositional behaviors. In this way, parent/child relationships that were already problematic as a result of the earlier attachment problems deteriorate further. It also allows the child to indulge in fantasies of being the opposite sex and thereby reinforces the child's cross-gender interests and behavior.

Zucker and Bradley (1995) consider avoidance of rough-and-tumble play in boys and a preference for sports and rough-and-tumble play in girls to be a specific factor contributing to children's GID. Also, the boys' feminine appearance and the girls' masculine appearance facilitate the adoption of cross-gender behavior in the children and shape the parents' responses. Two examples of specific maternal factors are a fear of male aggression and an intense need for nurturance. Typical paternal behaviors that would contribute to boys' GID development are acceptance of mother's tolerance of their son's cross-gender behavior and inadequacy feelings. According to Zucker and Bradley, the mother's fear of aggression leads to discouragement of male-typical behavior in sons while their need for nurturance results in unconscious encouragement of their son's nurturing qualities (which these mothers equate with femaleness). The fathers' qualities make it difficult for them to connect with their sons and they distance themselves from the family. Zucker and Bradley believe that fathers of girls with GID view females as less adequate and encourage masculinity in their daughters. They may also be overly aggressive or abusive, which creates fantasies in the girls that they have to protect their mothers and an identification with the aggressor.

Thus, in Zucker and Bradley's theory, a cross-gender identity may be reached through different pathways, and a broad range of factors may contribute to the disorder. Because there is also individual variation in vulnerability, in exposure to and impact of certain risk factors, the ultimate outcome may vary widely.

Some support has been found for a role in GID development of the factors that are considered crucial by Zucker and Bradley. In a few studies, evidence of elevated psychopathology in *parents* of gender-disordered boys was found. Relatively high rates of parental contact (80% of the mothers, 45% of the fathers) with mental health professionals, which could be taken as an indication of psychological or marital problems, were reported by Rekers, Mead, Rosen, and Brigham (1983). In this study it was also found that fewer male role models were living in the environment of boys with more extreme cross-identification as compared with the mild-to-moderate cross-gender identified boys. This finding may be interpreted in two ways. Though, in Zucker and Bradley's terms, all the boys had sought "cross-gender solutions," the absence of role models may have led to less limit setting in the most extreme group. The finding may also reflect that parents of the more extremely cross-gendered children had more problematic personalities and therefore more problems with staying in an enduring relationship. Wolfe (1990) reported that of 12 fathers of children with GID, all received an Axis I diagnosis for either a current or past diagnosis on the Structured Clinical Interview for *DSM-III* and 8 of them also received an Axis II diagnosis. Unfortunately, Wolfe had no control group.

Marantz and Coates (1991) found that the mothers of boys with GID showed more psychopathology. As compared to none of 17 normal control mothers, 25% (4 of 16 mothers) met the criteria of the Diagnostic Interview for Borderline Patients for borderline personality disorder, but this high percentage was not found by Zucker and Bradley (1995). Using the Structural Clinical Interview for *DSM-III*, Wolfe (1990) found that of 11 GID mothers all had at least one psychiatric disorder. No borderline personality disorder was found among the mothers. Zucker and Bradley, however, did find problems in social adaptation and affect regulation, which are aspects of the borderline configuration. Both Zucker and Bradley's and Wolfe's samples were from a higher social class background than the Marantz and Coates sample, which may have accounted for the differences in outcome. Marantz and Coates (1991) and Wolfe (1990) state that the mother's emotional unavailability may lead to anxiety and thus cross-gender identification in their sons. Though emotional unavailability alone does not seem to be a sufficient condition for the development of GID, the anxiety it creates may lead to the "solution seeking" of the child that Zucker and Bradley refer to.

To test the idea that emotionally preoccupied mothers are less able to limit their sons' cross-gender behavior, Zucker and Bradley (1995) related a composite measure of maternal psychopathology to maternal ratings of reinforcement of sex-typed behavior. They found that maternal psychopathology was more strongly related to the tolerance or encouragement of feminine behaviors and less strongly to the encouragement of masculine behaviors. These findings suggest that (certain types of) psychopathology of mothers influences the cross-gender development of sons by their lessened capacity to set limits.

In both Coates's and Zucker and Bradley's theories, an anxious temperament of the *child* is put forward as an element that makes the child constitutionally vulnerable to developing GID. When boys with GID were compared with controls they showed, on average, behavioral problems that were comparable in degree to those of demographically matched clinical control boys and higher than those of same-sex siblings and nonreferred controls (Bates, Bentler, & Thompson, 1979; Coates & Person, 1985; Zucker & Bradley, 1995). Zucker and Bradley (1995) also found that girls with GID had more general behavioral problems than same-sex siblings. Regarding patterns of behavioral problems, a large group of Canadian and

Dutch children with GID ($N = 488$) had a predominance of internalizing, as opposed to externalizing, behavioral difficulties, as measured by the CBCL (Achenbach & Edelbrock, 1983; Verhulst et al., 1996; Cohen-Kettenis et al., in press). The study was based on parent reports and supported the idea that children with GID have more internalizing problems (anxious and depressed) than controls. The data, however, do not make clear whether their internalizing behavior at home corresponds with physical response patterns under conditions of stress.

To test whether children with GID are actually vulnerable to high arousal patterns in stressful situations, they were stressed under experimental conditions (Cohen-Kettenis, van Goozen, & Snoek, 2000). Interpersonal stress was induced using a method involving frustration, provocation, and aggression in a general setting of competition between the real subject and a videotaped opponent of similar age and sex who competed for best performance over the session. Frustration was induced by asking the child to solve an unsolvable task under time pressure, while the opponent was watching the performance. Provocation was standardized by using the prerecorded videotape of the competitor. This competitor criticized the performance of the subject in a derogatory way. At the end, some questionnaires were completed. Cortisol, saliva, and heart rate were measured. It appeared that with the exception of their skin conductance levels, children with GID did not react in a typically anxious way with regard to physical correlates of anxiousness, physical responses to interpersonal stress, and self-reported emotion under stress. So, despite the repeated finding of internalizing problems as reported by parents, anxious reaction patterns do not seem to be present on all levels of functioning in children with GID.

Biological Theories

Organizational Effects of Sex Hormones

Hormones that are produced by the gonads affect behavior in two possible ways. One is that they act on the nervous system and trigger certain behavior patterns. These effects are not permanent and are referred to as activational effects. In men, transsexualism has been associated with a deficiency of circulating "male" hormones and an excess of "female" hormones and vice versa for women. When techniques of hormone determination became available such associations were investigated, but no convincing evidence exists that peripheral sex steroids play a role in the development of transsexualism.

Hormones may also affect behavior as a result of the process of sexual differentiation, of becoming male or female. This process refers not only to the formation of the internal and external genitals. The brain too undergoes a differentiation into male or female. Pre- or perinatal exposure of the brain to sex hormones leads to more permanent changes in the development of the nervous system and therefore behavior. These effects are referred to as organizational effects. A supposed discrepancy between genital differentiation on the one hand and brain sexual differentiation on the other has been invoked as an explanation for the most extreme form of GID, transsexualism.

To test the assumption that prenatal sex hormones have an influence on the development of transsexualism, biomedical research on transsexualism has addressed the areas we describe below. Though similar work has also been done on adult homosexuals, we do not report the results of these studies here. Overviews of biological research on homosexuality have been published elsewhere (e.g., Ellis & Ebertz, 1997; Gooren, 1988; Zucker & Bradley, 1995).

Individuals With Abnormal Prenatal Endocrine History. Genetic females exposed to abnormally high levels of testosterone (as in girls with CAH; see Chapter 3) would be expected to develop a male gender identity, even if they had been raised as girls, if androgens were a decisive factor in the formation of gender identity. A few of such cases have been reported (Meyer-Bahlburg et al., 1996). As Meyer-Bahlburg (1993) pointed out, individuals with sexual differentiation disorders may be at risk for gender problems (e.g., because of genital ambiguity or social reactions to this ambiguity). In most cases, however, CAH girls who were assigned and consistently raised as girls do not become transsexuals. This also seems to be the case for partial androgen-insensitive individuals who were raised as girls (Collaer & Hines, 1995; Zucker, 1999). A wish to live in the role of the opposite sex has rarely been observed in men and women exposed in utero to compounds which have (de-)masculinizing or feminizing properties (Collaer & Hines, 1995), although Dessens et al. (1999) found three transsexuals in a sample of 243 men and women exposed to maternal antiepileptic medication during pregnancy. Given the rarity of transsexualism, this is a remarkably high rate. Also, in many of the studies, some aspects of gender role behavior have been found to be atypical (see Chapter 3).

The Neuroendocrine Regulation of Luteinizing Hormone. In the second type of studies, it has been assumed that in humans, just as in lower mammals, the neuroendocrine regulation of luteinizing hormone (LH) is a reliable indicator of the sexual differentiation of the brain. Based on this assumption, it was postulated that MFs, like females, would show a rise in LH levels after estrogen stimulation (estrogen positive feedback effect) as a consequence of prenatal exposure to imbalanced sex steroid levels. The opposite was expected to occur in FMs. This hypothesis was based on animal research and supported in two other studies (Dörner, Rohde, Seidel, Haas, & Schott, 1976; Seyler, Canalis, Spare, & Reichlin, 1978). In other studies, however (Goodman et al., 1985; Spijkstra, Spinder, & Gooren, 1988; Spinder, Spijkstra, Gooren, & Burger, 1989; Wiesen & Futterweit, 1983), the results could not be replicated. One study by Dörner, Rohde, Schott, and Schnabl (1983) suggests that among transsexuals the estrogen positive feedback effect that was reported in some studies was more related to sexual orientation than to transsexualism. In this study, the phenomenon was found in transsexuals attracted to sexual partners of the same biological sex, but not in transsexuals attracted to opposite biological sex partners. Because the response had also been encountered among nontranssexual homosexuals, it seems to be associated with sexual orientation rather than with transsexualism. Whether the finding actually refers to prenatal brain sexual differentiation remains to be seen. Gooren (1986) demonstrated that MF transsexuals showed the estrogen positive feedback effect not before but only after estrogen treatment (when testosterone levels are depressed). He therefore questioned the idea that the neuroendocrine regulation of LH secretion is a reliable indicator of the sexual differentiation of the brain. In his study the earlier finding of an estrogen positive feedback effect in homosexuals was not corroborated.

Sexually Dimorphic Brain Nuclei. A third line of research on biological determinants of GID is reflected in studies on sexually dimorphic brain nuclei in transsexuals. In lower animals, the presence or absence of testosterone at the time of a critical period of brain sexual differentiation appeared to influence the morphology of certain brain nuclei (Breedlove, 1994). In humans, a number of hypothalamic nuclei have been reported to be sexually dimorphic with respect to size and/or shape (for an overview see Gorski, 2000; see also Table 4.4). These sex differences in the hypothalamus are thought to underlie sex differences in gender identity, reproduction, and sexual orientation. It has been found in six MFs that the central part of the bed nucleus of the stria terminalis (BSTc) was not only significantly smaller (based on the number of neurons) than in males but also completely in the size range of females. The opposite was found for an FM (Kruijver et al., 2000; Zhou, Hofman, Gooren, & Swaab, 1995). Nontranssexual males who

TABLE 4.4 Putative Structural Sex Differences in the Human Central Nervous System

Larger in the male than in the female

- Central component of the bed nucleus of the stria terminalis
- Darkly staining component of the bed nucleus of the stria terminalis
- Second interstitial nucleus of the anterior hypothalamus
- Third interstitial nucleus of the anterior hypothalamus
- Sexually dimorphic nucleus of the preoptic area
- Onuf's nucleus in the spinal cord

Larger in the female than in the male

- Anterior commissure (midsagittal area)
- Corpus callosum (midsagittal area)
- Isthmus of the corpus callosum (compared only with that of consistently right-handed men)
- Mass intermedia (incidence and midsagittal surface area)

Greater asymmetry in the male

- Planum temporale

Shape differences

- Splenium of the corpus callosum (more bulbous in females)
- Suprachiasmatic nucleus (elongated in females, more spherical in males)

SOURCE: Gorski (2000). In Kandel, Schwartz, & Jessell (Eds.), (2000). *Principles of Neural Science.* Reprinted with permission of McGraw-Hill. ©2000.

had taken estrogens for medical reasons did not show the smaller BSTc, making it unlikely that the size differences had been caused by the transsexuals' hormone treatment. In animals, the BSTc is known as a hormone-regulated structure. In the human thus far no direct evidence exists of a direct relationship between sex hormones and the sex dimorphism of the nucleus.

Sex-Related Cognitive Abilities, Functional Cerebral Asymmetry, and Handedness. A fourth line of research concerns sex-related cognitive functioning, functional cerebral asymmetry, and handedness in individuals with gender identity disorder. It has been fairly well established that sex differences exist in these areas, be it that the differences in functional asymmetry are fairly modest (Bryden, 1988; Harris, 1992; Hiscock, Inch, Jacek, Hiscock-Kalil, & Kalil, 1994). In general, men tend to process verbal stimuli in a more lateralized way than women do and show a weaker right-hand preference. With respect to specific cognitive functions, it has been found that women tend to outperform men on particular verbal tasks, whereas men tend to outperform women on certain visual-spatial tasks (e.g., Halpern, 1992; Linn & Peterson, 1985). There is evidence for a relationship between prenatal hormonal influences, on the one hand, and functional cerebral asymmetry, sex-related cognitive abilities, and handedness, on the other. This comes from pre- and postpubertal clinical samples, such as women suffering from congenital adrenal hyperplasia, and from studies in normal children (for a review: see Collaer & Hines, 1995). If cross-gender identity is (partially) determined by prenatal brain exposure to unusual sex hormone levels, one would expect more male-typical outcomes in FMs and more female-typical outcomes in MFs.

Regarding female-favoring cognitive abilities that differ between males and females, effeminate boys and adolescents had higher verbal than performance IQs (VIQ and PIQ) on Wechsler Intelligence scales. Also, the verbal comprehension factor was higher than the perceptual organization factor (Money & Epstein, 1967). Although Zucker and Bradley (1995) found no differences between Wechsler VIQ and PIQ in 164 prepubertal boys and 25 girls with GID, they report that the boys did better on two verbal subtests (vocabulary and comprehension) that load high on the verbal comprehension factor than on two more "spatial" subtests (block design and object assembly). When compared with clinical and normal control boys, it appeared that the boys with GID had a relative deficit in spatial ability, but not a relative advantage in verbal ability. However, their findings were not replicated in another child sample. In a Dutch sample of 71 boys and 21 girls, the VIQ/PIQ and verbal/spatial differences (as computed by Zucker and Bradley, 1995) were nonsignificant (unpublished results). Moreover, in an adult TS group of 17 MFs and 5 FMs, Wechsler scores were not sex-atypical (Hunt, Carr, & Hampson, 1981). So in some samples of individuals with GID, a pattern of cognitive functioning was observed that is not in line with the biological sex. The results, however, are too inconsistent to draw definite conclusions. Moreover, the Wechsler scales were not developed to measure constructs that show large sex differences. Therefore attempts have been made to compare transsexual and nontranssexual samples with other instruments. The scores of 8 MFs on an embedded figures test differed significantly from a male control group, but not from a female control group (La Torre, Gossmann, & Piper, 1976). Among 10 male controls, lateralization patterns for nonverbal (but not verbal) stimuli were stronger than among 13 MFs and 10 female controls (Cohen & Forget, 1995). Female patterns of cognitive functioning and functional cerebral asymmetry in MFs were also reported by Cohen-Kettenis, van Goozen, Doorn, and Gooren (1998). In their study, 44 MFs showed less functional cerebral asymmetry when processing auditory verbal stimuli and less lateral preference on a questionnaire, and they performed better on a verbal memory test than male controls. Only on a mental rotation test were no differences found. Because the standard deviations were large and the sex differences in the TS groups were less strong than the sex differences in the control groups, it might be that significant findings would have been found if larger samples had been tested. Unexpectedly, the 34 FMs appeared to be less instead of more lateralized than the female control group. On a verbal memory test, the FMs did show the predicted pattern of gender-atypical cognitive functioning. No differences were found in visual-spatial ability, but, again, it is conceivable that larger samples would have yielded significant findings. However, when testing lateralized processing of visually presented verbal and spatial stimuli, differences between 12 FMs and controls were not found (Herman, Grabowska, & Dulko, 1993).

Whether handedness differs between cross-gendered individuals and controls has been investigated both in children and adults. In these studies the assumption was that prenatal hormone brain exposure explained both the GID and the non-right-handedness, despite the fact that other mechanisms have been postulated to explain (non-)right-handedness (e.g., Annett, 1985; Coren, 1995). More left-handedness was indeed found in 205 boys with GID than in a clinical control group and in three population studies of nonreferred boys (Zucker, Beaulieu, Bradley, Grimshaw, & Wilcox, 2001). Elevated percentages of non-right-handedness in adult MFs and FMs were also found in six other studies (Cohen-Kettenis et al., 1998; Green & Young, 2001; Herman et al., 1993; Orlebeke, Boomsma, Gooren, Verschoor, & van den Bree, 1992; Slabbekoorn, van Goozen, Sanders, Gooren, & Cohen-Kettenis, 2000; Watson & Coren, 1992).

Birth Order and Sibling Sex Ratio

In men, homosexual orientation and the number of older brothers are correlated, whereas sexual orientation and the number of older sisters are not (for a review see Blanchard, 2001). Blanchard called this effect the "fraternal birth order effect." In women, this effect does not exist. The fraternal birth order effect was also observed in three studies, including children, adolescents, and adults with gender problems. In these samples, all adolescents and adults were attracted to members of their own biological sex. Blanchard (1997, 2001) has postulated that the effect reflects the progressive immunization of mothers to Y-linked minor histocompatibility antigens (H-Y antigens) that are, from very early in male fetal development, present on cell surfaces. He supposes that the mothers' antibodies cross the placental barrier and enter the fetal brain, thus preventing the brain from developing in the male-typical direction. As each succeeding male fetus increases the strength of the maternal immunization, the probability of homosexuality also increases in later born sons. Nonhomosexual cross- gendered individuals do not show the fraternal birth order effect, so it seems to be more related to homosexuality than to a cross-gender identity.

In contrast to boys, girls with GID were significantly more likely to be early born (Zucker, Lightbody, Pecore, Bradley, & Blanchard, 1998). Moreover, there was evidence for a sororal birth order effect, meaning that the early birth order was accounted for by an excess of younger sisters, but not of younger brothers. However, in adult women with or without gender identity disorder the results are much more inconsistent. In an attempt to explain the findings in girls, Zucker et al. (1998) mention that early born girls are more active than later born girls (Eaton, Chipperfield, & Singbeil, 1989) and that older siblings are more verbally and physically aggressive than younger siblings (Abramovitch, Corter, Pepler, & Stanhope, 1986). They suppose that these temperamental characteristics predispose early born girls to masculine behavior and interests.

Sibling sex ratio is the ratio of brothers to sisters in a given group. In White populations, the ratio of male to female live births is 106:100. In most of the studies on birth order the sibling sex ratio was also calculated. No strong evidence was found concerning the sibling sex ratio in girls with GID or women. However, taking the results of 13 studies on men together, Blanchard (1997) found that the sibling sex ratio differed significantly from 106 only in a combined homosexual feminine/transsexual sample ($N = 896$) and not in homosexual ($N = 2.365$) or heterosexual ($N = 5.308$) samples. By calculating the ratios of older and of younger siblings, he showed that the high sibling sex ratio did not merely reflect an excess of older brothers. The feminine/transsexual men also had more younger brothers relative to their younger sisters. So the sibling sex ratio findings may be unrelated to sexual orientation and only associated with cross-gender identification. It may also indicate a specific developmental pathway to gender problems, involving both a late birth order and an excess of brothers. Post hoc explanations for this finding are given by Blanchard (1997). As a psychosocial explanation he proposes that there may be less parental effort to "masculinize" an already feminine son, when there are more siblings in the family. This may happen consciously, for example, by rewarding masculine sons for their masculine activities, or unconsciously, for example, by giving sons in larger families more nontraditional tasks. Alternatively, the high sibling sex ratios may, according to Blanchard, result from strong maternal immune reactions to H-Y antigen, as zygotes that elicit stronger maternal immune reactions are favored at implantation. Thus, strong immune reactions to H-Y antigen may generate cross-gender identity and high sibling sex ratios, whereas weak immune reactions may generate homosexuality only.

SUMMARY

Historically, three terms have been particularly relevant in the field of gender problems: the term *transsexualism*, coined in 1923; the term *gender dysphoria syndrome*, coined in 1974; and finally the term *gender identity disorder*, which is the commonly used term in clinical contexts today. In response to a variety of criticisms, diagnostic criteria for GID in the subsequent editions of *DSM* and *ICD* have changed considerably. Although the *DSM* criteria are now similar for children, adolescents, and adults, the phenomenology is not. Moreover, it has become clear from follow-up studies that childhood GID and adult transsexualism do not show a one-to-one relationship. Current prevalence data of GID in adults vary greatly between countries. For children and adolescents such data are not yet available, but only estimates from clinical samples.

Theories about atypical gender development can be subdivided into psychological, biopsychological, and biological theories. There is increasing, but still largely indirect, evidence that the brains of certain types of cross-gendered individuals (MFs who are sexually attracted to men in particular) have been prenatally exposed to atypical levels of sex hormones. However, such exposure alone is almost certainly not enough to develop a cross-gender identity. For instance, despite certain masculine interests and behaviors in 46,XX CAH women, the majority does not develop a gender identity disorder. On the other hand, for certain types of cross-gendered individuals, for example, MFs who are sexually attracted to women, evidence that prenatal brain exposure to hormones are a factor of significance is weak. For women, the picture is even less clear, even for FMs who are attracted to women. For them, evidence regarding the hormonal hypothesis is more mixed than for their male counterparts. It should not be excluded that biological factors, other than organizational hormone effects, also result in a cross-gender development or in certain types of cross-gender development. The exact nature of these factors is, however, still largely unknown. For men, another mechanism, the progressive immunization of mothers to H-Y antigens, has been proposed. Though the existing empirical data are in line with such a mechanism, direct evidence for this mechanism is still lacking.

Support for environmental influences, parental functioning in particular, comes from studies in children with GID. So there is reason to believe that parental functioning plays a role in childhood GID. However, most of these children will be prehomosexual instead of pretranssexual. The significance of the childhood findings for the understanding of adolescent and adult GID thus is yet unclear. It is conceivable that environmental characteristics such as child-rearing practices that are associated with parental pathology and family constellation lead to some, but not all, kinds of gender identity disorders. For the development of certain, perhaps mild, forms of gender disturbance they may be a sufficient condition. For the development of others, environmental factors may not be sufficient or even necessary.

5

CLINICAL MANAGEMENT OF INTERSEX CONDITIONS

IMPORTANCE OF PARENT COUNSELING

Most parents are deeply shocked when discrepancies between the sex characteristics of their child are discovered. This is not only the case when they have a newborn with ambiguous genitals. They may be equally upset when, at later ages of the child, the chromosomes or gonads of the child appear not to be in accordance with the external genitals and sex of rearing (Slijper, Frets, Boehmer, & Drop, 2000). Interventions should never be only medical. When the children themselves are too young to understand their situation, the first psychological care concerns the parents.

Parents need emotional support and adequate information. They struggle with emotions like grief, shame, anxiety, and guilt and try to understand the full meaning of their child's condition. They worry about their child's future. Often there are no friends or relatives with whom they can or want to share this confidential information; professional support is imperative. Professional assistance should help them to appraise the situation in a realistic way, to deal with practical matters, and to get over disconcerting emotions. A thorough understanding of the situation may prevent needless fears. At our clinic we regularly encounter clear examples of such fears. For instance, despite the fact that it was explained repeatedly to parents of a complete androgen-insensitive, even gonadectomized, girl that she would grow up looking completely female, they kept asking whether she would grow a beard after puberty. Invariably the question arises who should be informed and about what aspect of the condition (see below). Usually parents worry about their child's chances of a happy life. They wonder about partnership, sexual orientation, sexuality, and infertility, but may feel embarrassed to discuss such matters. So timely and appropriate counseling of the parents is essential (Slijper et al., 2000).

When the children grow up, a broad range of condition-related problems may arise. As described in Chapter 3, a delay in language, motor, or emotional development; vulnerabilities in their intelligence profiles (e.g., low verbal IQ); weak school performance; poor executive functioning; social relationship problems; temper tantrums; and gender identity problems are not uncommon. In some conditions, however, the risk of developing one or more of these problems is much higher than in others. Clinicians need to monitor the child's development on a regular basis and parents need to be well aware what signs of developmental arrest they have to take seriously. Knowledgeable parents will be better able to detect potential problems in an early stage. When problems do arise, timely referral to relevant agencies can prevent further escalation. The child can be treated or counseled, additional problems can be kept within bounds, and/or the family can be supported in coping with permanent limitations of the child.

IMPORTANCE OF CHILD COUNSELING

Children with intersex conditions obviously need adequate counseling. Children who are diagnosed at birth cannot be immediately informed. Instead, professionals and parents will have to discuss and agree upon a policy regarding timing and type of information and support the child should receive when growing up.

When children are diagnosed at older ages, for example, at the elementary school age, they are usually aware that something is going on at the time the diagnosis is made. When (some of) the results of their medical examination have been explained to them, they may, like their parents, be shocked and distressed. For the children, as for their parents, counseling that is focused on cognitive comprehension, emotional acceptance of their situation, and coping with the consequences of the condition is of utmost importance (see below).

Depending on the needs and possibilities of the child, any type of psychological intervention can be useful. But unlike their parents, the children undergo cognitive changes when they grow older. New developmental phases may generate new questions or emotional needs. For instance, an atypical appearance of the genitals or the importance of infertility are often denied before puberty, but usually become a source of concern in adolescence. It is no exception if a child seeks help as an adolescent, though he or she has not been very eager to receive psychological assistance as a child. In a Dutch study it was shown that, in a sample of 59 children with intersex conditions, 19% had mild psychological problems and 39% had psychiatric problems meeting *DSM-IV* criteria (Slijper et al., 1998). Psychopathology occurred twice as often among children who received no counseling as among children who did.

NEONATAL APPROACH

The birth of a child with ambiguous genitals is a rare and unexpected event for all parties. If such a child is born in a hospital with few diagnostic facilities, the family should be referred to a specialized clinic. There an interdisciplinary team will, as quickly as possible, make a diagnosis on the basis of a comprehensive (genetic, hormonal, and physical) examination of the child and estimate which sex assignment will give the child the best possible chances of a healthy psychosexual development. Before such a decision is made, it often happens that doctors, especially in clinics that are not experienced in handling children with ambiguous genitals, attempt to reassure the parents. They draw hasty conclusions as to the "true sex" of the child. Yet it is important that parents are not wrongly informed about the sex of their child. It is better to tell parents that the cause of their child's genital appearance has to be further examined than to give them speculative answers. Most parents find it hard to change their image of the sex of their baby, once it has been established. When parents have used a nickname for the baby during pregnancy they can use that name a little longer until they know whether their child will be raised as a boy or as a girl. If clinicians refrain from referring to the baby as "he" or "she" until it is clear that the child will be assigned the male or female sex, it will also help parents not to prematurely draw conclusions as to their child's sex.

Another question that comes up immediately after the discovery of a child's genital ambiguity is to what extent parents should disclose their child's condition to others during the time that they do not yet know whether their child will have a female or male sex assignment. It has been argued that not revealing the situation to others creates an atmosphere of secrecy. This could eventually harm the children, because they mistakenly infer that they suffer from something shameful. Harmon-Smith (1998) even formulated "10 commandments" of how to openly deal with neonates who are born with atypical genitals. However, in our Western societies the chances that people in the child's environment will not understand and accept the phenomenon of genital ambiguity are still considerable. It seems right to inform parents about two possible causes of harm: one that may result from openness and one that may result from secrecy. In most circles, teasing by other children and stigmatization are likely to occur when the outside world knows about the condition. This already happens when people in the child's environment do not know the complete story. It creates feelings of being an outcast and loneliness. On the other hand, feelings of shame and insecurity may also occur when the child is told to keep his or her condition a secret. It is not always possible to know beforehand which children (and parents) will be able to handle complete openness. Currently, many parents want their children to make the choice themselves about who, besides close relatives, should know of their situation. Once the information is given, it cannot be reversed. So they do not inform the people in the child's environment before the child is old enough to make the decision. Despite the need parents have to share their feelings with others, they fear the long-term consequences of disclosure for their child (see also Slijper, Drop, Molenaar, & Scholtmeijer, 1994).

There is no discussion about medical interventions, including surgery in infancy if the child's life is in danger or if there are other medical reasons to intervene. There is, however, great disagreement regarding the necessity of surgical interventions to "normalize" the genitals (see below).

INFORMATION AND SUPPORT

Parents

If the condition is diagnosed at birth, naturally only parents can be informed. In any case the parents need information about the condition and about treatment aspects or phenomena that will occur with certainty (e.g., infertility). When phenomena are discussed that are associated with the condition, but not invariably occur, the variation between children with the same condition should be stressed. It is good for the parents to know what to expect, but it is not necessary to make them worry about events that may never occur.

It will be difficult for parents to raise their children if they do not have adequate information. Parents need this information to give them support and to help them prevent potential problems. No matter how well-educated parents may be, they are usually incapable of digesting all facts at once (because they lack education, are overwhelmed by the message, or both). Yet, the first session is crucial. The way the message is conveyed and the unity of information between team members can make the experience either difficult but tolerable or impossible to cope with. A consistent team approach is therefore important. The person who will counsel the family for a longer period of time is preferably present at the first session, when the parents are informed about their child's condition. In such a way, the family counselor will know how the parents have learned about their child's condition and what their first reactions had been. Continuity in content and style is thus more likely when, in later sessions, more specific aspects of the condition, its treatment, and the child's (psychosexual) development are discussed more extensively with the family counselor. Ample attention has to be given to the parents' emotions and questions about upbringing. In the case of denying or rigidly rejecting parents, it may require much therapeutic skill to help parents accept their child's situation. Complete acceptance of the child's condition is extremely important. If parents continue to consider their daughter a "failed son" or, worse, a "freak," this will obviously harm the child's development.

If parents struggle with the issue of disclosure of the condition to family and friends, it can be helpful to point out that most people do not have to know the whole story. Some facts (e.g., about medication) need to be given to certain adults, such as day-care center caretakers. Other facts (e.g., karyogram), however, do not have to be disclosed until the child is old enough to make his or her own choices.

Occasionally, children brought in from less specialized clinics have to be reassigned, provided that the diagnosis is not made too late. For instance, a virilized "baby girl" who appears to be a 46,XY child with an idiopathic hypospadias has much better chances of functioning socially, sexually, and reproductively as a man than as a woman. It goes without saying that parents going through such a double uncertainty regarding the sex of their child need extra attention. They have to deal with repeated shock and confusion. The legal sex change (or sex reannouncement) cannot be hidden from the environment. In our experience, however, the environment may react very positively when simple but accurate information is given about why a reannouncement sometimes occurs.

Children

Parents and clinicians should have one policy and try to avoid giving contradictory information. Even when the condition is discovered at a later age, it is impossible for children to understand all the facts at once. Breaking the message into little pieces and giving it to the children piece by piece is usually more effective.

It is important that clinicians and parents cooperate when they inform the child about aspects of his or her condition. They need to agree upon who will inform the child and about timing. In our opinion it is preferable if parents, whenever possible, inform their children, but this is not always possible. Sometimes clinicians have to give some assistance. For instance, if parents have problems intellectually understanding the condition, it may be helpful if a clinician is present when they inform their child. In this way, the giving of wrong information can be prevented. For similar reasons the professional who takes care of the long-term counseling of the child may regularly check the child's understanding of his or her condition and correct it when necessary. Though parents and clinicians should take the child's developmental level and intellectual capacities into account, when they explain aspects of the condition, they will not always find it easy to do so.

If a clinician feels a child has to be told about a new aspect of his or her condition but the parents are emotionally not yet ready for it, it can be helpful if some work is first done with the parents. Only if they are able to cope with their own feelings is it likely that they can discuss and explain sensitive topics with their child in a realistic and down-to-earth way. Independent of the type of condition, it is always helpful if children are timely and adequately informed about biological and psychological aspects of sexual development in general, before specificities about the condition are discussed (Slijper et al., 2000).

In childhood and adolescence, a child may encounter a variety of phenomena:

1. Need for (genital) surgery
2. Need for medication
3. Learning (language) problems
4. Social problems (due to subassertiveness, inappropriate social skills, or cross-gender role behavior)
5. Precocious or delayed puberty
6. Extreme shortness or tallness
7. Absence of menses
8. Need for feminizing or virilizing hormones
9. Need for nonsurgical genital treatment (e.g., vaginal dilators)
10. Infertility
11. Need for technical aids when having sexual contact
12. Sex reassignment

Fortunately, not every child with an intersex condition will encounter all the phenomena when growing up. For instance, a complete androgen-insensitive girl may need a gonadectomy (1), will not menstruate (7), will need hormones at puberty to feminize her body (8), will have to decide if, when, and how she will deepen her vagina (1 and 9), and will have to cope with infertility (10). A girl with CAH may have genital surgery shortly after birth (1), will need medication (e.g., cortisone therapy) to restore the hormonal balance (2), may have problems with acceptance by other children because of her tomboyism (4), may have a precocious puberty (5), and may become a very short adult (6). A boy with KS may develop language or general learning problems (3) and social problems (4), may have a delayed puberty (5), will probably become very tall (6), and will be infertile (10).

Phenomena That Are Known From Early Onward

It is absolutely necessary to give a child an adequate explanation for early, unavoidable, or already known phenomena (e.g., medication for CAH girls) (Table 5.1). If they are very young (e.g., kindergarten age), such an explanation does not have to be very detailed. Developmental level and intellectual capacities always have to be taken into account. The first explanations should be given as soon as the child starts asking questions or when unavoidable events are about to occur. Giving such partial information is usually not very hard for parents, though they may have difficulties finding the right words. Sometimes, smart children draw their own conclusions from the partial information given to them, as did one of our 8-year-old girls with CAIS who had heard that she did not have a uterus. She checked with her parents whether she was right in that she would never be able to have children of her own. In such a case it would not be sensible to deny this. Unfortunately, parents who want to give their child a completely carefree childhood are inclined to deny painful facts. They do not always realize that, by doing so, they will make it harder for the child to cope with the truth at a later moment.

Phenomena That Will Occur With Certainty

These phenomena or events have to be explained or announced at the right time (see Table 5.1). A boy with KS of school age may wonder why he performs so poorly at school. For the acceptance of his level of academic performance, it may be helpful if he understands that this is related to his condition, not due to laziness. Girls with CAH sometimes wonder why they are so extremely tomboyish and find it reassuring to know where their boyish behavior and preferences come from.

TABLE 5.1 Ages at Which Explanations About the Condition Can Be Given

Preschool and kindergarten age (about 3–5)

- Early surgery (scars)
- Medication
- Hospital visits
- Physical exams
- Atypical appearance of genitals

School age (about 6–12)

- Learning and language problems
- Social problems
- Precocious puberty
- Short stature, extreme tallness
- Additional information about medication (growth hormones)

High school age (about 12–18)

- Need for feminizing or virilizing hormones
- Absence of menses
- Delayed puberty or incomplete pubertal development
- Need for genital treatments (e.g., vaginal dilators and surgery)
- Infertility
- Need for technical aids when having sexual contact

Around 18 years

- Karyotype

Around puberty some children have to be prepared for hormone therapy. They need to know why they cannot enter puberty without help from this type of medication. Sometimes they are not yet aware what "entering puberty" actually means, so this should be included in the preparatory discussions. Girls have to know that estrogens will give them breasts, but no menstruation. When they do not realize that this implies that they will not be able to bear children, they will have to be told explicitly that this is the case. Boys who will need androgens must know that these hormones are important for their genital growth, lowering of their voice, body and facial hair growth, and muscle development. They should be prepared that sexual thoughts and feelings will be much more prominent than before they took hormones and that they may feel cranky more often than they used to.

For various reasons choices regarding surgical interventions have to be made in adolescence. Girls with a shallow vagina can choose between dilatation, surgery, or not doing anything. Some girls indeed wait until they have a boyfriend and want to have sexual intercourse. Boys with severe penile malformations, genital scars, or absent testicles have to choose whether and when they want to have surgery. Naturally they should have all relevant information before they can decide upon such matters.

At the beginning of legal adulthood, which is 18 years in many countries, patients should know the whole truth about themselves, including their karyotype. Adult patients who discovered the truth long after they reached adulthood usually found the truth far more preferable to the guessing and not knowing what they had for many years (Kemp et al., 1996).

Parents and clinicians struggle most with information about the karyotype. For long, it was felt that it was in the best interest of the child not to reveal this fact. It was expected that a girl, even when told in late adolescence, would be too confused if she learned about her having 46,XY chromosomes. In our experience, confusion results only if the information has been given in a thoughtless manner. Well-known unfortunate phrases of inexperienced clinicians are "you (your child) should have been a boy," "you are (your child is) partly a boy, partly a girl," or "your (your child's) origins are male." One of the reasons why family doctors preferably cooperate with specialized teams is that, in some countries, they play a central role in the medical care of the family. They also should know how to deal with this sensitive issue and may thus facilitate acceptance of the condition by the family. Instead of focusing on "what you (your child) should have been" or "basically are (is)," it is less confusing for the child and parents when it is stressed, *"you are (your child is) what you feel (he/she feels), no matter what chromosomes or gonads you have (he/she has)."* In other words, gender identity defines who "one really is," not chromosomes or gonads. We usually explain that people's feelings about themselves largely depend on how they consider their condition. For instance, androgen-insensitive girls may feel a relief discovering that they feel much better when they consider themselves as "superfeminine" or a "superwoman" (because their bodies react to "male hormones" even less than the bodies of other girls) than when they consider themselves as "basically male."

By the time the children learn the "whole truth and nothing but the truth" of their condition it is practical to have written information available. It is very useful if such information covers biological as well as psychological aspects.

Phenomena That May or May Not Occur

Phenomena that do *not* necessarily occur can be mentioned when a substantial amount of information about the condition is given to the child (see Table 5.1). In this stage, one should, however, avoid too much detail.

It may unnecessarily worry the child. If the phenomenon actually occurs more specific information can still be given.

The above ages are no more than a rule of thumb. Children who seem to understand that there is more to their condition than has been explained or keep asking questions can be told more and at earlier ages than children who are not particularly interested or are even somewhat reluctant to learn about themselves.

Psychological Interventions

Although giving youngsters complete information about their condition is of utmost importance, it is often not enough. Fortunately, not all children have a hard time integrating this information into their self-concept and to learn to live with limitations, if there are any. But many struggle sooner or later with issues that are specifically related to their condition. As a consequence of the physical differences between them and their peers, they may develop a low self-esteem and be insecure in their social relationships. Poor school performance or certain obvious physical characteristics, such as extreme shortness, may enhance this lack of confidence. They may have to overcome negative feelings about their genitals, which they consider weird or ugly. When they grow older, some have to learn how to emotionally deal with their infertility. Adolescents may rebel against their parents or their fate by "unhealthy behaviors." For instance some do not drink enough fluids (which is rather easy to do but may hurt their kidneys in the long run), do not catheterize often enough, or "forget" to take their medication. They may be shy in romantic and sexual relationships and they often fear the moment that they have to tell their potential partners about their condition. If parents are understanding and supporting, it can be of great help to the children. But even then professional support is often necessary, because adolescents usually do not want to discuss intimate matters with their parents. If a child chooses to live in the opposite gender role after a number of years, professional guidance is essential.

Which type of intervention is suitable will largely be dependent of the specific problem of the individual child. For children, treatment may be aimed at coping with teasing, establishing a satisfying body image, and enhancing social skills and self-esteem. Treatment for adolescents is more often focused on feelings of grief or rage, as they begin to realize that their bodies will not change. Boys typically try to deal with this insight by denying and rationalizing, whereas girls tend to react with hopelessness and depression. Heterosexual adolescents usually need some heterosocial and heterosexual skills training, which has to be somewhat adjusted for homosexual youngsters. They need sexual education more than their peers. They usually consider it a great relief if they have learned to talk about their genitals and about sexuality realistically and in a down-to-earth way. For children who were raised as girls but want to continue their lives as boys a manualized cognitive behavior therapy approach is in development. It includes how to deal with the gender reassignment within the peer population, within school, and within the family's social spheres. Psychosexual education is also incorporated in the approach. As a part of this, it specifically deals with how to be sexually interactive with girls without having a penis (Reiner, 2000).

CRITICISM OF CLINICAL POLICY

For long, decisions on sex assignment, timing and type of surgery, and the decision to inform or not to inform patients about their condition have almost exclusively been in the hands of medical professionals. In the past decade, the clinical management of intersex conditions has received a lot of disapproval (e.g., Chase, 1997; Dreger, 1999a; Kessler, 1998). The criticism is partly a result of new evidence on the influence of hormones on brain development. This evidence has raised doubts regarding criteria that are relevant for sex assignment. Also, adult individuals with intersex conditions started to criticize the lack of information. Many of them only coincidentally – and often not earlier than in adulthood – discovered what their condition was. After discovering the decisions that had been made in their lives, they expressed strong opposition against cosmetic genital surgical interventions on children.

Sex Assignment at Birth

In most modern societies, a choice has to be made regarding sex assignment when genital ambiguity is evident at birth. The criteria for this decision have changed over the years and, as mentioned, are still a matter of hot debate among clinicians. In the 1950s, Money and his coworkers at Johns Hopkins University Hospital published several studies on psychosexual outcome of intersexed individuals (Money, Hampson, & Hampson, 1955, 1957). They concluded from these very first studies that assigned sex and gender of rearing instead of chromosomal, gonadal, or genital sex were the best predictors for adult gender identity. This led to an "optimal-gender policy," in which sex assignment was based on the expected optimal outcome in six areas: reproductive potential (if possible), good sexual function, minimal medical procedures, an overall gender-appropriate appearance, a stable gender identity, and psychological well-being (Meyer-Bahlburg, 1998, 1999; Zucker, 1999). At the time nothing was known about sexual differentiation of the brain and the theory of "psychosexual neutrality at birth" prevailed. For many years, this policy was widely accepted among clinicians.

Since the demonstration of sexual brain differentiation in animals (Phoenix, Goy, Gerall, & Young, 1959), prenatal exposure of the brain to androgens has increasingly been put forward as a critical factor in gender identity development (Diamond & Sigmundson, 1997; see also Chapter 4). The renewed discussion on prenatal brain androgenization was partly based on the earlier mentioned case of identical twins (see Chapter 1). One of the boys lost his penis in a circumcision accident. Along the lines of the "optimal-gender policy," the boy was reassigned as a girl and at first was reported to function well in the female role, despite much tomboyish behavior (Money, 1975a). A follow-up in adolescence revealed that the child was very unhappy as a girl. At puberty, he strongly resisted taking estrogens, because he did not want to have breasts. Psychological treatment did not make him feel any better about his female role. After he heard that he had been born as a boy, he reassumed the male role at age 14. He had surgical reconstruction of the genitals and as an adult man married and was father to stepchildren (Diamond & Sigmundson, 1997). This case is in line with findings of a gender identity disorder in some women with CAH (Meyer-Bahlburg et al., 1996) and a wish for or actual sex reassignment after upbringing as a female in various other conditions, such as penile agenesis (Dittmann, 1998), partial androgen insensitivity (Gooren & Cohen-Kettenis, 1991; Slijper et al., 1998), cloacal exstrophy (Feitz, Van Grunsven, Froeling, & de Vries, 1994; Reiner, 1997; Stein et al., 1994), prenatal exposure to diphenylhydantoin (Phornphutkul, Fausto-Sterling, & Grupposo, 2000), 5α-RD (Hurtig, 1992; Imperato-McGinley, Guerrero, Gautier, & Peterson, 1974; Wilson, Griffin, & Russell, 1993), mixed gonadal dysgenesis (Birnbacher, Marberger, Weissenbacher, Schober, & Frisch, 1999), and 17β-HSD (Imperato-McGinley et al., 1979; Kohn et al., 1985; Rösler, 1992). So the existence of a wish to live as males in individuals who have been reared as females suggests that prenatal androgen exposure may be a more important determinant of gender development than has long been believed.

The suggestive but not conclusive evidence of relatively frequent sex reassignment requests among prenatally androgenized individuals who were raised as females led Diamond and Sigmundson (1997) to publish new guidelines on sex assignment. They recommend a *male* sex assignment of persons with

- 46,XY chromosomes and partial androgen insensitivity
- 46,XY chromosomes and 5α-RD
- 46,XY chromosomes and 17β-HSD
- 46,XY chromosomes and a micropenis
- 46,XY chromosomes and hypospadias
- Klinefelter Syndrome (47,XXY)
- 46,XX chromosomes and CAH with a penile clitoris and extensively fused labia

Their recommendation to also raise extremely virilized 46,XX CAH individuals as males is remarkable. Most clinicians are still reluctant to make such a decision. If the condition is discovered at birth, they are now usually raised as girls, because they have female internal genitals, the potential of becoming pregnant, and more often than not a female gender identity (Horowitz & Glassberg, 1992). So it is unclear why the first choice should be to raise these children as boys.

Diamond and Sigmundson recommend a *female* sex assignment of individuals with

- 46,XY chromosomes and complete androgen insensitivity
- 46,XX and 46,XY chromosomes and gonadal dysgenesis (defective or no ovarian or testicular development)
- Turner syndrome (45,XO)
- 46,XX individuals with CAH with a hypertrophied clitoris

For persons with mixed gonadal dysgenesis and true hermaphrodites, Diamond and Sigmundson recommend male or female assignment dependent on the size of the phallus, the extent of the labia/scrotum fusion, and testosterone levels.

Despite the above findings of gender identity disorder and a wish to live as men after having been raised as women, the majority of individuals with intersex conditions seem to develop a gender identity along with their gender of rearing. So clinicians would greatly profit from information from solid, prospective studies that collect detailed data on the condition itself, environmental parameters during upbringing, and their interaction in large, homogeneous groups of children with intersex conditions. Given the small numbers of children with ambiguous genitals and the large heterogeneity of the group it is unlikely, however, that such information will be available in the near future. One may even wonder whether we will ever have enough data to make a correct (that is, without regrets in adulthood) decision for every single individual. So what could be a solution for the time being?

Some state that "imposing" the male or female gender on children is in itself a wrong way to find solutions. For them, society should change and accept more gender (identity) variation. In such an accepting society, individuals who develop an identity in between a male and female identity would neither have to be psychologically or medically forced into one of only two categories (e.g., Elliot, 1998; McKain, 1996). Clinically we have come across adults who have chosen to live an "in-between" or "third-gender" life. All appeared to be intellectually, emotionally, and socially very capable of handling the many complexities they encounter daily. They also had the advantage of living in well-educated, tolerant social circles. It is the merit of such people that society is made more aware of different gender options. However, they had chosen such a life(-style) after reaching adulthood. They were not raised "without gender" or "forced" to live as a third gender. Without doubt more tolerance of gender variation is beneficial for all who do not fit into or do not want to live according to the male/female dichotomy. But even if more tolerance occurred in our societies, it would not automatically imply that a genderless or third-gender rearing of children was favorable. No matter how hard many of us try to change society, we are still very far from "gender irrelevance." For some time, raising children as neither a boy nor a girl would be an experiment that might do as much psychological harm as the early medical practices have done in some cases. So a "provisional" sex assignment is seen by some as an in-between solution. The idea is that only older children can make definite choices and that they will do so after their gender identity has become crystallized (e.g., Dreger, 1999b).

In most cases there will be no problems when it comes to sex assignment, but in a few there will be (e.g., partially androgen-insensitive children). At present, the best we can do is to make our decisions on a case-by-case basis and take both the available empirical knowledge and our clinical experience into account. When this is done by a multidisciplinary team, which also takes the opinion of parents seriously, it will prevent important consequences of a decision from being overlooked. But, despite careful clinical procedures, we will have to live with the fact that the ultimate psychosexual outcome still cannot completely be predicted in all children. Undoubtedly requests for a gender change will occur from time to time. This is unavoidable. But if we keep an open mind, help families not to consider this a complete disaster, and give appropriate counseling, we can minimize the negative impact of such gender changes for the individual.

Information

A second point of criticism of patients is that, certainly in the past, doctors often did not reveal the true nature of the patient's condition. This may have been due to a genuine concern for the patient, doctors' anxieties to discuss such matters, or both. As some form of treatment often had to be given, many patients have become aware only in adulthood that they had an intersex condition. Some were already in their late thirties or forties. As a consequence many felt resentful toward their doctors and parents. The secrecy surrounding their condition had created feelings of shame, anger, guilt, and confusion (e.g., Kemp et al., 1996). Since the early 1990s, intersex activists have themselves attempted to break this secrecy and shame surrounding intersex conditions. In 1993, they formed the Intersex Society of North America (ISNA), an organization offering support and information to persons with intersex conditions and their families. They publish a quarterly, *Hermaphrodites With Attitude,* and have an interactive site on the Internet. They fight shame not only by creating an atmosphere of openness, but also by promoting changes in clinical practice. They hope that education of the public will help individuals not to feel unnecessarily ashamed and prevent social stigmatization.

Despite all these efforts, some clinicians still feel that it is in the best interests of the patient to withhold sensitive facts, such as karyotype. In most professional and other writings, however, such a lack of disclosure is no longer considered acceptable for ethical and practical reasons. For instance, usually the ability to cope with whatever difficulty in treatment (e.g., compliance) is greater when patients are informed about their situation. Also, doctors and other professionals understand that the trust between clinician and patient (or parent and child) will be seriously harmed if a patient finds out that fundamental information about himself or herself has been withheld. Overcoming this may be even more painful than being informed about the condition itself.

Surgery

Genital surgery in intersexes has been performed for about a century (Neugebauer, 1908), but the number increased considerably in the second half of the 20th century. The purpose of genital surgery has long been to give the children a genital appearance that was in line with their gender of rearing. It was felt that this surgery should be done as early as possible. One expected that, by creating this concordance between assigned sex and external genital sex, psychosexual development would be in agreement with both the external genitals and the gender of rearing (Money & Ehrhardt, 1972). When 46,XX children with ambiguous genitals were raised as girls, they underwent a reduction, or even removal, of the enlarged clitoris, a labioscrotal reduction, and vaginoplasty. In addition to these surgical procedures, 46,XY children, raised as girls, also had a removal of the Wolffian structures and a removal of the testicles. 46,XY children who were raised as boys had a removal of the Müllerian structures and dysgenetic gonads (if present) and a correction of hypospadias.

Over the years technical advances have made it possible to perform most of these surgical interventions at progressively younger ages. Nowadays, many types of surgery are possible neonatally (De Jong & Boemers, 1995). The earlier recommendations regarding timing of surgery concentrated on technical pros and cons of surgery at different times in childhood or adolescence (e.g., Sotiropoulos, Morishima, Homsy, & Lattimer, 1976). A more fundamental issue regarding surgery is currently being debated. Consumer organizations state that, unless medically necessary, surgery should not be performed before individuals are old enough to make their own decisions (Chase, 1997). They have several arguments to support this position. First, the long-term outcome of early surgery is far from satisfactory. There are reports of chronic pain, scarring, loss of sexual sensitivity, inability to achieve orgasm, distress about the cosmetic appearance of having no clitoris and the necessity of multiple operations (Alizai, Thomas, Lilford, Batchelor, & Johnson, 1999; Creighton, Minto, & Steele, 2001; Schober, 1998, 1999). Second, later in life a person may have the wish to live in the opposite gender role or want to adopt an intersexual identity. In such cases, a change of the already-present sex characteristics would impede this person's opportunities to fully live in the desired way. Third, it is not the right of parents or medical professionals, but only the right of the individual, to decide on cosmetic surgical interventions. As a result of this opposition medical professionals have become more open to these arguments. They now seem to be more careful in their approach when it comes to early surgery (Creighton, 2001; Schober, 1998, 1999; Wilson & Reiner, 1999; see also the Statement of the British Association of Paediatric Surgeons Working Part on Surgical Management of Children Born with Ambiguous Genitalia by Rangecroft et al., 2001).

Regarding early surgery, it has also been suggested that society could play a role in the psychological health of children with intersex conditions. An acceptance of greater genital variation would create a situation where it is not a medical emergency or social disaster to have characteristics of both sexes and early surgical adjustment would be superfluous (Dreger, 1999a; Elliot, 1998; Kessler, 1998). In this chapter, we already commented on the feasibility of a genderless or gender irrelevant society as a solution for those who do not fit into one of the two gender categories. Here, we wish to add that true acceptance of genital variation, though perhaps more attainable, also has a long way to go. Despite agreeing with the desirability of greater acceptance of genital variation, clinicians continue to struggle with the translation of these ideas into daily practice. The argument that genital surgery addresses physical differences that are not visible to others in the course of normal social interaction does not apply for surgery of the external genitals (Schober, 1998). First, caregivers other than parents will see the genitals of very young children when changing diapers or helping them when they go to the toilet. Second, in hot weather it is not uncommon for parents to let toddlers paddle about naked. Often other children are present. Third, in some countries, such as the Netherlands, children undress together when they have swimming lessons or when they shower after sports activities. It is these moments that children with atypical genitals fear the most, even after teachers and parents have put great effort into creating an atmosphere of tolerance in the classroom and on sports teams. Some persist in refusing to undress in the presence of others. For them, being genitally different is a great burden no matter what their parents or doctors say (Mureau et al., 1995). How far should professionals go in stressing that the ambiguity or different appearance of their genitals is not something to be ashamed of, despite the children's own feelings?

For the moment we should again acknowledge that it is not always possible to predict whether and what type of surgical interventions are in the best interest of the child. If surgery takes place it is also unclear what the best age to perform surgery is. The unfavorable outcomes most opponents now refer to are the result of a mixture of bad techniques, feelings of shame due to the underlying message that one's genitals are shameful, and multiple traumata (e.g., many painful operations, attitudes of doctors, multiple humiliating genital exams, and negative attitudes of parents). No interventions or late interventions may create new traumata as severe as those derived from early interventions (see also Daaboul & Frader, 2001). Again, the most careful way seems to be to decide on a case-by-case basis. In making decisions on individual children, the criticism of adults with bad experiences, insights from clinical and fundamental research, and the individual situation of child and family have to be taken into account. For now, if it is chosen to raise a child with ambiguous genitals, the likelihood of a positive outcome seems to be the greatest in families that have no emotional or cultural barriers to doing so and that are able to handle practical matters easily.

SUMMARY

Learning that a child's sexual differentiation has not occurred completely in the female or male direction comes as a shock to the parents of affected children, to the children themselves, and to clinicians who rarely encounter a child with an intersex condition. An adequate handling of the situation right from the beginning is crucial for a healthy psychological and psychosexual development of the child. Sometimes the condition is discovered at birth. In this case, only the parents will have to be informed immediately; the child will be informed later. As the information is complex and parents are usually emotionally overwhelmed, it often takes several sessions before they begin to understand the implications of their child's condition. Parents vary widely in their reactions and their ability to cope with the situation. Because it is crucial that they understand what they can do to positively influence their child's development, they usually need support or counseling. If they were already unstable before the birth of their child, they even may need psychotherapy to cope with the feelings of guilt, anger, anxiety, shame, and confusion they invariably have.

Even when the diagnosis is not made at birth, children themselves may be too young to fully understand their condition. Yet they need an explanation for the events they experience, such as doctor visits, hormone treatments, absence of menstruation, and so on. For this reason it is necessary to convey the information in pieces. If particular events will happen with certainty (e.g., hormone treatments) they must know this well in advance. Informing the child is preferably done by their parents, but some assistance by clinicians may be necessary. Depending on the cognitive and emotional maturity of the child, the complete story, including karyogram, can be told at a younger or older age. It seems important to start informing the children during childhood and adolescence and not to wait until they have reached adulthood. Thus they can gradually integrate aspects of their condition (e.g., infertility) into their sense of self. However, this does not always come by itself. To accept the condition and cope with problems that most other children do not have is no easy task. Many children, especially children with chromosomal conditions, will need social skills training, remedial teaching, speech or language therapy, occupational therapy, or medication. Nearly all may want and need emotional support, counseling, or, at times, psychotherapy to learn to live a balanced life despite their vulnerabilities.

For decades, sex assignment in children with ambiguous genitals depended more on surgical possibilities than on other criteria. Because children were viewed as psychosexually neutral at birth, there seemed to be no objection against assigning and raising most children (46,XY children included) with intersex conditions or severe genital malformations as girls. Early surgery was considered to contribute to a healthy psychosexual development, because it helped avoid ambiguity in the way children experienced themselves and were experienced by others. Sometimes information about the condition was not disclosed to the family for similar reasons. Since the early 1990s, however, adults with intersex conditions and professionals in the field have expressed their criticism of these issues.

First, the assumption that children are psychosexually neutral at birth has been challenged by fundamental and clinical research. Prenatal brain exposure to sex hormones and perhaps other biological factors probably influence gender development to a greater extent than has long been assumed. Although it is unlikely that biological factors entirely determine gender identity, they should be taken into account when it comes to sex assignment decisions. In some individual cases, for instance, when it is unclear how androgen-exposed a child was prenatally, it will still be hard to know whether a child will have a happier life as a boy or as a girl. Considering all parameters and including the opinions of all relevant persons, a decision has to be made. The possibility that the child will later regret the decision cannot be overlooked. If the persons involved keep an open mind and parents are adequately counseled, the consequences of a sex reassignment need not necessarily be a disaster. Though there are proponents of raising such children as a third sex, we believe that our society is not ready for the acceptance of third gender in children. We doubt that this solution is in the best interest of the child.

Second, noninformation and misinformation regarding their condition has been very damaging for many individuals. Consumer organizations have made clear that knowledge about their situation would have prevented much confusion and emotional suffering. Also, it makes more sense to properly inform parents than to withhold information, as they will have to monitor the development of their children. Only when they know what signs to take seriously can they timely warn clinicians. This of course also applies to the children when they grow older.

Third, from formal studies in which aspects of sexual behavior, sexual functioning, and sexual satisfaction were measured in detail and from individual testimonies of adults who underwent early genital surgery, it appears that the long-term outcome of this surgery is not very positive. Although surgical techniques are improving, these studies have made us aware that surgical success cannot be measured by cosmetic appearance alone. Because early surgery may have long-term disadvantages, consumer organizations stress that children should have the opportunity to make their own choices. They argue that no cosmetic surgery should be done before children are able to give truly informed consent. Although professionals generally agree on using more caution for hardly visible (e.g., mild hypospadias) or invisible (e.g., vaginal agenesis) conditions, there is still disagreement about the management of clearly visible genital ambiguity. As it is unclear how growing up with truly ambiguous genitals will affect a child's well-being, many are reluctant to abstain from surgical interventions. It is conceivable that growing up with ambiguous genitals is, under favorable conditions (e.g., capable parents and a tolerant environment), not as traumatic as most clinicians fear. So decisions should be made on a case-by-case basis.

Unfortunately, many children with intersex conditions will first be seen by inexperienced clinicians. These clinicians may be as emotionally and cognitively perplexed as the parents and may not know how to inform and support the parents. Chances are higher that harm is done by an inappropriate or confusing way of informing the parents and child. This is why the children are better referred to specialized teams. Intersex conditions are complicated and an adequate quick diagnosis and treatment requires the input of specialists from many disciplines, including child psychologists or psychiatrists. Close cooperation with the family doctor is necessary as he or she will often know the family quite well and be the first person the family will turn to in case of problems.

6

CLINICAL MANAGEMENT OF GENDER PROBLEMS IN CHILDREN

INTRODUCTION

Between the various *DSM* versions, *DSM* criteria for GID have changed considerably. For children, the *DSM-III-R* criteria have been criticized because they were rather confusing and unbalanced (Zucker, Bradley, & Lowry Sullivan, 1992). This was, first, because there were different criteria for boys and girls; second, because cross-gender identification and same-gender aversion characteristics were included in one criterion; and, third, because a stated desire to be of the opposite sex was necessary for the diagnosis (for boys only), which probably led to an underestimation of GID diagnoses in older boys. Older boys have indeed been found to be less inclined to express the wish to be a girl than younger boys (Zucker, Finegan, Doering, & Bradley, 1984). In the *DSM-IV*, the criteria were adjusted to repair these inadequacies, but for the *ICD-10* the critique still largely applies. However, after the publication of the *DSM-IV*, new critical articles appeared. The focus now was on other aspects. In the *DSM-IV* children do not have to express a desire to be of the opposite sex to meet criterion A (cross-gender identification) (Bartlett, Vasey, & Bukowksi, 2000). Furthermore, discomfort with gender role is given the same diagnostic significance as discomfort with one's biological sex. As a result, children who are gender deviant but do not want to be of the opposite sex and do not have an aversion to their own sex characteristics can meet GID criteria. Bartlett et al.'s conclusion was that children who verbally express their wish to be of the opposite sex and have an aversion to their physical sex characteristics need clinical attention, whereas the other group does not. Richardson (1999, p. 49) argues that, for boys, a revised criterion A would be that "cross-gendered interests be employed in a pathological way. Cross-dressing or cross-gender play could be required to be joyless, compulsive, fraught with rage or anxiety, or frankly dissociative to qualify for inclusion." He further considers criterion B "conceptually confused, identifying as a symptom of a disorder [aversion to rough-and-tumble play] a non-pathological factor that predisposes to its development – a temperamental trait that more commonly appears in those without GID [healthy non-conforming boys] than in those with the disorder." Regarding criterion D, he proposes that the child's observed distress is "not attributable solely or principally to rejection or harassment because of his gender atypicality." The concern with pathologizing healthy functioning gender-atypical children thus is an important reason for both authors and others to conclude that the diagnosis of GID for children should be removed from DSM in its current form (Bartlett et al., 2000; Richardson, 1999) or even altogether (e.g., Isay, 1997).

The above criticisms should make clinicians aware that there are referred children who are cross-gendered in some, but not all, possible aspects and that one should be cautious in classifying a child as having a GID on the basis of mere gender-atypical behavior. Depending on the outcome of the diagnostic process, clinical management may vary from intensive interventions to counseling activities. Treatment goals will vary accordingly.

DIAGNOSIS

When children with gender problems are referred for diagnosis, the first goal of clinicians is to assess whether a child actually meets the criteria for GID. In the more extreme cases this will not be a very difficult task. However, children may take a position anywhere between "typical for boys" or "typical for girls" on various dimensions (Table 6.1). When not only the current situation is taken into account, the picture can be even more complex. Cross-gender profiles may change over time because of true changes or be the result of the growing awareness of older children of the social undesirability of cross-gender behavior. Retrospective accounts of adolescents with GID make clear that cross-gender feelings, fantasies, and sometimes even behaviors have persisted until after puberty without others being aware of it. Especially when children do not state they want to be of the opposite sex and do not show an aversion to their bodies, it can be hard to know whether their cross-gender behavior and preferences are manifestations of gender dysphoria or just atypical, albeit still in the normal range. But even if all information is accessible, there is no easy algorithm that can help us infer a diagnosis of GID from a cross-gender profile (see Table 6.1).

TABLE 6.1 Dimensions of Cross-Genderedness

	(typical for) boys		*(typical for) girls*
Identification			
Identity statements	•	....	•
Identification figures	•	....	•
Role play	•	....	•
Fanatasy play	•	....	•
Experience of physical characteristics			
Wants sex characteristics of	•	....	•
Cross-dressing?			
Prefers dressing in clothes of	•	....	•
Energy expenditure			
Rough-and-tumble play	•	....	•
Active play	•	....	•
Peer, object, and activities preference			
Peer preference	•	....	•
Toy prefrence	•	....	•
Play and games preference	•	....	•
Preference for activities	•	....	•
Motor behavior/speech			
Mannerisms/speech	•	....	•

The second goal of the diagnostician is to understand what factors might have influenced the gender development of the child and what factors perpetuate the child's GID. Several factors have repeatedly been put forward in the literature as contributing to or conserving cross-gender identification (see Chapter 4). Although the ultimate significance of most of these factors as determinants of GID is not (yet) known, they may have heuristic value when used to try to understand an individual child's development. They may also give a clue as to the potential aims of psychological interventions. As has been indicated earlier, parental factors may be linked to atypical gender development. So it is useful to pay particular attention to often reported factors, such as the mother's emotional or physical availability at the time of GID onset, gender issues in the individual parents' family of origin (e.g., sexual abuse of mother by males), gender issues in the child's family (e.g., father's contempt of women and mother's strong preference for a child of the opposite sex), certain family dynamics (e.g., a vulnerable mother and/or an aggressive, dominant father in the case of a girl with GID or problematic relationships with sibs). Also, child factors have to be considered. The child may have other psychiatric problems (see below). Anxiousness, making the child exceptionally vulnerable to the above-mentioned environmental influences, may be another, temperamental, risk factor. Life events of the child (e.g., serious illness of the child or parents, adoption, divorce of parents, and sexual abuse) are additional possible sources of vulnerability.

A third goal of the clinician in the diagnostic phase is to put the information about the child's cross-genderedness in a broader perspective. This means that more general aspects of the child's functioning also have to be evaluated, such as cognitive level, socioemotional functioning, and school performance. The observation of vulnerability of children in certain areas may help the clinician to interpret certain cross-gender behaviors. For instance, a boy who often plays with (younger) girls and with girls' toys and girls' games may do so not because he is unhappy about being a boy. Instead, limited cognitive abilities and immaturity may make him no match for other boys.

In addition to a GID, other psychopathology may be present. The relationship between such pathology and the gender problem can take any form. First, cross-gender symptoms may primarily be a component of another disorder. A boy with a pervasive developmental disorder can be very preoccupied with cross-gender toys (e.g., repeatedly dress and undress Barbie dolls) and at times even say he wants to be a girl. At other times, however, this preoccupation may have a completely different content. Second, other disorders, such as ADHD or Tourette syndrome, may exist that are entirely unrelated to the GID. Such disorders can, however, have a negative impact on the gender problem. They may undermine a boy's social status, making him more prone to flee into the less threatening girls' world. Third, certain disorders or problems may be a consequence of the GID. When a girl with GID enters puberty she may try to stop her breast growth by developing anorectic eating patterns. Teasing or bullying may lead to poor school functioning, low self-esteem, or a depressed mood. Stigmatization will be even more disastrous in children with other vulnerabilities, such as poor cognitive abilities or a repressive environment.

The broader perspective not only includes the child's functioning but comprises family functioning as well. Family functioning may have a direct impact on the child's gender feelings and behavior or generate negative feelings on the part of the child. For instance, feelings of shame may be caused by the shame of sibs about their brother's femininity or sister's masculinity. Or parental conflicts, due to differences in emotional reactions to the child's cross-gender behavior, may cause feelings of guilt. For similar reasons it is relevant to know about attitudes of the wider environment toward the cross-gender behavior of the child.

In sum, proper understanding of the extent of the gender problem itself, the child's development and current functioning, the functioning of the family, and the attitudes of the child's wider environment is necessary when making a decision as to what types of interventions will benefit the child.

Types of Cross-Genderedness

The subtypes of children that we mentioned in Chapter 4 referred to a division based on psychosexual outcome. Such a classification can thus far only be made retrospectively. Yet there is heterogeneity within the young children who show cross-gender behavior.

Boys who are only occasionally interested in girls' toys or girls' play, or tomboys who also have some girls' interests, are probably rarely seen in clinics unless they have highly homophobic parents. Children who are referred to our clinic usually show a fair amount of cross-gender behaviors and interests. Whether all these children need clinical attention is debatable. As Meyer-Bahlburg (1985, p. 682) noted, within this group one may encounter behaviors that belong to a "zone of transition between clinically significant cross-gender behavior and mere statistical deviations from the gender norm."

Within the clinically referred children, Zucker and Bradley (1995) distinguish the four following subgroups.

First, there are children who develop symptoms in reaction to a life event or traumatic experience, such as parental divorce or sexual abuse. The onset can be as early as in the "true" GID group but is usually later. Before the event gender behavior was usually not atypical. In our experience, such cross-gender behaviors are less pervasive (e.g., only fantasy play and cross-dressing) and sometimes already decrease before treatment has started. Instead of "flying into femininity" in reaction to life events, boys can also be preoccupied with cross-dressing or cross-gender play for other reasons. For example, one boy in our clinic with a very rejecting mother and overly aggressive father often played sadistic games with Barbie dolls, tying them up and hanging them. One day, his mother caught him cross-dressed, tying his sister's hands. The motives for his cross-gendered "play" clearly do not correspond to the pattern that is seen in most children with GID.

Second, there are boys who fulfill some of the *DSM-IV-B* criteria, but hardly the *DSM-IV-A* criteria. When they play girls' games and play with girls, they seem to do so because they are incapable of maintaining relationships with other boys or because they are not comfortable with their company. When they cross-dress, they seem to do it to please their girl friends, rather than enjoying it themselves. Their lack of assertiveness is evident not only when they are in the company of boys but also when they play with girls. They dislike some boys' games, sports, and rough-and-tumble play and rarely play with boys, but they do not dislike their bodies. Friedman (1988) used the term *juvenile unmasculinity* to characterize the behavior of this group. Richardson (1999) expects that most boys in this group will belong to the healthy functioning gender-atypical boys. One would expect that a similar phenomenon would exist in girls. However, in our clinic, we never come across masculine girls who seek the company of boys and prefer boys' activities only because they feel uncomfortable in the company of girls or have poor relationships with girls.

Third, there are boys who are not particularly feminine in their behavior and preferences, but like to wear female undergarments. They have a clear preference for soft fabrics such as nylon and silk. As in the first group, this attraction to soft fabrics may emerge after certain life events. Wearing soft clothes appears to have a calming and comforting effect. Boys who show these types of interests, however, are fairly rare. Of over 150 children under 12 at our clinic, they accounted for less than 3%. Again, we never encountered a similar phenomenon in girls.

Fourth, there are children with intersex conditions who may show the same cross-gender behavior, interests, identification, and anatomic dysphoria as other children with GID. Because it is an exclusion criterion according to *DSM-IV*, these children cannot be given a GID diagnosis (just a diagnosis of GID not otherwise specified, or GIDnos). Indeed, they are probably different from non-intersex children with regard to etiology (Meyer-Bahlburg, 1994). Treatment, however, that already varies greatly within non-intersex children with a GID diagnosis will not be very different from treatment given to children with GID only.

Diagnostic Procedure

At the gender clinic of the Department of Child and Adolescent Psychiatry of the University Medical Center in Utrecht, the Netherlands, a standard procedure applies when a child under 12 is referred. The purpose of this procedure is to assess the severity of the gender problem and other potential behavioral or emotional problems and to identify factors that might have influenced the gender development of the child and factors that may interfere with treatment.

The procedure consists of at least five sessions, but may take longer in complex cases. At the first session, the parents and child are seen together and separately. We ask parents why they have decided to come to the clinic and to give some information about the development and behavior of the child and their own responses to this behavior. The family situation is explored to see whether we have to take any special circumstance into consideration. The parents' expectations of the assessment and possible treatment are discussed and the procedure is explained. After this, they have to fill out several questionnaires, while we talk with the child to estimate the meaning of the assessment for the child, to create a working alliance, and to gather some first information regarding the gender problem.

After this first session, we have another interview session with the child and, in a different session, the child is psychologically tested. Usually there are separate interview sessions with each parent. The gender development and current functioning of the child are discussed with the parents, and behaviors, preferences, and statements of the child that are referred to in the *DSM-IV* are addressed. Also, specific attention is paid to the parents' own family history and any gender issues that might have played a role in their lives. Furthermore, feelings of both parents about their child's cross-gender behavior, their child-rearing practices, and marital or family conflicts regarding the cross-gender behavior are explored.

Apart from the gender behaviors, interests, and identity, we measure general psychological functions such as intelligence and various aspects of socioemotional development and current functioning. We concentrate specifically on aspects that are reported to be more often present in children with GID, such as anxieties, problematic social relationships, separation/individuation problems, low self-concept, and awareness of stigmatization. We also try to gain insight into themes that are central in the child's life and his or her ideas and feelings about his or her family.

Instruments

A testing session with a child starts with an interview in order to get some relevant information in an open way. This interview covers many areas, such as play, games, toy and peer preference, preference for rough-and-tumble play, gender role in play, cross-dressing, identification figures, identification with adult gender roles, interest in nurturing, body satisfaction, and choice of gender at birth. The number and formulation of the questions will depend on the age of the child (see Table 6.2). Very few children have problems with these questions, whereas they find questions

TABLE 6.2 Gender Preference Interview

1. Who are your best friends?
2. What games do you usually play with your friends?
3. What are your own favorite games?
4. What are your favorite toys?
5. Do you have any hobbies? Which ones?
6. What are your favorite movies /books/TV programs?
7. Do you like romping? Who are your favorite romping partners?
8. Do you like to play “father and mother” (“play house”); what is your role in this game? Can you tell me what is fun about this role?
9. Do you like to dress up? What is your favorite outfit? [If not,] What do you usually wear at carnival or costume parties?
10. Are there any people you admire a lot?
11. When you are grown up, would you like to become like them? Can you tell me what is so good about him/her?
12. What do you want to be when you are grown up? What profession do you want to have when you grow up?
13. Do you want to marry when you are grown up? Any idea who will be the lucky person?
14. Are you already in love with someone? Can you tell me more about him/her?
15. Is someone in love with you?
16. When you are grown up, do you want to have children? How many? Boys or girls?
17. Do you like to take care of babies?
18. If you look in the mirror, are there any parts of you that you are happy with?
19. If you look in the mirror, are there any parts of you that you are unhappy with? What is wrong with these parts of you?
20. If I were a fairy and I could change you with my magic wand, what parts of you do you want me to change?
21. If my magic stick could fulfill your greatest wish, what would that be?
22. Suppose you weren’t born yet, and I, the fairy, asked you whether you would like to become a girl or a boy, what would you choose?

regarding their gender identity (from the Gender Identity Interview) usually much harder to answer.

To gather information on cross-gender behavior and feelings of the child, various instruments are available. At the gender clinic of the Department of Child and Adolescent Psychiatry of the University Medical Center Utrecht, the standard battery consists of the tests in Table 6.3. In addition to these instruments, a few other instruments have been published (for an overview, see Zucker & Bradley, 1995, pp. 60-61). Depending on the individual case, the battery is expanded with additional tests.

For young children there are instruments that test the ability to identify men and women and the understanding of gender as a characteristic that is

TABLE 6.3 Test Battery for Children Younger Than 12 with Gender Dysphoria

---

Specific instruments

For children under 6

- Gender labeling task (Leinbach & Fagot, 1986)
- Gender constancy task (Slaby & Frey, 1975) consisting of subtasks regarding:
  - Gender labeling
  - Gender stability
  - Gender consistency
- Toy preference (photographs)
- Playmate preference (photographs)

For all children under 12

- Gender Preference Interview (see Table 6.2.)
- Gender Identity Interview (Zucker & Bradley, 1995)
- Gender Role Questionnaire (Ijntema & Cohen-Kettenis, unpublished)
- Play and Games Questionnaire (adapted from the Child Game Participation Questionnaire, Bates & Bentler, 1973)
- Play Observation (except for "mature" 11- to 12-year-olds) (Rekers & Yates, 1976; Zucker et al., 1985)
- Draw-a-Person test (Rekers, Rosen, & Morey, 1990)

General instruments for children <12

- IQ test
- Sentence Completion Test For Childern Under 7
- Kinetic Family Drawing Test (Burns & Kaufman, 1972)
- Self-perception Profile (Veerman, Straathof, Treffers, Van den Bergh, & ten Brink, 1997) for children older than 7

Specific instruments for parents

For children <6:

- Preschool Attributes Inventory (PAI; Golombok & Rust, 1993)
- Child Behavior and Attitude Questionnaire (Bates et al., 1973; modified by Meyer-Bahlburg, Sandberg, Yager, Dolezal, & Ehrhardt, 1994)
- Child Game Participation Questionnaire (Bates & Bentler, 1973; modified by Meyer-Bahlburg, Sandberg, Dolezal, & Yager, 1994)
- Gender Identity Questionnaire (Elisabeth & Green, 1984, modified by Zucker & Bradley, 1995)

General instrument for parents

- Developmental History Questionnaire (unpublished)
- Child Behavior Checklist (CBCL; Achenbach & Edelbrock, 1983)

General instruments for teachers

- Teacher version of the CBCL (TRF, Achenbach & Edelbrock, 1986)
- School Questionnaire (unpublished)

---

stable in time (gender stability) and independent of superficial changes (gender consistency) (Leinbach & Fagot, 1986; Slaby & Frey, 1975). These are useful instruments to determine whether a young child has a basic understanding of the concept of gender. Young children with GID tend to be more cognitively confused than controls about gender (Zucker et al., 1999).

In older children, cross-gender interests and behaviors can be measured through standardized interviews or questionnaires. These are the Gender Identity Interview (Zucker & Bradley, 1995), the Play and Games Questionnaire (adapted from the Child Game Participation Questionnaire, Bates & Bentler, 1973), and the Gender Role Questionnaire. The Gender Role Questionnaire (Ijntema & Cohen-Kettenis, unpublished) is a self-developed 32-item questionnaire with questions regarding hobbies, sports and games, friends, clothing, identity, and self-attribution of gender characteristics. The questionnaire shows large gender differences and has a Cronbach's α of .92. Except for the Gender Preference Interview, whose psychometric properties have not been investigated, the gender tests in the battery contain only instruments with some discriminant validity. Both the Gender Identity Interview and the Gender Role Questionnaire gather relevant data in a structured way. If necessary, the data can be used as a starting point for further qualitative examination of the meaning of gender in the child's life.

When children are too young to fill out questionnaires, we use two sets of pictures to assess toy and peer preference. One set consists of typical girls' and boys' toys, the other of pictures of boys and girls. Combinations of a girls' toy (e.g., Barbie doll) and a boys' toy (e.g., soccer ball) or combinations of a picture of a girl and a boy are presented. By pointing their finger to the selected picture, children have to indicate the toy they like most or the child they would like to play with. The advantage of the method is that the children do not need to have very advanced verbal skills to express their preferences. They only need to comprehend the instruction. This ability is first appraised with test items of other objects, such as a balloon or a bear. This task shows clear gender differences in children without GID.

Zucker, Bradley, Doering, and Lozinski (1985) describe a standard set of stereotypical girls' and boys' toys and dress-up apparel that can be used for observing (cross-)gender play (modified from Rekers & Yates, 1976). The set was tested in children with and without GID. As compared to Zucker et al.'s (1985) procedure, we use a shortened version. Children are observed only at two play sessions, one while playing for 5 minutes with the toys and one while playing for 5 minutes with the clothes. A testing assistant, sitting behind a one-way screen, records the number of seconds that the child is in physical contact with the material. We have shortened Zucker et al.'s procedure, because children tended to get bored or become restless in the third session. Obviously, the play observation session gives much more than only quantitative information. Some 11- and 12-year-olds consider the free play test too childish. They will either not engage in play or refuse to follow the instructions. When this is because they are more mature than other children of the same age, they tend to express their thoughts and feelings in a more sophisticated way in the interviews.

In addition to giving information about object preference, the play observation creates the opportunity to observe the children's mannerisms and gestures. Rekers and Morey (1989) found that feminine boys tend to make certain gestures (e.g., "limp wrists") more often than controls. When a boy indeed makes such gestures, it becomes understandable why he is an easy target for teasing, even when he is not open about his cross-gender preferences to other children. Masculine-typed gestures do not seem to negatively influence the position of girls with GID among peers.

The Draw-a-Person test can be used for most age groups except for the very young. Children with GID tend to draw opposite-sex persons first. They also tend to draw the opposite-sex person taller and with more detail than the same-sex person (Zucker & Bradley, 1995) (Figure 6.1a and 6.1b). However, the rates are far from 100%, so the value of this measure lies more in the qualitative than in the quantitative information (Figure 6.2a and 6.2b).

We use several questionnaires that measure the gender behavior at home and at school. For parents, there are, in addition to two CBCL items (5 and 110; Achenbach & Edelbrock, 1983), some instruments that specifically ask for gender role behavior, identity statements, and the child's expression of feelings about his or her sex characteristics (Bates & Bentler, 1973; Bates, Bentler, & Thompson, 1973, modified by Meyer-Bahlburg, Sandberg, Yager, Dolezal, & Ehrhardt, 1994; Golombok & Rust, 1993). For school, only one item of the Teacher Report Form (Achenbach & Edelbrock, 1986) can be used, but teachers also spontaneously report gender-atypical behavior on our open school questionnaire. This questionnaire asks for learning problems, the motivation of the child to learn, the ability of the child to concentrate on academic activities, the general behavior of the child in and outside the classroom, peer contacts, contacts with adults at school, contacts between teachers and parents, and possible reasons for teachers to pay special attention to the child.

Regularly, a family therapist assesses family functioning. This is done when family dynamics seem to greatly influence the child's gender problem and family therapy is considered.

Figure 6.1a First Drawing of an 8-Year Old Boy With GID. Note the difference in height with Figure 6.1b.

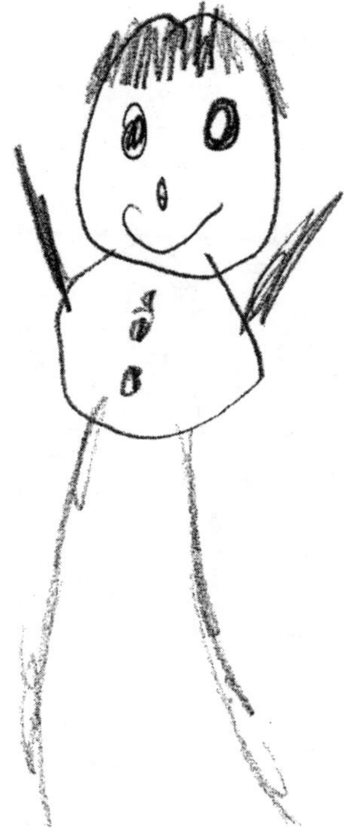

Figure 6.1b Second Drawing of an 8-Year-Old Boy With GID. Note the difference in height with Figure 6.1a.

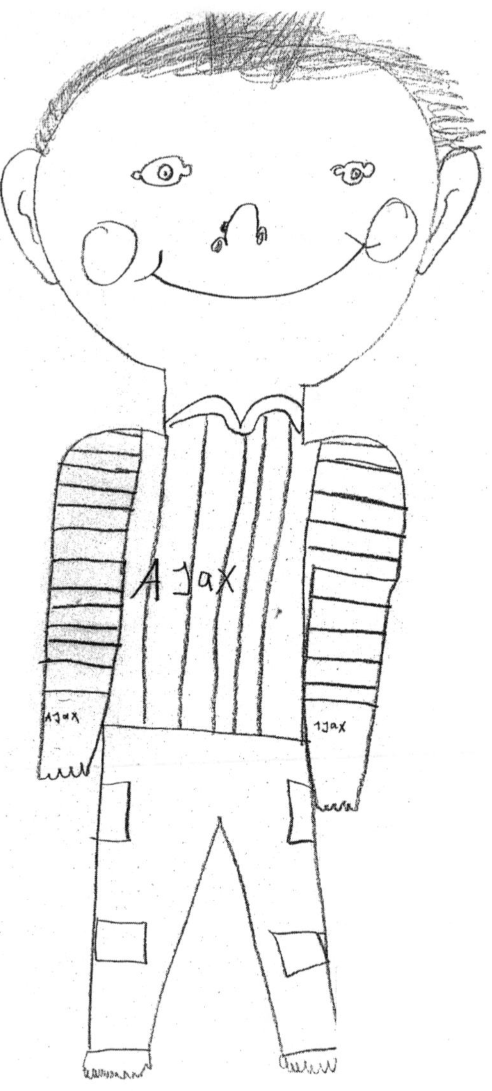

Figure 6.2a First Drawing of an 11-Year-Old Girl With GID. Note that the boy in this drawing is smiling and the name of a famous soccer club (AJAX) is on his shirt. Compare with Figure 6.2b. The girl cries and has "huilen" ("crying") written on her shirt.

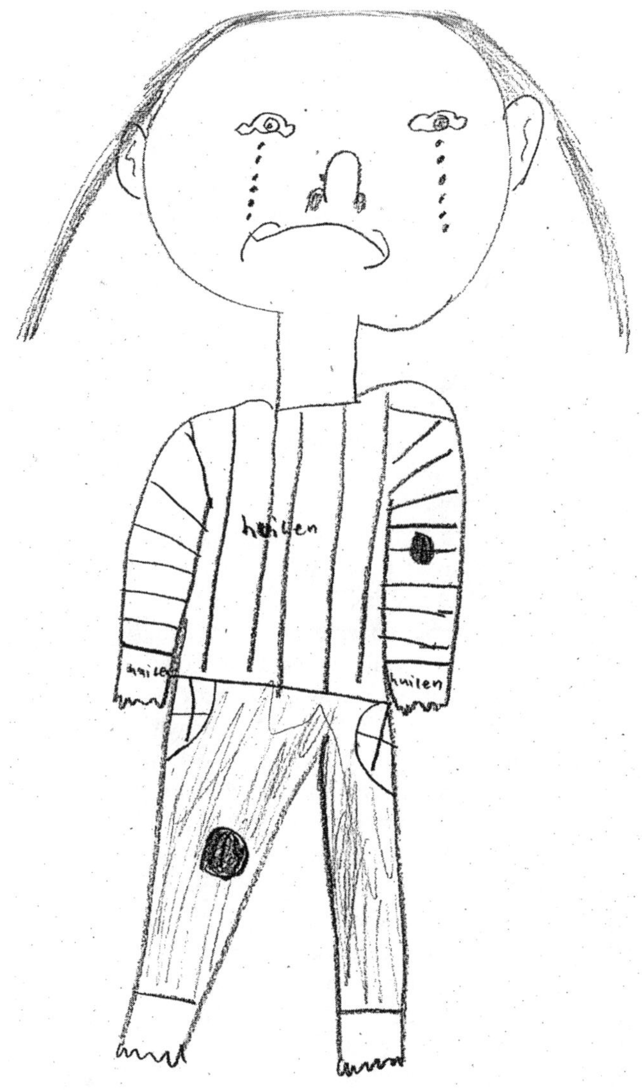

Figure 6.2b Second Drawing of an 11-Year-Old Girl With GID. Note that the girl in this drawing cries and has "huilen" ("crying") written on her shirt. Compare with Figure 6.2a. The boy is smiling and has the name of a famous soccer club (AJAX) on his shirt.

INTERVENTIONS

Treatment Rationales and Treatment Goals

Moral or religious motives, and perhaps also a genuine concern about problems associated with a homosexual lifestyle, have led some therapists to treat cross-gendered children in order to prevent homosexuality or, as Rekers and Kilgus (1995) call it, sexual deviance (e.g., Haber, 1991; Rekers, 1982; Silverman, 1990). Others treat children with GID, because they feel that having a psychiatric disorder is inherently stressful and needs clinical attention. There is, however, strong opposition to such treatment rationales. Arguments are (1) that attempts to prevent homosexuality are unethical, because homosexuality is not a psychiatric disorder, (2) that there is no evidence whatsoever that treatment actually prevents homosexuality, and (3) that GID in children is not necessarily a psychiatric disorder (if one disagrees with the current *DSM* criteria). This resistance is probably directed more toward therapeutic interventions of children who have "mild" forms of GID (according to Bartlett et al., 2000) and do not express discomfort with their bodies and do not have a desire to be of the opposite sex) than toward children with "extreme" forms of GID (e.g., Feder, 1997; Menvielle, 1998; Pleak, 1999). An intermediate position in this debate is taken by Meyer-Bahlburg (2002). He pragmatically refers to the decrease in cross-genderedness in the majority of the children with GID who approach puberty. Taking the serious social and emotional problems children with GID may encounter into consideration, hc states, "These sequelae of GID are our primary reason for its treatment. We expect we can diminish this problem if we are able to speed up the fading of the cross- gender identity which will typically happen in any case" (Meyer-Bahlburg, 2002, p. 361).

Relatively little dispute exists regarding the prevention of transsexualism, though evidence about the effectiveness of treatment in preventing adult transsexualism is also virtually nonexistent.

Among those who consider treatment of children with GID justified, short-term treatment goals depend on the etiological theories of gender identity disorder. Clinicians who consider GID to be the result of an underlying developmental psychopathology and/or a defense to deal with distress, which is generated by early life experiences, aim at modifying the supposed causal and/or perpetuating factors. In doing so they try to attain a gender identity change (e.g., Bradley & Zucker, 1998; Coates & Wolfe, 1997; Karush, 1993; Shane & Shane 1995; Silverman, 1990). Clinicians who regard GID as a result of inappropriate learning experiences aim at extinguishing cross-gender behaviors and reinforcing same-gender behaviors and skills (e.g., athletic skills in boys), either within therapy sessions or at home, assuming that these changes imply a cross-gender identity change (Meyer-Bahlburg, 2002; Rekers, 1995). Although the etiological explanations of these clinicians differ, all assume that changing a cross-gender identity in children is possible (Bradley & Zucker, 1998; Rekers, Kilgus, & Rosen, 1990). Clinicians who consider childhood cross-gender identity and behavior primarily as manifestations of later homosexuality and do not consider homosexuality a psychiatric disorder do not try to change gender identity and cross-gendered behavior per se. These therapists focus instead on acceptance of the child's cross-genderedness by parents and child and try to support the child in establishing a healthy self-esteem and adequate coping mechanisms (Menvielle, 1998; Pleak, 1999). However, even therapists of opposing backgrounds will agree that certain forms of suffering should be alleviated under all circumstances. Such distress may come from social ostracism, non-GID psychiatric or family problems, or intense unhappiness about one's sex characteristics and being a boy or a girl.

Types of Interventions

Behavior Therapy

The primary target of behavior therapists obviously is the cross-gender behavior of children. The majority of these treatments were done by Rekers (1995) and his coworkers. They worked primarily with boys. Their techniques include reinforcement of gender-typical behavior during therapy sessions and extinction of cross-gender behavior, gradual shaping of gender-typical behavior, and desensitizing fear of failure. They also try to accomplish gender behavior changes by mediation therapy. They encourage the same-sex parent (or other same-sex role models within the family) to invest time in positive play and interaction with the child. They not only recommend that parents ignore the cross-sex-typed behaviors and praise same-sex typed and neutral play and behavior but also teach the parents how to do it. They encourage parents to provide their sons with nonthreatening training experiences to develop athletic skills. Differential (social) attention and reinforcement are also used by the therapists.

With older children, Rekers and his colleagues use self-monitoring techniques. The children have to press a wrist counter when playing with same-sex typed toys. When they have earned a certain amount of points they exchange them for rewards or privileges. A "bug-in-ear" device is used to instruct and verbally reinforce the child while playing.

As feminine gestures and mannerisms are a source of rejection and ridicule, Rekers and colleagues devote particular attention to these behaviors. They first obtain a baseline. Then they verbally explain to the child or show him on videotape which gestures will be the target behaviors. The child then receives a number of tokens. During a play session he loses a token every time he shows a specific target gesture. The gestures are treated one by one. After a number of gestures have actually disappeared, similar procedures are followed at home and at school in order to foster generalization of the results to other settings.

In their treatment, Rekers and colleagues also try to remediate athletic skills defects. They start with easy tasks and reward the boys for successful performance. In this way they shape a number of ball game abilities. If possible, the father is included in the training. In therapy sessions, the fear of failure that these boys often have is desensitized. Rekers (1995) states that these procedures are quite effective in helping the child enjoy success in his increasing abilities.

Psychoanalytic Therapies

Treatment with psychoanalytic psychotherapy, psychoanalysis, or other forms of individual psychodynamic psychotherapy is reported in a great number of case studies. Depending on their theoretical orientation and assessment of the literature on GID, therapists have formulated a wide range of treatment goals (e.g., Haber, 1991; Shane & Shane, 1995; Silverman, 1990; Stoller, 1970). Their focus is obviously on the assumed underlying child or family pathology in order to influence the cross-gender identity. The reported causal factors in much of the psychotherapy literature do not necessarily overlap with the factors reported in the research literature. Paternal aggression, weakness, and unavailability; extreme maternal closeness ("blissful symbiosis," Stoller, 1975); and maternal physical and emotional absence leading to attachment problems are all mentioned as determinants of cross-gender identification.

Combined Approaches

A few reports exist on treatments of boys that combine elements of behavioral, psychodynamic, milieu, or family therapy (Di Ceglie, 1998; Green, 1974; Green, Newman, & Stoller, 1972; Lim & Bottomley, 1983). Green and his coworkers focus on the overcloseness of the relationship between mother and child and an appreciation of male-typed activities.

They try to establish a trusting relationship with a male therapist in order to give the boy a positive role model. They further encourage positive bonds with males by increasing the involvement of the boy's father in his life. In therapy they encourage engagement in male-typed activities and stress the advantage of such activities. Finally, they educate the parents as to how they may be influencing the child's gender problem and advise them how to reward masculine behavior and disapprove the child's feminine behavior. Lim and Bottomley (1983) worked along similar lines. They describe how they did individual work with a child to create insight and enhance masculine behaviors. At the same time they worked with the family to overcome their resistance to change, with mother allowing separation from the child and with father encouraging assertive and masculine behavior of the child.

Meyer-Bahlburg (2002) describes an eclectic approach for 4- to 6-year-old boys that primarily focuses on the environment of the child. Key components of this approach are (1) gender ideology and sensitization, (2) father/son relationship, (3) responding to cross-gender behavior, and (4) peer relations. It consists of weekly treatment sessions with the parents only. In the gender ideology and sensitization part of the treatment, parents and therapist have to come to an agreement about what gender-typical behaviors in young children are and the desirable degree of sex-typing. Parents may need cognitive restructuring, sensitization, or information in this respect. In order to enhance the relationship between father and son, the therapist tries to change intrafamilial alignments. The father is encouraged to spend more active time with his son and the mother to let go of her son and to support his male role taking. Furthermore, parents are instructed how to respond to the cross-gender behavior. Instead of prohibiting and responding critically, they are taught to pay positive attention to gender-neutral or masculine activities and no attention to cross-gender activities. Finally, parents have to arrange five play dates per week with other boys that have to be attained in 6 weeks. These boys should be neither cross-gendered, nor too rough. Once the boy has become comfortable with other boys, group activities and extracurricular activities, such as clubs or camps, have to be initiated.

Di Ceglie (1998) describes a treatment model that is used at the Portman Clinic in London. Di Ceglie and his coworkers note that the etiology of GID is still largely in the dark and probably multifactorial. Therefore, in their management of GID, altering cross-gender identity is not a primary objective. In this respect, their approach differs from most other treatment approaches. Instead of aiming directly at gender identity change, they focus on developmental processes that may have negatively influenced the child. They also stress the importance of recognition and nonjudgmental acceptance of the gender identity problem. Di Ceglie's treatment model concentrates on amelioration of emotional, behavioral, and relationship difficulties; on breaking the secrecy around GID; and on activation of the child and family's interest in exploring impediments in development (e.g., mourning processes and insufficient separation/individuation). In order to attain their goals, Di Ceglie and his coworkers use therapeutic interventions such as individual, family, and group therapy and social and educational interventions. All these activities are integrated into a comprehensive management plan. In some cases, the interventions diminish or solve the gender problem; in others they do not. Di Ceglie emphasizes the importance of close collaboration among different professionals, such as psychologists, psychiatrists, social workers, psychotherapists, and (particularly for children with GID who enter puberty) pediatricians.

The Dutch treatment approach resembles the approach in England in several ways. Depending on the outcome of the diagnostic phase, therapy can be focused on any characteristic of the child, the family, or both that seems to be related to the child's suffering or malfunctioning. Treatment is meant to strengthen the child to overcome his or her vulnerabilities, alleviate distress, and remove obstacles to a healthy development. Gender identity disorder, among other factors, may make the child vulnerable and be a source of distress and an obstacle to a healthy development. If there seems to be a relationship between problematic child or family factors encountered in the diagnostic procedure and the gender dysphoria of the child, the treatment will first focus on these factors. To parents it is explained that the child needs treatment anyway, because of the observed problems. The gender identity problem may or may not change as a result of treatment. It is also made clear that the final psychosexual outcome, with or without treatment, cannot be predicted.

When the child and family appear to function reasonably well, a counseling contact is offered to the parents, as they often find it hard to deal with certain practical or emotional matters. This approach allows the clinician to remain involved in the development of a child with GID. The most commonly used forms of therapy are (cognitive) behavior therapy social skills training, mediation therapy (parent training), play therapy, and family therapy (see the vignette for "Family Therapy"), but psychodynamically oriented therapies are also offered.

When a child is seen for individual therapy, parents are always counseled separately. In these sessions the question of how they should react to the child's cross-gender behavior invariably comes up. We believe that it is beneficial for children, especially as they grow older, to be able to have social relationships with both boys and girls. In order to have a good time when they play with same-sex peers, it is also necessary that they have at least a few common interests. Because it does not come naturally, children with GID need some encouragement to play with same-sex peers. Children could be stimulated to develop broader, perhaps neutral, interests other than dolls (in the case of boys) or soccer (in the case of girls). With regard to cross-dressing we recommend setting limits in place and time. Allowing cross-dressing only in their own room or at certain times may serve several purposes. For instance, in certain neighborhoods, children would meet much aggression when seen cross-dressed. To keep the cross-dressing away from the eyes of others protects the child from being harassed. If children tend to completely lose themselves in their fantasies, a restriction of cross-dressing keeps them in the reality of their daily world. When the rationale for this restriction is explained, children are much better able to understand why this happens to them and are thus more compliant. Entirely forbidding children to cross-dress may not work out very well. Parents who do not allow their children to have opposite-sex toys or clothes often tell us that their children manage to get what they want behind their parents' backs.

VIGNETTE: Family Therapy

Marc, an intelligent and attractive boy, was 6 years old when his parents came to our clinic. His family consisted of his father (37 years), his mother (30 years), himself (6 years), and his sister, Jill (4 years). His parents were well educated. They were both rather rational people and also tried to raise their children in a rational and responsible way.

It appeared that, from babyhood, Marc loved external stimulation, but found it hard to amuse himself. When he could not yet walk or crawl he easily became frustrated. He often wanted to achieve things that were outside his range. As Marc was his mother's eldest child, she gave him, from birth on, oceanic amounts of attention. His mother was a competent but insecure woman. She felt increasingly inadequate as a mother because Marc was demanding and difficult to please, and received little support from her husband in the upbringing of the children. When Marc's sister, Jill, was born, Marc continued demanding as much of his mother's attention as he did before. However, it was no longer physically possible for her to give

Marc what he wanted. The mother was very happy with her little daughter; Jill happened to be a very easy child. For the first time she experienced that taking care of a child was not necessarily a hard job. Marc developed an extreme jealousy. He occasionally showed sadistic behaviors toward his sister, which made the mother afraid to leave the children without her supervision. The mother constantly tried to fulfill her children's wishes, but primarily functioned as a peacekeeper. She developed angry and aggressive feelings toward her son, because he increasingly spoiled the atmosphere at home with his demanding and envious behavior. This also made her feel guilty. The father felt redundant and concentrated on his work. On the weekends, he sometimes took one child out (while the mother went away with the other child) to prevent the many scenes and quarrels that occurred when the family was together.

Because Marc's cross-gender behavior had started shortly after his sister was born, it was hypothesized that the two events were related. Marc might have come to the conclusion that being a girl was the best way to get his mother's love and attention.

Before therapy started it appeared that the father and mother had different ideas about the extremeness of their son's cross-gender behavior. The mother was very anxious about Marc's femininity and feminine interests and feared he might become a transsexual. In the father's opinion, Marc was not a genuine cross-gender boy because Marc also showed an interest in some boys' objects and activities. Like his mother, his father too was worried about Marc's extreme jealousy, but he had fewer problems handling Marc's difficult behavior. He felt that Marc's extreme jealousy was also a way of manipulating his mother.

Both parents recognized the importance of addressing Marc's jealousy rather than his feminine behavior. Therapy became a joint responsibility in changing interaction patterns. Both parents, but the mother in particular, had to make a major change in thinking about Marc's problems. Instead of focusing on the cross-gender behavior, she had to focus on her general child-rearing problems. She increasingly understood the importance of allowing the father to be more involved with the children and after a while she even enjoyed it. The father became more sensitive to his children's feelings. He started doing things with his son alone, such as sailing and cooking. The father's hobby was cooking and Marc very much enjoyed working in the kitchen with his father. This change in the father's involvement made the mother feel more supported by her husband. In the course of therapy, the mother could admit to herself that she was very tired of spending all her energy on her family. She decided to stop working for a while and, for the first time in years, she had some time to herself. When Marc's jealousy of Jill resumed normal proportions, the children started playing together. For the first time this could take place without constant quarreling. Marc's interest in girls' toys and clothes diminished drastically. This was still the case at a follow-up 6 months after therapy had ended.

Parent Organizations

In the Netherlands, parents of children with GID can also meet regularly at meetings of a parent support group, "Berdache," which was established in 1998. The group organizes educational or supportive meetings for parents a few times a year. Not every parent is equally interested in these meetings, but many parents come once or twice. A few stay for longer periods. Because the threshold for these meetings is low, many parents seek contact with this organization before coming to our clinic. Berdache also takes care of parents if they need advice while still on the waiting list.

Berdache not only provides services for parents and families but also has contacts with schools. They send information to schools, give talks, and advise teachers. As a result of their activities (often in the national media), teachers are now more aware of the phenomenon and feel more comfortable handling the daily matters they are confronted with. We receive many positive reactions from parents and children about the school activities of Berdache. One is that, in schools with "antiteasing programs," children are indeed not teased. Often the reason for starting such a program is the presence of a child with GID.

To our knowledge only England has a similar nationwide organization in Europe. The English support group is called "Mermaids." They do not organize meetings, but offer services through the Internet.

Effectiveness of Psychological Interventions

As no well-controlled treatment studies exist, it is unclear to what extent and until what age which type of gender identity disorder can be influenced by psychological interventions. It is also unclear whether certain forms of treatment are more effective than others. According to some clinicians, gender identity is more malleable in very young (<6 years) children (Coates & Wolfe, 1997; Meyer-Bahlburg, 2002; Zucker & Bradley, 1995), whereas in adolescence and adulthood a cross-gender identity is very difficult to change. Whether changes of gender identity that are reported in the literature are the result of the described psychological interventions, maturation only, or a combination of both remains to be demonstrated. However, from the above it should be clear that, even if there are no short-term or long-term changes in gender identity, many children with GID could profit from psychological interventions.

SUMMARY

When a child is seen because of his or her cross-gendered behavior, the first goal of the clinician is to assess whether a child actually meets the criteria for GID. Several authors have criticized the current *DSM* criteria. They believe that the criteria do not sufficiently make a distinction between healthy functioning gender-atypical children and children who clearly suffer because of their cross-genderedness. They fear that the healthy group will needlessly be pathologized and treated accordingly. Besides this type of cross-genderedness, other forms have also been distinguished. Cross-gender behavior may be the response of a child to a traumatic life event, (in boys) an inability to maintain oneself among same-sex peers, (in boys) limited to interest in wearing women's undergarments, or present in children with intersex conditions who cannot have a *DSM-IV* GID diagnosis because an intersex condition is an exclusion criterion.

Apart from deciding whether a child meets diagnostic criteria, the clinician also has to understand what factors (in the past or at the time of referral) may have influenced the cross-genderedness of the child. Factors that have repeatedly been put forward in the literature as contributing to or conserving cross-gender identification can be used heuristically. The information about the child's gender behavior and feelings then has to be appraised against a broader background, such as general aspects of the functioning of child and family. A proper understanding the gender problem, evaluated in this wider perspective is necessary when a choice about appropriate treatment interventions has to be made.

Especially for English-speaking countries a variety of instruments are available to assess gender understanding, behavior, and feelings. These are cognitive tests, parent and child questionnaires, child interviews, play observations, and projective methods.

Great disagreement exists regarding the treatment of children with GID. Some therapists treat the children to prevent homosexuality. Many consider this to be unethical, because homosexuality is not a psychiatric disorder. They also point to the fact that there is no evidence that treatment actually prevents homosexuality. Opponents of the current *DSM* criteria are also against treatment of children with GID (at least of children with less extreme forms of GID), because they do not see GID as a psychiatric disorder. Yet, in most clinics some form of treatment is offered.

A variety of methods are used to treat children with GID. Behavior therapists explicitly focus on an enhancement of gender-typical behavior and a reduction of cross-gender behavior. Psychodynamic psychotherapists focus on the assumed underlying child or family pathology, assuming that treatment of this pathology will change the child's cross-gender identity. In the work of some eclectic therapists the primary focus is on any factor that may negatively influence the child's functioning, not the cross-genderedness per se, whereas some do try to influence the child's cross-gender behavior. Treatment will sometimes, but not always, diminish or solve the gender problem.

Despite the many treatment approaches, controlled studies do not exist. It is therefore still unclear whether (an extreme) GID in childhood can truly be cured. Whether homosexuality or transsexualism can be prevented by psychological interventions before puberty also remains to be demonstrated. Nothing is known about the relative effectiveness of various treatment methods. Studies on GID in children are accumulating, but the field is still in its infancy. Pending controlled studies, psychotherapy directly aimed at curing GID has no place in the treatment arsenal. Fortunately the numbers of specialized centers, where large groups of children with GID are seen, is increasing. This makes it more likely that the much needed intervention studies will become possible in the near future.

7

CLINICAL MANAGEMENT OF GENDER PROBLEMS IN ADOLESCENTS

DIAGNOSIS

Most cross-gendered adolescents come to clinics with a straightforward wish for sex reassignment. Some are not certain whether SR is the solution to their problems and have more open questions regarding their identity. Usually, the adolescents are eager to come to a gender identity clinic. Occasionally, it is the parents' rather than the child's initiative to seek clinical help. For example, one couple was worried about their daughter, who had been clearly cross-gendered since early childhood. When she entered puberty she seemed to suffer deeply from the physical changes. She started to walk with a stoop when her breasts were developing. She also stopped swimming because she could no longer wear shorts. Even when the weather was extremely hot she was wearing large sweaters. She withdrew from contacts with her peers and did not want to play soccer any longer when she had to move from a mixed to a girls' team. Her mood became depressed. She was jealous of anything her brother did. Her appearance was extremely masculine. Yet she did not want to talk about her feelings with anybody and adamantly denied a wish for SR. If someone mistook her for a boy, it made her furious. In this case, her parents, who were convinced she was a transsexual and ashamed of her transsexualism, forced her to come to the clinic.

In the diagnostic phase, the gender problem as well as potential underlying or related problems have to be examined comprehensively. It is impossible to diagnose transsexualism on the basis of objective criteria (e.g., hormone levels). There are no medical instruments that reliably show who is a transsexual and who is not. Psychometrically sound psychological instruments to measure transsexualism do not exist either. Yet it is extremely important not to misdiagnose and thus mistreat applicants for SR. So, in order to make a diagnosis, mental health professionals are largely dependent on the information given by the applicants. Fortunately, parents almost always accompany their children when they apply for SR. Even if they unconsciously or deliberately distort their life histories or reported gender feelings, their story can be checked. Because of the importance of the decision to be made, the diagnostic procedure is extensive and takes time (see below).

The recommended procedure in the Standards of Care of the International Harry Benjamin Gender Dysphoria Association (Meyer et al., 2001), an international professional organization in the field of transsexualism, is to come to the SR decision in various steps. In the first phase, an applicant has to fulfill *DSM* or *ICD* criteria for gender identity disorder or transsexualism. The next phase, which is sometimes labeled triadic therapy, includes three elements (Meyer et al., 2001). The elements consist of real-life experience in the desired role, hormones of the desired gender, and surgery to change the genitals and other sex characteristics.

The First (Diagnostic) Phase

Procedure

In this phase, information must be obtained from both the adolescent and the parents. The information concerns various aspects of the general and psychosexual development of the adolescent. The diagnostic team further needs information on current cross-gender feelings and behavior, current school functioning of the child, peer relations, and family functioning. With regard to sexuality, the subjective meaning of cross-dressing, the type of cross-dressing, sexual experiences, sexual behavior and fantasies, sexual attractions, and body image have to be explored.

Obviously, adolescents are unable to give accurate information about their very early development. Some cannot even give a realistic picture of their current functioning. So information given by parents is important in order to get a comprehensive view of the child's situation. Yet, parents too may, intentionally or unintentionally, distort facts. They may deny their child's GID symptoms out of fear that acknowledging them would too quickly open the door to SR or they may simply not accept the fact that their child is a transsexual. If children have not or have hardly been raised

TABLE 7.1 Test Battery for Gender Dysphoric Adolescents

For adolescents
General instruments:
- Intelligence test
- MMPI for adolescents
- Youth Self-Report version of the Child Behavior Checklist (Achenbach & Edelbrock, 1987)

Specific instruments:
- Biographic questionnaire for transsexuals (self-developed; see Cohen-Kettenis & van Goozen, 1997)
- Utrecht Gender Dysphoria Scale (Cohen-Kettenis & van Goozen, 1997)
- Body Image Scale (Lindgren & Pauly, 1975)
- Draw-a-Person test (Rekers, Rosen, & Morey, 1990)

For parents and teachers
- Child Behavior Checklist (CBCL, Achenbach & Edelbrock, 1983)
- Teacher Report Form (TRF, Achenbach & Edelbrock, 1986)
- school questionnaire (self-developed, see Chapter 6)

by their parents, it is helpful to have even more sources of information, such as grandparents or other relatives, to get a broad view of the child's past and current functioning.

This diagnostic phase focuses not only on gaining information. In order to prevent unrealistically high expectations as regards their future lives, the adolescent also has to be thoroughly informed about the possibilities and limitations of sex reassignment and other kinds of treatment. This information should be given soon after the first sessions. The way a patient responds to the reality of SR can also be informative diagnostically.

Instruments

For adults, many treatment centers use standardized instruments to appraise the intellectual and emotional coping mechanisms of the person and to detect psychopathology. In an overview of 19 clinics in North America, Europe, and Australia, Petersen and Dickey (1995) report that, in addition to self-developed instruments, combinations of the following tests were included in a standardized testing battery: MMPI, WAIS-R, Rorschach, Thematic Apperception Test, Draw-a-Person test, Symptom Check list-90-R, and Bem Sex Role Inventory. Table 7.1 indicates which instruments are included in our standard test battery for adolescents.

TABLE 7.2 Utrecht Gender Dysphoria Scale (FM Young Adolescent Version)

1. I preferably behave like a boy
2. Every time someone treats me like a girl I feel hurt
3. I love to live as a girl
4. I continuously want to be treated like a boy
5. A boy's life is more attractive for me than a girl's life
6. I feel unhappy because I have to behave like a girl
7. Living as a girl is something positive for me
8. I enjoy seeing my naked body in the mirror
9. I like to behave sexually as a girl
10. I hate menstruating because it makes me feel like a girl
11. I hate having breasts
12. I wish I had been born as a boy

The biographic questionnaire is a semistructured interview schedule with questions regarding the development of the gender problem, current cross-gender feelings and behavior, peer relations (teasing and bullying), family functioning, prior and current (medical and psychological) treatments, and various aspects of sexuality.

The gender dysphoria scale is a short questionnaire with questions regarding the distress persons feel when confronted in daily life with the fact that they belong to their biological sex (Table 7.2). As can be expected most nontranssexuals score close to the minimum score, which is 12. Most transsexuals score close to the maximum score, which is 60. In our experience, difficult applicants in terms of eligibility for SR and in terms of a problematic treatment course score in the middle range of the scale.

The body image scale simply lists 30 physical characteristics. The respondents indicates their (dis-)satisfaction with each body part on a 5-point scale. They can also express a wish to change the particular body part. Three subscores can be obtained: a primary and secondary sex characteristics score and a neutral body part score.

Like children, adolescents with GID also tend to draw an opposite-sex person first and one that is larger than the drawing of a same-sex person. However, the Draw-a-Person test is used for its qualitative rather than quantitative information (Figure 7.1).

Differential Diagnosis

As noted before, not all transgendered adolescents have a clear and explicit wish for SR. Some may simply be confused regarding aspects of their gender. For example, young male homosexuals may have a history of

Figure 7.1a First Drawing of a 15-Year-Old Girl With GID.

Figure 7.1b Second Drawing of a 15-Year-Old Girl With GID.

stereotypical feminine interests and cross-dressing. As a child they may have had a GID diagnosis. During puberty, they discover their sexual attraction toward men. In some cases they mistake their homosexuality for GID, despite a drastic reduction or disappearance of their cross-gender interests and activities. In ego-dystonic homosexuals, it is not confusion but lack of acceptance of their homosexuality that makes them consider SR a solution to their problem.

Transvestic fetishism occurs in heterosexual or bisexual male adolescents who become sexually aroused by cross-dressing. Boys with transvestic fetishism may also be confused about their wish to cross-dress. Usually they hope that SR will "solve" their sexual excitement when cross-dressed. Gender Identity Disorder and transvestic fetishism may co-occur, but in our adolescent patients this has been hardly encountered. In that case both diagnoses should be given.

A wish for SR may further exist in persons who prefer to be sexless, but have no cross-gender identity, such as Scoptic Syndrome patients (Coleman & Cesnik, 1990). These men want to be rid of their sex organs, but do not wish to acquire the sex characteristics of the other sex. Even in adults Scoptic Syndrome is extremely rare.

Last, boys with transient stress-related cross-dressing may mistake their interest in cross-dressing for a need for SR. This may also happen in patients suffering from severe psychiatric conditions (e.g., schizophrenia), accompanied by delusions of belonging to the opposite sex. In rare cases, GID and schizophrenia coexist. As preschizophrenic youngsters are usually not very stable psychologically, medical interventions will never be considered before they are adults.

When *DSM-IV* GID criteria are not completely met, the classification Gender Identity Disorder Not Otherwise Specified (GIDNOS) is used. *ICD-10* has three categories in addition to transsexualism: "Dual-Role Transvestism," when someone wears opposite sex clothes to experience temporary, but not permanent, membership of the opposite sex, without a sexual motivation for the cross-dressing; "Other Gender Identity Disorder"; and "Gender Identity Disorder, Unspecified." Neither of the last two has specific criteria.

Some individuals with gender problems do not seek complete SR. Instead they try to integrate masculine and feminine aspects of the self. Some seek partial medical treatment, either hormones or some forms of surgery.

INTERVENTIONS

Psychotherapy or Sex Reassignment?

Nowadays many clinicians with experience in the field will consider the question, as formulated in the heading of this paragraph, as outdated. However, it played an important role in the development of treatment models for GID. The desirability of SR as a resolution for the psychological suffering of transsexuals has been controversial since the first sex change operations were performed. Many psychotherapists view transsexualism as a delusion, something close to psychosis, a narcissistic disorder, a psychological defense against homosexual feelings, a psychological defense against anxiety-provoking gender role incompetence, and/or a result of unsuccessful separation/individuation from the mother, and so on, but hardly as a phenomenon in itself (e.g., Chiland, 2000; Kavanaugh & Volkan, 1978-1979; Kubie & Mackie, 1968; Lothstein, 1984; Meyer, 1982). They feel that one should try to help transsexuals to resolve emotional conflicts underlying their wish for sex change by no other means than psychotherapy. By doing so the discrepancy between gender identity and body characteristics would be eliminated.

However, the existing case reports do not provide convincing evidence for complete and long-term reversal of cross-gender identity by means of psychotherapy. This is, first, because operationalizations of gender identity differ considerably from report to report. Consequently, treatment successes have been evaluated on the basis of diverse and sometimes vague (e.g., the clinicians' global impression) criteria. Second, clinicians also encounter a stated disappearance of the wish to undergo SR when no psychotherapy has been given. Applicants may refrain from SR because they fear losing significant persons or becoming a social outcast, but, many years later, return to continue the procedure (Marks, Green, & Mataix-Cols, 2000). So even the few claimed cures (e.g., Barlow, Abel, & Blanchard, 1979) might in fact have been postponements of SR. Third, the case studies describe patients who were highly motivated to "change" their gender identity, a characteristic rarely encountered in most applicants for SR.

Outcome studies on extremely gender-dysphoric SR applicants who have been randomly assigned to either SR or psychotherapeutic treatment, and with very long-term follow-ups, do not exist. Considering the lack of motivation of most transsexuals for psychotherapy, one may wonder whether it will ever be possible to conduct such studies. The absence of evidence that psychotherapy is the treatment of choice has led mental health professionals to look for other solutions to the problem. Because a once-firmly established cross-gender identity appeared virtually impossible to change, the only rational solution to the problem seemed to be the adaptation of the sex characteristics to the cross-gender identity. This solution was supported by the results of some early studies showing no apparent psychological disturbance in transsexuals, which would make SR a hazardous enterprise (e.g., Green & Money, 1969; McCauley & Ehrhardt, 1977; Roback, McKee, Webb, Abramowitz, & Abramowitz, 1976; Strassberg, Roback, Cunningham, McKee, & Larson, 1979). Later, more attempts were made to assess the pretreatment psychological condition of the transsexual group. Today, many studies are available (e.g., Beatrice, 1985; Bodlund & Armelius, 1994; Brems, Adams, & Skillman, 1993; Cohen, de Ruiter, Ringelberg, & Cohen-Kettenis, 1997; Cole, O'Boyle, Emory, & Meyer, 1997; Derogatis, Meyer, & Boland, 1981; Greenberg, & Laurence, 1981; Haraldsen & Dahl, 2000; Kuiper, 1991; Leavitt, Berger, & Hoeppner, 1980; Mate-Kole, 1988; Miach, Berah, Butcher, & Rouse, 2000; Murray, 1985; Pfäfflin, 1993; Sundblom, Bodlund, & Höjerback, 1995). In some, evidence of psychopathology was found, whereas in others it was not. These contradictions may be partly a result of differences in methodology and quality of measuring instruments, but they could perhaps also be explained in other ways. Lothstein (1984), for instance, conceptualizes transsexualism as a variant or subtype of borderline disturbances (Kernberg, 1975). According to Kernberg, this condition is characterized by identity diffusion, primitive defense mechanisms, and weak reality testing. So Lothstein expected transsexuals to primarily exhibit psychopathology when unstructured projective tests were used or when they were in stressful situations, but not when structured questionnaires were used. Studies using projective tests, however, do not seem to point unequivocally toward borderline pathology (Brems et al., 1993; Cohen et al., 1997; Fleming, Jones, & Simons, 1982). A more likely explanation for the conflicting results is that, thus far, most investigators have treated transsexuals as a homogeneous group. The results, however, might have varied, depending on the composition of the group of subjects under study. For instance, Leavitt et al. (1980) found that psychological functioning depended on the duration of hormone treatment. Better psychological adjustment was associated with longer use of feminizing hormones. In another study psychological functioning appeared to be related to living in the desired social role. Male-to-females living as women functioned better than those still living as men (Greenberg & Laurence, 1981). Also, SR applicants who met the *DSM-III* criteria of transsexualism demonstrated no psychopathology, whereas a group with gender identity disorder of adolescence and adulthood nontranssexual type (GIDAANT) showed moderate psychopathology (Miach et al., 2000). In Chapter 4 we already described other distinctions made between subgroups of transsexuals: homosexual (early onset, core, primary) and nonhomosexual (late onset, noncore, secondary) transsexuals. The homosexuals appeared to function before treatment somewhat more favorably than the heterosexuals (Smith, 2002). So it might well be that the studies that found psychopathology in transsexuals included subjects from other transsexual subgroups, whereas other studies found no psychopathology in transsexuals. As young applicants are more likely to belong to the homosexual (early onset, core, primary) group, their psychological functioning will be relatively favorable compared to that of the heterosexual (late onset, noncore, secondary) group.

Because transsexualism is not necessarily associated with psychopathology, an extreme cross-gender identity in most individuals seems to be fixed after puberty, and psychological treatments are not particularly successful in solving the problems of these individuals, SR seems to be the treatment of choice for very gender-dysphoric adults. This does not imply that psychotherapy is of no use to applicants of SR (see below). It is one element of a multifaceted approach of different treatments that should be coordinated.

The Desirability of Sex Reassignment for Adolescents

Even if one agrees with SR as a (palliative) treatment form for adult transsexuals, one could argue that adolescents should never be allowed to start sex reassignment, because they are still in a rapidly changing developmental process. At present, this is the policy in many countries. However, clinicians are faced with increasing numbers of youngsters who powerfully express that they find their lives unbearable without hormonal interventions.

One argument in favor of early treatment is that an eventual arrest in emotional, social, and intellectual development can be warded off more successfully when the ultimate cause of this arrest has been taken care of. Another is that early treatment might be beneficial in adolescents because their secondary sex characteristics have not yet fully developed. For instance, young MFs will, as adults, pass much more easily as females when they have never grown a beard or developed a low voice. In contrast, when MFs are treated several years later, their voice will always keep a male-like quality, and many years of painful and expensive depilation are involved to remove their facial hair. When breasts of FMs remain small, breast reduction will be an easier intervention, with less scar tissue. If the bodily changes of puberty are not interrupted and an adolescent still wants SR after he or she has reached adulthood, major physical interventions will be required to remove the unwanted physical characteristics. Yet, despite these obvious advantages, early treatment for adolescents with GID touches sensitive strings. Disapproval is common among professionals and laypeople. As Wren points out, "The debate about early physical treatment for transgendered adolescents will be passionately held. It throws up a host of issues that directly challenge thinkers and practitioners in the fields of endocrinology, medical ethics, child development, politics, and human rights. These young people challenge our definitions of masculinity and femininity and our ideas about the meaning of gender differences. They challenge our view of 'pathological' and 'normal' developmental processes. They challenge our capacity to celebrate difference and diversity. Debates about fair and ethical treatment for these young people can never be a matter for specialists in psychological medicine alone" (Wren, 2000, p. 229). In the absence of evidence that transsexualism can be treated in adolescence by psychotherapy alone and that transsexualism is necessarily associated with severe psychopathology and the presence of the arguments in favor of early treatment, a few centers have started, in carefully selected cases, with hormonal therapy before adulthood (see also Chapter 8).

Psychological Interventions

Persons who are merely gender-confused or whose wish for SR seems to originate from factors other than a genuine and complete cross-gender identity are served best by psychological interventions. Such interventions may help them to better understand and cope with gender issues and to try out alternative solutions to their problem. One could be part-time cross-gender living (in the desired role only in an accepting environment). Another could be to identify stressors leading to the desire to cross-dress and deal with them in nonmaladaptive ways.

For individuals who want to explore their options for coping with gender dysphoria group therapy has also been advocated (Althof & Keller, 1980; Stermac, 1990; Yüksel et al., 2000). The information coming from members who are in different phases of understanding their gender problem, and the support in finding ways to deal with the problem, seems to be particularly beneficial to group members.

Family therapy may help to solve conflicts between family members rather than intrapsychic conflicts. These conflicts are quite common in cross-gendered adolescents. Of 69 adolescents who were seen at a specialist gender identity development service in the UK, 75% appeared to have relationship difficulties involving parents or caretakers (Di Ceglie et al., 2002). It regularly happens that a transsexual adolescent wants to be more open about his or her condition than the other family members. Conversely, when they already live permanently in the opposite gender role, parents are sometimes concerned that their children will get into trouble because they do not disclose their situation to boyfriends or girlfriends. In particular, they fear aggressive reactions when these friends discover the truth. Another frequent cause of intrafamilial conflicts is that parents have trouble treating their sons as daughters and vice versa. Also, some adolescents perform poorly at school or behave badly at home, blaming everything on their difficult situation. Although family therapy is very useful for families with adolescent transsexuals, in our experience, family therapy never actually "cured" an extreme GID in adolescence.

Psychotherapy, combined with pharmacotherapy (low doses of lithium carbonate), has been reported to be successful in cases of Scoptic Syndrome, because the medication made patients more amenable to psychotherapy (Coleman & Cesnik, 1990). In-patient treatment in psychiatric hospitals may be needed for persons suffering from severe psychiatric conditions. If the psychiatric disorder has been treated properly by medication or another method the request for SR will have to be reevaluated. In the case of adolescents with severe psychiatric comorbidity, hormone therapy will not be prescribed before adulthood, even if the adolescent is transsexual and has recovered from the psychiatric illness.

The efficacy of all these interventions, however, has not been investigated in formal outcome studies. Outcome studies in which specific forms of therapy for homogeneous subgroups of persons with mild or atypical forms of GID are evaluated would undoubtedly contribute to our knowledge on appropriate treatment of GID persons. The relative rareness of the condition and diversity within the group with respect to relevant treatment goals make it unlikely that such studies will be conducted in the near future.

Psychotherapy for Sex Reassignment Candidates

From the UK study it appeared that more than half of the referred adolescents suffer from feelings of depression (Di Ceglie et al., 2002). These feelings do not always disappear without additional therapy. They are a matter of concern by themselves, but should also be taken care of in order to optimize the situation for further diagnostic work.

For adolescents, the first (diagnostic) phase is lengthy and intensive. So, in addition to gathering information to make the diagnosis, any relevant issue that comes up in the first phase has to be explored. This means that the diagnostic phase often contains therapeutic elements. Patients need time to reflect on any unresolved personal issues or doubts regarding SR before embarking on somatic treatment. It is paramount that any form of psychotherapy offered to GID patients is supportive. The more the patient is confronted with doubts on the part of the therapist, the less chance he or she has to explore his or her own doubts if they exist. Therapists also need to be knowledgeable about hormone treatment, surgery, and the legal consequences of the treatment to compare the SR solution in a balanced way with other options for living with the gender problem (e.g., part-time living in the opposite role or, for males, cross-dressing unobtrusively under male garments).

Other issues that may come up in the first phase are anxieties concerning the loss of important people as soon as they learn about the patient's SR wish or uncertainties whether passing in the opposite role is feasible. Long before the SR procedure actually starts, patients may need support when "coming out" or need social skills training to make the forthcoming changes easier to handle. When hormone treatment has started, psychotherapy may still be of use. Some patients indeed have to deal with loss, or negative reactions from the environment. Others can work on certain personal issues only after they no longer need to worry about masculinizing or feminizing their bodies. For these reasons, some clinics offer postsurgical psychotherapy. Whether patients accept this depends largely on the individual needs of the patient and the quality of earlier therapist/patient contact.

For adults, the standards of care do not require a minimum number of psychotherapy sessions before SR is started. This is because patients differ widely in their abilities to attain similar goals in a specified time and because a minimum number of sessions tend to be construed as a hurdle, which discourages the genuine opportunity for personal growth. The therapist can be an important support to the patient throughout all phases of gender transition (Meyer et al., 2001). For adolescents, the clinician has to be involved with the patient and family for a minimum of 6 months before hormones can be prescribed.

Triadic Therapy: The Second SR Phase

Real-Life Experience

In the real-life experience (RLE) phase, one has to live permanently in the role of the desired sex. Significant persons have to be informed about the impending changes. The HBIGDA Standards of Care (Meyer et al., 2001) describe six parameters to assess the quality of a person's RLE: (1) to maintain full- or part-time employment, (2) to function as a student, (3) to function in community-based volunteer activity, (4) to undertake some combination of items 1–3, (5) to acquire a (legal) gender-identity-appropriate first name, and (6) to provide documentation that persons other than the therapist know that the patient functions in the desired gender role. For adolescents this means that they live in the desired role not only at home but also at school and within organizations they belong to as well, such as sports clubs. If there is a close contact with parents and school, there is usually no need for documentation.

The underlying idea of this requirement is that applicants should have had ample opportunity to appreciate in fantasy or in vivo the familial, interpersonal, educational, and legal consequences of the gender role change. Feelings of dysphoria usually decline as a result of both the first bodily changes and the possibility to live in the new social role (see below). During the real-life experience the social transformation is a major focus of the discussions, when the adolescent starts to live in the desired role after the diagnostic phase. This is obviously less the case when they already lived in the desired role before applying for SR.

Physical Interventions: Hormones and Surgery

For adolescents, the guidelines of the Royal College of Psychiatrists (Di Ceglie, Sturge, & Sutton, 1998) as well as the HBIGDA Standards of Care (Meyer et al., 2001) make a distinction between three stages of physical intervention: (1) the fully reversible interventions, (2) partially reversible interventions, and (3) irreversible interventions.

Eligibility for Physical Interventions In practice, it appears that a diagnosis of GID alone is not sufficient for the decision to start the next treatment phase (RLE and hormones). This applies not only to adolescents but also to all SR applicants. This is, first, because in the *DSM-IV* a "strong and persistent cross-gender identification" is not operationalized in terms of duration or scores on certain instruments. Mental health professionals may thus disagree on the extremeness of a patient's GID. Clinicians who have seen few GID patients might be more inclined to consider someone's cross-gender identification as strong and persistent than clinicians who have seen large numbers of patients with GID. So, despite the fact that formal *DSM-IV* criteria are applicable to an individual patient, the actual extremeness of the GID may vary. Second, Bower (2001, p. 2) correctly points out that, in the *DSM-IV*, the preoccupation or the overwhelming desire of the patient to acquire the anatomical sex characteristics of the chosen gender is underemphasized. He proposes, in the following sentence in the *DSM-IV*, that "This preoccupation may be manifested as an intense desire to adopt the social role of the other sex *or* to acquire the physical appearance of the other sex through hormonal or surgical manipulation," the word "or" should be replaced by the word "and." When applied to adolescents we believe that only those applicants for SR who have from very early on (toddlerhood) shown a clear and extreme cross-gender identification in all social environments and want to adopt both the social role of the other sex and SR should be eligible for SR.

But even extremely cross-gender-identified persons may not be able to handle the drastic life changes that accompany SR. In the literature on adults, certain factors, such as psychopathology, are reported as a risk for poor outcome. Especially when making decisions on the eligibility of early interventions one should take potential risk factors into consideration (see below).

Eligibility for Fully Reversible Interventions As soon as pubertal changes have begun, adolescents with extreme forms of GID may be eligible for puberty-delaying hormones. However, adolescents should be able to make an informed decision about pubertal delay. Therefore it is preferable if they experience the onset of puberty, at least to the second phase of pubertal development, Tanner Stage Two (Meyer et al., 2001).

Allowing adolescents with GID to take puberty-delaying hormones is justified by two goals. One is to gain time to further explore the gender identity and other developmental issues in psychotherapy. The second is to make passing easier if the adolescent continues to pursue SR. Naturally one wants to minimize an unfavorable outcome. It is therefore wise to require that, as a rule, GID adolescents eligible for hormone treatment meet the following criteria: (1) throughout childhood the adolescent has demonstrated an intense pattern of cross-gender behaviors and identity, (2) gender discomfort has significantly increased with the onset of puberty, and (3) the family consents and participates in the therapy.

It should be said that, thus far, the value of these additional criteria has not been empirically tested. The criteria have been developed through consensus among experienced clinicians (Di Ceglie, 1998; Meyer et al., 2001).

Puberty-delaying hormone treatment should not be viewed as a first step of the cross-sex treatment, but as a diagnostic help (Cohen-Kettenis & van Goozen, 1998). Therefore, a period of cross-gender living, the RLE, is not necessarily required, when only these hormones are taken. It is difficult to give a general rule for the start of the RLE, as the personalities and life circumstances of adolescents are so different. Some wait until they are 16 and have graduated from school. They start the RLE when they start to take cross-sex hormones, because they want to look "really convincing" at the moment of their social role change. Some think, correctly, that they already look convincing enough and begin living in the desired role even before they have started with puberty-delaying hormones. Others start the RLE some time after they have taken the puberty-delaying hormones and are relieved that their masculinization or feminization is not progressing.

Eligibility for Partially Reversible Interventions Adolescents may be eligible for estrogen or androgen therapy as early as age 16 (see Chapter 8 for a discussion on age limits). Although in many countries 16-year-olds are legal adults for medical decision making and do not require parental consent, parental consent is preferred. Adolescents need the support of their parents in this complex phase of their lives.

Mental health professional involvement, for a minimum period of 6 months, is another eligibility requirement for hormonal interventions of adolescents. The objective of this involvement is that treatment is thoughtfully and recurrently considered over time.

Eligibility for Irreversible Interventions Surgical interventions should not be carried out prior to adulthood or, if hormone treatment started shortly before adulthood, prior to an RLE of at least 2 years in the desired gender role. The Standards of Care emphasize that the "threshold of 18 should be seen as an eligibility criterion and not an indication in itself for active intervention" (Meyer et al., 2001, p.10). If the RLE supported by the cross-sex hormones has not resulted in a satisfactory social role change or if the patient is not satisfied with or is ambivalent about the hormonal effects, the applicant should not be referred for surgery.

Effects of Fully Reversible Interventions Lutein hormone-releasing hormone (LHRH) agonists block further progress of puberty. These compounds bind so strongly to the pituitary that the secretion of luteinizing hormone (LH) and follicle-stimulating hormone (FSH) no longer takes place. Eventually the gonadal production of sex steroids discontinues and a prepubertal state is (again) induced (Gooren & Delemarre-de Waal, 1996).

Pediatric endocrinologists prefer LHRH agonists over other compounds, such as progestins or antiandrogens (blocking testosterone secretion or neutralize testosterone action) for boys or progestins for girls, because LHRH agonists are more effective and have fewer side effects. As a result of the progestin or antiandrogen treatment in boys, body hair growth diminishes. Penile erections and sexual appetite may disappear or become less frequent. In girls, progestins block the production of estrogens and progesterone. They are given only to stop menstruation.

Adolescents that have gone into puberty at a very young age or have started with LHRH agonists or cross-sex hormones at a relatively late age will already have developed certain secondary sex characteristics. Some cannot be reversed by hormone treatment. Because facial hair growth is very resistant to antiandrogen therapy, additional mechanic hair removal techniques may be necessary. Speech therapy is sometimes needed, because the vocal cords will not shorten once they have grown, and the MF has to learn to use his voice in a female fashion. Surgical techniques to shorten the vocal cord exist but are as yet rarely employed. There are still concerns about the safety and effectiveness of such voice modification techniques.

Effects of Partially Reversible Interventions To induce female sex characteristics in MFs, such as breasts and a more female-appearing body shape due to a change of body fat around waist, hips, shoulders, and jaws, estrogens are used. Other physical effects are decreased upper body strength, softening of the skin, decreased testicular size and fertility, and less frequent and less firm erections. Little can yet be said about effects on emotion. In one study it was found that, in MFs, after 3 months of treatment, there was an increase in indirect angry reactions at the expense of aggression and assertiveness. Sexual arousability also decreased (van Goozen, Cohen-Kettenis, Gooren, Frijda, & van de Poll, 1995). Individual MF patients report that they cry more easily when they watch moving television scenes or feel more calm after the start of their treatment, but this was not found in two studies on emotional functioning of transsexuals after 3-4 months of hormone treatment (Slabbekoorn, van Goozen, Gooren, & Cohen-Kettenis, 2001; van Goozen et al., 1995).

In FMs, androgens are used for the induction of male body features, such as a low voice, facial and body hair growth, and a more masculine body shape. Other physical changes are a mild breast atrophy and clitoral enlargement, though the clitoral size will never reach the size of a penis by means of androgen treatment only. Reversible changes are increased upper body strength, weight gain, and decreased hip fat. With respect to psychological effects, van Goozen et al. (1995) found that FMs after 3 months of androgen treatment reported an increase in anger- and aggression-proneness and in sexual arousability, whereas affect intensity diminished (Slabbekoorn et al., 2001).

Irreversible Interventions In MFs female-looking external genitals are created by means of vaginoplasty, clitoroplasty, and labiaplasty. In cases of unresponsiveness of breast tissue to estrogen therapy, breast enlargement may also be performed, but usually is not needed.

For FMs a mastectomy is often performed as the first surgery to successfully pass in the desired role. When skin needs to be removed, this will result in fairly visible scar tissue. Considering the still-continuing improvements in the field of phalloplasty, some FMs do not want to undergo genital surgery until they have a clear reason for it or choose to have a neoscrotum with a testicle prosthesis with or without a metaidoioplasty, which transforms the hypertrophic clitoris into a microphallus (Hage & Mulder, 1995). Other genital surgery consists of removal of the uterus and ovaries.

EFFECTS OF SEX REASSIGMENT

Since the first sex change operations, many studies have been carried out in order to investigate the therapeutic effectiveness of SR. Pfäfflin and Junge (1992, 1998) extensively reviewed 79 follow-up studies published between 1961 and 1991. A total of approximately 2000 postoperative patients were included in their survey. Since 1991 several more have appeared. (Bodlund & Kullgren, 1996; De Cuypere, 1995; Rakic, Starcevic, Maric, & Kelin, 1996). Only three studies report on postoperative functioning of transsexuals treated in adolescence (Cohen-Kettenis & van Goozen, 1997; Smith, Cohen, & Cohen-Kettenis, 2002; Smith, van Goozen, & Cohen-Kettenis, 2001). In most, but not all, studies relatively small samples were investigated. Moreover, the studies vary considerably with respect to methodology, number of subjects, and outcome criteria. Postoperative success was often defined by a combination of factors, sometimes including "objective criteria" such as employment or housing. Improvement in such conditions, however, should be considered secondary to the main treatment goal: diminution or resolution of gender dysphoria. Despite these differences between studies, the general conclusion can be drawn that SR effectively resolves the gender dysphoria experienced by transsexuals. Depending on methodology, number of subjects, and criteria, varying success percentages are mentioned. Early reviews report satisfactory results in 71.4% of the MFs and 89.5% of the FMs (Lundström, Pauly, & Wålinder, 1984; Money & Ehrhardt, 1970; Pauly, 1968, 1981). In a more recent review, the numbers are 87 and 97% respectively (Green & Fleming, 1990).

In two studies on adolescent transsexuals investigating gender dysphoria (Cohen-Kettenis & van Goozen, 1997; Smith et al., 2001), a substantial decrease in postoperative gender dysphoria was found. None of the patients showed regrets. Psychologically and socially, they functioned fairly favorably and better than adult transsexuals tested with partly the same instruments in an earlier study (Kuiper, 1991) (Table 7.3).

Negative results, like severe postoperative regrets, are also described. Pfäfflin and Junge (1992, 1998) found that, among the approximately 2000 transsexuals, 18 MFs and 5 FMs returned after SR to their original gender role because of postoperative regrets. Many of the evaluation studies are reports on increasing numbers of applicants, treated at the same gender clinics. Therefore the 1-2% of their sample who felt regret are still an estimation. Weitze and Osburg (1998) report in their study on applications for legal sex change that of the 733 persons who applied for a legal change of sex status at courts in West Germany and West Berlin between 1981 and 1990, one person reapplied for legal sex reassignment. When requests for reversal of first-name changes only were included, 0.4% of the total sample of 1422 applied for legal retransformation. Weitze and Osburg (1998) believe, however, that not all individuals with regrets might want to go through a second legal procedure. They therefore expect that the actual number may be somewhat higher than 0.4%.

After analysis of a number of extensive case histories, Pfäfflin and Junge (1992, 1998) conclude that most cases of postoperative regret could have been avoided by means of a careful differential diagnosis, an adequate real-life experience, and a reasonable quality of surgery. In another study, Pfäfflin (1992) added poor psychological functioning and lack of professional guidance during treatment as risk factors. Five risk factors (higher age at assessment, criminal activities, inadequate social support, more masculine-appearing physical appearance, and more sexual contact with women) were identified in an early Swedish study (Wålinder, Lundström, & Thuwe, 1978) that had compared five MFs voicing postoperative regrets with nine MFs who expressed no regrets. In another Swedish study 4 of 13 MFs were judged to regret their treatment openly or indirectly (Lindemalm, Körlin, & Uddenberg, 1986). Four of 35 (!) factors seemed to be associated with

TABLE 7.3 A Comparison of Scores on the Dutch Short MMPI (NVM) of Postoperative Adult (Kuiper, 1991) and Adolescent Transsexuals (Smith et al., 2001) With Normative Samples

	Adult FMs	*Adult MFs*	*Adolescent FMs+MFs*
Negativism	high	high	average
Somatization	average	high	average
Shyness	high	high	average
Psychopathology	high	high	average
Extraversion	average	average	average

postoperative regrets. These unfavorable factors were (1) a high age at first request about SR (after age 32), (2) traumatic separation from parents before age 6, (3) having completed military service, and (4) having done heavy physical labor. However, their findings were not confirmed in the large samples covered by the reviews of Pfäfflin (1992) and Pfäfflin and Junge (1992, 1998). When percentages of regretful patients in homosexual and heterosexual transsexual groups were compared, none of 97 homosexual FMs and MFs showed any regrets, whereas 4 out of 14 (28.6%) heterosexual MFs consciously regretted the decision to undergo SR (Blanchard et al., 1989). In a recent Swedish study, with a retrospective cohort design, a non-regretful group of 205 transsexuals and a regretful group of 13 (9 MFs and 4 FMs) were compared (Landèn, Wålinder, Hambert, & Lundström, 1998). Here, two factors predicted regret of SR, namely lack of support from the patient's family, and the patient belonging to the *noncore* group of transsexuals (i.e., transvestites and effeminate homosexuals). In a Dutch study among 10 regretful patients it was concluded that in most cases combinations of a very late onset of gender dysphoria, fetishistic cross-dressing, psychopathology, and social isolation were present (Kuiper & Cohen-Kettenis, 1998).

Factors that were associated with relatively poor postoperative functioning, in empirical studies that did not include regretful transsexuals were "noncore transsexualism," SR application late in life, poor surgical results, psychological instability, inadequate social functioning, unfavorable physical appearance, loss of work and family, and a lack of compliance (Eldh, Berg, & Gustafsson, 1997; Lundström et al., 1984; Ross & Need, 1989).

Group sizes in these studies, however, were very small, making it impossible to calculate which risk factors or combination of factors are the most decisive. A recent prospective study among 162 adult transsexuals, revealed that, at posttest, only one male applicant regretted his decision to the point of returning to a male social role (Smith, 2002). Therefore comparisons could not be made between regretful and nonregretful applicants. Instead, the level of postoperative (social and sexual) functioning was measured by means of a questionnaire. The factors that predicted relatively poor postoperative functioning were sexual orientation (nonhomosexual), severe psychopathology, and dissatisfaction with secondary sex characteristics at assessment. In the above studies, however, it is repeatedly noted that the presence of a risk factor is not an absolute contraindication for SR.

Despite the sometimes poor quality of the studies some applicant-related factors are consistently reported. These are a late onset age and/or age at assessment, poor social support, (severe) psychopathology, unfavorable physical appearance, and poor surgical results. Most of the other factors are probably closely related to those mentioned.

In adolescents age of onset is invariably extremely early. Although no specific comparisons have been made between adolescent and adult transsexuals, it is likely that the younger group is less dissatisfied with their secondary sex characteristics than the older group. For adolescents, severe psychopathology and poor social support might be the most relevant risk factors, known before treatment, for poor postoperative functioning. Persons with (combinations of) these risk factors deserve extra clinical attention in every phase of the process and, in some cases, an adjusted treatment procedure. Clearly, professional guidance during the SR procedure also plays an important role. This is not only true for mental health professionals, whose most important tool is interaction, but also for endocrinologists and surgeons. Instead of attributing poor outcome solely to patient characteristics, health care professionals should realize that the quality and quantity of their interventions also contribute to the outcome of SR.

SUMMARY

Most adolescents with gender problems come to clinics with a straightforward wish for sex reassignment. Some are just uncertain and confused about their gender identity. Currently it is impossible to diagnose transsexualism on the basis of objective measures. Yet a correct diagnosis is of utmost importance. Therefore the diagnostic procedure is lengthy and extensive. Specialized clinics usually follow the recommended procedures in the Standards of Care of the International Harry Benjamin Gender Dysphoria Association (Meyer et al., 2001), an international professional organization in the field of transsexualism, which is a guide for the diagnosis and treatment of applicants for SR in various steps. In the first phase, an applicant has to fulfill *DSM* or *ICD* criteria for GID or transsexualism. The next phase includes three elements: a real-life experience in the desired role, hormones of the desired gender, and surgery to change the genitals and other sex characteristics.

In the first phase information is obtained from the adolescent, the parents, and, if possible, the school. The information concerns various aspects of the adolescent's development, current cross-gender feelings and behavior, sexuality, body image, peer relations, school functioning, and family functioning. Psychological assessment is necessary to evaluate cognitive and emotional coping abilities and psychopathology. Not many specific instruments for the assessment of gender dysphoria in adolescents are available. This first phase is also used to inform the child and the parents about the possibilities and limitations of SR.

Applicants for SR may have gender problems other than transsexualism, such as transvestic fetishism, transient stress-related cross-dressing, or a wish to be sexless rather than of the opposite sex. A wish for SR may also be a part of a broader psychiatric disorder or a manifestation of ego-dystonic homosexuality. Some individuals with GID do not seek complete SR. Still others attend clinics to explore their gender feelings and do not have a clear wish for SR.

Sex reassignment as a solution to the psychological suffering of transsexuals has been controversial since the first sex change operations were performed. However, transsexualism does not appear to be inherently associated with psychopathology, and psychotherapy has not been particularly successful in solving it. Therefore SR seemed to be the treatment of choice for transsexual adults. Opposition to SR for adolescents is even stronger than for adults, because they are still developing. Arguments in favor of early treatment are that early SR may avert negative social and emotional consequences of the GID more successfully than late SR and make passing as a member of the opposite sex relatively easy, because the secondary sex characteristics have not yet fully developed. This, however, does not imply that SR is a solution for every adolescent who applies for SR.

Psychological interventions are the treatment of choice for youngsters whose wish for SR is related to factors other than a genuine and complete cross-gender identity. For them individual psychotherapy, group therapy, family therapy, and psychiatric treatment are better options than SR. Psychotherapy before, during, and after SR may also be useful for SR candidates who need time to explore unresolved personal issues or need support.

When a SR applicant is considered to be eligible for SR, he or she has to live permanently in the role of the desired sex, the so-called real life experience. An increasing number of adolescents, however, already live in the desired role when they are first seen at clinics. With regard to physical interventions for adolescents, a distinction is made between three stages: fully reversible interventions, partially reversible interventions, and irreversible interventions. The fully reversible hormones block further progress of puberty. This creates time to further explore the gender identity and other developmental issues in psychotherapy and makes passing as the desired gender easier if the adolescent continues to pursue SR. The partially reversible interventions consist of cross-sex hormone treatment. To induce female sex characteristics in MFs, estrogens are used, whereas in FMs, androgens are used for the induction of male body features. Irreversible interventions include various types of surgery. In MFs female-looking external genitals are created and sometimes breast enlargement is performed. In FMs a mastectomy, removal of the uterus and ovaries, and some form of genital surgery are performed.

Many follow-up studies have been carried out to evaluate the effectiveness of SR. Most studies concern treatment effects in adult groups. Success percentages in relatively recent studies are 87% for MFs and 97% for FMs, but outcomes differ greatly between studies. This is probably due to methodology, number of subjects, and outcome criteria. Postoperative regret to the point of a second role reversal is estimated to be 1–2%. In the few follow-up studies on adolescent transsexuals there were no participants with regrets, gender dysphoria had virtually disappeared, and psychologically and socially the adolescents functioned fairly favorably. Extrapolating from studies on adult transsexuals it seems that psychopathology, poor social support, and physical appearance may be the factors that are most likely associated with poor postoperative functioning.

Based on our experience with gender-dysphoric adolescents, we believe that some can be treated by psychological interventions only. For others, however, psychotherapy is not enough. If the diagnosis and treatment decisions are made by an experienced and interdisciplinary team, it is possible to select candidates for early SR. It would seem that young transsexuals who do not show severe psychopathology and are well supported by their environment are better off when they are treated as soon as the diagnosis can be reliably made than when they have to wait until they are adults. The results of follow-up studies make clear that alleviation of the gender problems is not equivalent to a life free of conflicts. That is why involvement of the mental health professional is not only important before and during SR. Even after surgery, there may be a need for psychotherapy or counseling.

8

LEGAL ISSUES OF INTERSEXUALITY AND TRANSSEXUALISM

LEGAL SEX ASSIGNMENT OF INTERSEXES

Ancient History

In history, most intersex conditions could not be recognized and the children were thus not treated differently from other children. The definition of the sex of a newborn with ambiguous genitals, however, has been a problem from ancient times. Although ancient Roman traditions glorified androgyny in art and in philosophy, babies with ambiguous genitals were seen as monsters (*monstra*) and as a bad omen, and they were killed in a purifying ceremony (Wacke, 1989). Only in the 6th century did Emperor Justinian suggest letting such children live and deciding their sex according to the predominant aspect of their genitals as either male or female. As this decision was not always possible, medieval legislation applied an additional rule: At the time of baptism, the father of the child preliminarily declared the sex of the child. When grown up, and before getting married, the offspring had a choice of his or her future sex, which had to be corroborated by a publicly sworn "promissionary oath," renouncing one sex and adhering to the other for the rest of his or her life. When civil legislation gradually replaced canonic (church) legislation, in cases where a predominance of male or female genital characteristics could not be decided upon at birth, the rule was to decide in favor of the male sex (*"in dubio pro masculo"*; Hirschauer, 1993) to guarantee privileges which the person, if male, might be endowed to. If a person broke the promissionary oath, this was regarded as sodomy, and it was punished with capital punishment until the late 17th century. In the course of the 18th century such cruel rules were slowly loosened. Instead of having to swear an oath, the person only had to demonstrate his or her decision by unambiguous behavior with respect to the chosen sex. Later, choosing one's own sex in adulthood was increasingly replaced by the judgments of medical doctors. It was generally doubted that true hermaphroditism existed. It was argued that there might be individuals whose sex was dubious at first glance, but in effect they would really belong to one of the sexes. The French *Code Civil* of 1804, which influenced most of the legislation of continental Europe, therefore left the decision of the sex of a person mainly to medical judgment, not to the person himself or herself, and medical judgment focused on the appearance of the external genitals only. For the law, this external appearance was the decisive criterion for legal sex determination.

Errors of sex assignment based on this tradition of evaluating the sex of the external genitals as either male or female did not pose a serious legal problem for the following 2 centuries. Usually, such errors could easily be repaired by presenting a medical document explaining the error in the previous sex determination. The error was thus rectified, a new birth certificate was issued by the registrar, and courts did not have to be involved in this procedure. At present this holds true for intersexes (as measured by external genitals) in practically all cultures.

Recent History

In the 20th century, medical research explored the concept of intersex in much more depth. Neugebauer (1908) was the first scientist to systematically collect cases of "true" hermaphroditism. The author of a classic work of the 1960s stated that hermaphroditism, formerly an exotic phenomenon, had become a major research field, analyzing chromosomes and hormones: "Between 1952 and 1958 approximately the same number of cases of true hermaphrodites were published as in the years 1900-1951" (Overzier, 1961, p. 537). Including cases of pseudohermaphroditism, he estimated the prevalence of intersex states in the population as 2–3 in 1000. A large number of new forms of intersex were described. Money (1968) called them *Sex Errors of the Body,* thus indicating that some of these conditions also might require the correction of the legal status of an individual once the error was detected and medically corrected. This background may explain one of the reasons why even some researchers in transsexualism, as well as transsexuals themselves, craved so much for somatic explanations of the condition. Such explanations might have allowed circumnavigation of the rigid cliffs of the law, which acknowledge only errors of sex assignment based on the morphology of external genitals.

LEGAL IMPLICATIONS OF TRANSSEXUALISM IN ADULTS

The main scope of this book is the understanding and management of GID in childhood and adolescence, including its legal implications. As yet there are not many specialized centers for the treatment of such children and adolescents, and there is practically no scientific literature on the legal implications of their treatment. Therefore, it may be useful to shortly outline the most important aspects of the legal discussion of adult transsexualism.

Surgical Sex Reassignment Preceded Legal Considerations

The First Sex Reassignment Surgeries in Female-to-Male Transsexuals

The first (incomplete) surgical sex reassignment surgery (*ablatio mammae and hysterectomy*) was performed on an FM in Berlin in 1912. The psychiatrist and surgeon involved apparently doubted that the treatment was in accordance with the law, as it took several years before the treatment was published. At that time not even the term *transsexualism* was available. The German sexologist Hirschfeld (1918) mentioned this first operation in passing as late as 6 years after the operation, the surgeon Mühsam (1926) 14 years later. Mühsam saw this patient, who made his living as a painter in 1921, 9 years after the first operations, and he performed an additional ovariectomy on him as he kept complaining about his ovaries as foreign bodies. The patient continued to live as a male until he died of tuberculosis in 1924.

The First Sex Reassignment Surgeries in Male-to-Female Transsexuals

The first (incomplete) MF sex reassignment surgery was performed in Berlin in 1920 (Mühsam, 1926). The patient had been referred to the surgeon by Hirschfeld. The patient was first surgically castrated. One year later, in 1921, an ovary was implanted. The surgeon did not dare to comply with the patient's wish to get a penectomy. Instead, he hid the penis subcutaneously below the perineum and formed a pouch from scrotal flaps to serve as a vagina. Interestingly enough, the patient later lost his transvestic and transsexual urges, returned to a male lifestyle, had the surgery redone, lived and cohabitated with a woman, went abroad, and worked as a physician.

In 1922, Hirschfeld referred a second MF patient to Levy-Lenz, one of his coworkers in his Institut für Sexualwissenschaft in Berlin, for surgical castration, followed by a penectomy in spring 1931. Finally, in fall 1931, a third operation was performed by the surgeon Gohrbandt, Urban Hospital, Berlin, to create a neovagina (cp. the first report of the surgical construction of a neovagina by Abraham, 1931, English translation Abraham, 1998). As a housekeeper in the institute, this patient, called by her first name, Dora, or Dorchen, became a well-known person in the field of sexual science and beyond (Herrn, 1995; Pfäfflin, 1997). This is also true for the famous Danish patient Niels Hoyer, alias Lilli Elbe (1932), who was operated on at Hirschfeld's recommendation in 1930 and who published her sensational and widely distributed autobiography in 1932. Patients as well as doctors experienced themselves as pioneers. Legal issues were not their primary concerns.

Terminology and Politics

Legal issues played, however, an important background role that is better understood when taking into account that in those days sexual relations between men was still a felony. Hirschfeld, one of the protagonists of the gay liberation movement at the end of the 19th and the beginning of the 20th centuries, conceptualized homosexuals as a "third sex" and tried to demonstrate the biological foundation of their condition. At the beginning of the 20th century, the gay liberation movement suddenly was at risk of breaking up when some noblemen with close connections to the German Kaiser Wilhelm II were convicted of homosexual acts. One faction, oriented toward an idealized Greek type of socially well-adjusted lifestyle, feared the failure of their attempts to abolish criminal sanctions against homosexuals if homosexuality also included so-called effeminate styles, drag queens, and so on. Hirschfeld reacted to this dangerous situation by coining the term *transvestism* and presenting a two-volume monograph containing biographies of persons of whom many would now be characterized as transsexual or transgendered (Hirschfeld, 1910), thus creating a new category apart from homosexuality. Hirschfeld (1923) also coined the term transsexualism (*psychischer Transsexualismus*) more than a quarter of a century before Cauldwell (1949), who is credited in most of the literature with having invented the term. Benjamin (1953), who knew Hirschfeld well and cooperated with him, would appear to have used the term even later "for the first time."

Publicity Shapes Conceptualization of Transsexualism

The spectacular case of Christine Jorgensen marked the sudden and rapid expansion of the history of transsexualism. Jorgensen, an American former GI whose family originated in Denmark, underwent a surgical castration in 1951 and penis amputation and the construction of a vulva in 1952, both performed in Copenhagen, and the construction of a neovagina in 1954, done in New Jersey. That these procedures drew public attention was mainly due to the *New York Daily News* headline "Ex-GI Becomes Blond Beauty: Operation Transforms Bronx Youth." The worldwide echo of this report—it was the time when TV was becoming widespread—resulted in a public discussion of whether sex change was possible (King, 1986). This widespread public reaction caused the doctors involved to reflect on and reevaluate their practice (Hamburger, Stürup, & Dahl-Iversen, 1953). Jorgenson got fan mail from all over the world, and Hamburger, the endocrinologist who had treated Jorgensen in Copenhagen, evaluated this mail in a remarkable publication with the heading "The Desire for Change of Sex as Shown by Personal Letters from 465 Men and Women" (Hamburger, 1953). This article as well as Benjamin's (1953) of the same year became trailblazers for the medical handling of transsexualism. Both authors explicitly commented on the public reaction to Jorgenson's case, and Benjamin used it to counter the "sensational" and "unscientific" (Benjamin, 1953, p. 12) public discussion, offering a fundamental discussion of the problems involved. Studying the files and interviewing Jorgenson as well as the doctors who had treated her, Hertoft and Sørensen (1979) attempted to reconstruct the primary intentions in Jorgensen's treatment. While the patient had wanted the operation to enable her to live as a woman, the doctors' intention, according to the authors, had been to reduce her "homosexual impulses" by administering cross-sex hormones and surgical castration (Hertoft & Sørensen, 1979). Jorgenson, they conclude, had gotten the operation due to motives other than her own. Only after the event had been interpreted publicly in the media as a sex change had its authors accepted it as such and recommended cross-sex hormone treatment as preparation for genital surgery. Hirschauer's (1993, 1997) lucid socio-ethnological investigation of the social construction of the sexes and gender and of the medicalization of gender migration emphasize the importance of this turning point for the further development of treatment programs for transsexuals.

The breakthrough within the North American academic world took place when, in 1965, the Johns Hopkins University Clinic in Baltimore, Maryland, established the first Gender Identity Program in the United States, which was soon followed by similar institutions or Gender Identity Clinics in Los Angeles and Minnesota. At the end of the 1970s there were about 40 such Gender Identity Clinics in the United States (Kando, 1973). The scientific debate concentrated on whether sex change was at all possible and whether sex reassignment was an adequate form of treatment. Doubts were mainly formulated by psychiatrists, psychologists, and psychoanalysts (e.g., Kubie & Mackie, 1968; Socarides, 1970). Psychiatrists started to become the gatekeepers for access to SR in the mid-1960s, whereas at the beginning of the transsexual "project" (Hirschauer, 1993, 1997) sexologists, endocrinologists, and surgeons clearly had the leading role.

That all these questions had been discussed extensively in Europe long before the American debate is hardly recognized in the Anglo-American literature. In Europe, surgery had been performed on a small scale for many years, mainly in Germany, Czechoslovakia, and Switzerland. Even legal sex changes had been admitted by Swiss courts (as early as 1931; Will, 1992) or by solitary decisions of German registrars or local administrations, even in Nazi Germany. This was something one would certainly not have expected as many homosexuals, transvestites, and transsexuals (then still described as transvestites) were put in concentration camps (Huelke, 1949; Bürger-Prinz & Weigel, 1940). In 1950, Boss, a Swiss psychoanalyst, presented to a renowned psychiatric audience the case of one of his patients, whom he had referred to a surgeon. Mitscherlich, the leading psychoanalyst in German-speaking countries after World War II, opened a broad debate on the legitimacy of the procedure, inviting all psychiatric chair holders in Switzerland, Austria, and Germany to voice their opinions (Boss, 1950-1951; Mitscherlich, 1950-1951; Mitscherlich et al., 1950-1951a, 1950-1951b). The debate covered mainly philosophical, moral, and therapeutic aspects and only marginally also legal ones. Of course, the opinions were split, and there were votes clearly stating that such operations should not be allowed.

A significant contribution to the political atmosphere was made in 1965, when Wålinder (1968) started a prospective study with transsexuals in Sweden, the same year the Gender Identity Clinic at Johns Hopkins University Clinic was founded. Unlike the development in the United States, which was hampered by Meyer and Reter's (1979) skeptical albeit, from a methodological point of view, flawed description of outcomes (for a critique see Abramowitz, 1986; Fleming, Steinman, & Bocknek, 1980; Lothstein, 1982; Pfäfflin & Junge, 1998), in a number of European countries the tradition of treating transsexuals developed continuously and steadily. It is therefore no surprise that European countries took the lead in solving legal problems connected with SR. As mentioned above, individual solutions were already found in Switzerland and Germany in the 1930s and 1940s, and Sweden was the first country to pass a specific law in 1972.

The Two Major Legal Questions

When Hirschfeld and Benjamin started their work, many of their patients still had a legal problem with cross-dressing, which, in some countries, was an offense that could result in arrest and other inconveniences. Effeminate behavior of males and wearing female attire made many such persons subject to suspicions of engaging in homosexual activities, which were criminalized, not only in North American states but also in many European countries. Local traditions of the police and courts differed widely as regards the factual prosecution of such behaviors. This is now history in western countries and no longer has to be legally dealt with. Much more important became the following two major legal questions: (1) Are cross-sex hormone treatment and SRS legitimate procedures? and (2) Should legal sex change be granted after SRS?

Legitimacy of Cross-Sex Hormone Treatment and Sex Reassignment Surgery

Interestingly enough, the legal implications of cross-sex hormone treatment were hardly ever discussed. Endocrinologists and sexologists just applied these treatments, and the patients were satisfied with the results. As the example of Christine Jorgenson demonstrates, hormone treatment was even justified as a means of tackling the transsexual experience of the patient. Initially, this was still interpreted as a variant of homosexual behavior, even though its effects turned out to be quite the contrary. Hormone treatment promotes gradual change and does not affect the appearance of the genitals. The legal profession did not seem to bother about that.

Surgical interventions in somatically healthy persons posed different challenges. The crucial questions were if they were *contra bonos mores* and if they had to be considered a "crime of mayhem." This offense is derived from early English common law, wherein mayhem was defined as an atrocious breach of the King's peace and as a "violent depriving of another of the use of such of his members as may render him less able, in fighting, either to defend himself or to annoy his adversary" (Holloway, 1974, p. 35). "Thus *contra* to the beliefs held by some of those knowledgeable in the field of transsexualism, removal of the gonads was, indeed, a mayhem at early common law, although the typical offence involved the removal of a hand, finger, or eye" (Holloway, 1974, p. 35). In some countries such surgical interventions were in breach of specific castration laws which either generally banned such interventions or reserved surgical castration for narrow indications only, for example, to prevent sex offenders from relapsing. In such cases these decisions had to be approved by a medical board or by state authorities, because transsexuals were not considered sex offenders. If someone came to a doctor and asked him to chop off his hand or gouge out his eye, taking the Sermon of the Mount all too literally, and if the doctor granted the request and really did so, he would be brought to court for grievous bodily harm. It would offend common decency and morals to thus injure a healthy person. Removal of genitals could certainly not be judged a purely cosmetic intervention but a serious attack on the integrity of the person. To justify SRS, doctors put the suffering of the patient to the fore, and they classified their doing as taking refuge to last resort (*ultima ratio*). Taking this reasoning into account, the step-by-step procedure with Christine Jorgensen gains plausibility.

Some of the follow-up studies on the outcome of SRS describe MF patients whose testicles were not totally removed during the SRS procedure, but transposed to other places of the body to protect the surgeon from the criminal prosecution for having castrated a man illegally. They come from different countries. Benjamin (1964, p. 108) described some patients whose testicles were displaced retroperitoneally "according to the method of Dr. Elmar Belt, Los Angeles." Randell (1969, p. 370) from England and Hoenig, Kenna, and Youd (1971) from England and Canada report a so-called "restribution operation" transposing the testicles under the abdominal wall; Alanko and Achté (1971) from Finland talk similarly of supraperitoneal implantation. When, in the 1970s, SRS was reactivated in Germany after World War II (in the 1960s, German transsexuals mainly traveled to Casablanca, Morocco), doctors first asked permission from the State Attorney to proceed.

There were two major ways of avoiding criminal prosecution when doing SRS. The first and most important was to establish research projects and Gender Identity Clinics and to publish beneficial results of treatment. This strategy, started in the mid-1960s, proved to be very successful. The second one was to issue standards of care for the treatment of transsexuals. The primary purpose of such standards of care was to protect surgeons from lawsuits of malpractice. At the same time they offered guidelines for organizing diagnostic and therapeutic procedures. This strategy was also very effective. The first such standards of care were published in 1979, and they have since been revised and updated several times. Paying reverence to the author of the first monograph on transsexualism, Harry Benjamin (1966), they are called *The Harry Benjamin International Gender Dysphoria Association's Standards of Care* (most recent edition: Meyer et al., 2001). In addition to these internationally very useful standards, there are now a number of similar texts issued by medical and psychological associations in different countries, for example, in Italy, Germany, and Russia. Sex reassignment surgery is now available in many countries of the world. Even in times when it was neither allowed nor available in some countries, for example, communist China during the leadership of Mao Tse Tung and Iran during the leadership of the Ayatollah Khomeini, individual patients from these countries could go abroad, receive the treatment, and come back and were accepted, at least in Iran, after treatment in their home country as a member of their "new" sex and gender.

The question of whether cross-sex hormone treatment and SRS were legitimate procedures found a short answer: Practice was faster and stronger than any doubts as to their legitimacy. They were accepted before a court or a legislator could effectively stop them. This holds true even though there were individual cases of doctors who actually were sentenced for grievous bodily harm after performing SRS, for example, in Buenos Aires, Argentina, in 1966 (Holloway, 1974). Such cases remained rare exceptions. Transsexuals first convinced their doctors that they needed SR. Together with their doctors they consequently convinced the public that they benefited from such treatment. This is what happened with adult transsexuals. For adolescent patients with GID one would wish to have a more reflected development of treatment decisions. Yet, it seems reasonable to learn from the needs of patients, even if they are still underage.

Legal Consequences of Sex Reassignment Surgery

Switzerland and Germany were the first countries to allow legal name and sex change in individual cases in the 1930s and 1940s. Such cases did not draw much public attention; they were solved more or less in silence. Thus it was possible not only to change one's legal status *ex nunc* (from the time of the surgery) but also *ex tunc* (retrospectively from birth onward). After World War II legal sex change in Europe was much more complicated. The argument of the invariability of the sex of a person was again strong in many countries that derived their law from Napoleon's *Code Civil* of 1804. In those countries, the birth certificate was and still is the source for all other personal documents. Therefore it is essential to change the sex in this document (*ex tunc*) to endow a person with the full rights of his/her new gender.

In Anglo-American countries it was easier to adopt a new first name, and registration was not centralized as in many European countries. Absurd situations arose when a person, after SRS, could change neither his or her first name nor his or her legal sex. The person then had an extremely hard time. But we also know of a remarkable number of patients who succeeded in convincing the registrar to turn a blind eye to legal restrictions and solve individual cases by using those procedures that were primarily for handling cases of somatic intersexuality. To a large extent such favorable outcomes usually were restricted to very skilled patients who were unusually successful in living their lives according to expectations of the new gender role.

Sweden was the trailblazer in 1972 with a law, and many other countries followed with either specific laws or administrative solutions. Some countries allow full recognition of the new legal status, including the right to marry as a member of the new sex, whereas others, for example, the United Kingdom, still had reservations against such consequences. Although one might understand old traditions and respect other people's fear of homosexuality, such reservations do not make sense and are counterproductive for a person after SRS.

Alternative Roads Toward Legal Sex Change

Will (1992, 1995) summarized the various routes to alleviate the suffering from legal restrictions that for so long a time had burdened transsexuals. Referring to European countries, he distinguished mainly three models, which demonstrate the variability of practical solutions found in other countries and cultures as well.

Smooth Solutions Such as Those in Switzerland, Sweden, and Austria

Although *Switzerland* is not known to be a country of hazardous reforms, it was the first country to offer practical solutions. The first approval of a legal sex change was ruled in 1931. In 1945 the judge of the court of Neuenburg stated: "It is not the body alone which determines the sex of a person, but also his soul" (Schweizerische Juristen Zeitung, 1946, Swiss court Neuenburg, July 2nd, 1945; 23 Journal des Tribunaux, 1946.1.122). In cases where the law does not supply specific rules, the Swiss Civil Code authorizes the judge to proceed according to the rule that he would establish if he were the legislator. The ruling is an *ex nunc* ruling endowing the person with all rights of the new gender.

In contrast to the practical Swiss solution that was hardly taken notice of in other countries, the *Swedish* law of 1972 attracted international attention and became the model for laws in other countries, for example, Germany and Italy. Sex reassignment surgery is not necessarily a prerequisite for changing one's first name in Sweden. If surgical treatment is, as in most cases, desired, the applicant has to attain official approval. Legal sex change is granted to unmarried Swedish citizens who are a minimum age of 18.

In *Austria*, neither a law nor a court ruling was needed. Since 1981 administrative channels regulate legal sex change for transsexuals. The applicant has to present a medical report confirming the surgical sex change. The administrative regulations do not list a minimum age or a restriction to Austrian citizens.

Remedy by National Laws as in Germany (1980), Italy (1982), The Netherlands (1985), and Turkey (1988)

In 1976, the *former East Germany* issued an administrative regulation allowing legal sex change after SRS for legally mature citizens. The regulation was never publicized, and thus many patients in the *former German Democratic Republic* were not aware of it and looked for help abroad. The *Federal Republic of Germany* (West Germany), after 20 years of intensive discussion, finally issued a specific law for transsexuals in 1980 (Pfäfflin, 1981). The law provided two solutions: The so-called small solution permits changing one's first name from unambiguously male to female or vice versa if two experts confirm that the person is transsexual and has seen himself or herself as a member of the opposite sex for at least 3 years and if it can in all probability be assumed that his or her sense of belonging to the opposite sex will not change. The so-called major solution permits a change in legal sex membership if the requirements are met for a change in first name and, additionally, the applicant is not married, sterile, and has had SRS. The decision is taken by a district court. Initially, the law had fixed an age limit for both variants of 25 years, which later was dropped. At present there is no longer a fixed age limit. The law is reserved for German citizens.

In 1982, *Italy* issued a specific law for legal sex change, including intersexes. Surgical interventions have to be approved of by the judge before being performed. Hereafter, the judge will rule the legal sex change. There is no age limit and no restriction to Italian citizens.

In *the Netherlands*, the National Health Council (Gezondheidsraad) played, for quite a while, an important role in the delay of a practical solution. In reaction to an SRS performed in 1960 in the city of Arnhem, the Gezondheidsraad issued a report in 1965 aiming at banning SRS and declaring it a severe bodily injury that had to be sanctioned by criminal law. Due to that, SRS was not performed in the Netherlands for many years, and patients went abroad for treatment. In 1977 a second commission issued a new report, this time in favor of SRS, which finally, in 1985, led to the insertion of four new paragraphs in the Civil Code (paragraphs 29a–29d). The district court decides in favor of the applicant once he has demonstrated being unmarried, sterile, and convinced of belonging to the opposite sex, to which he has been adapted as far as possible from a medical as well as from a psychological point of view. The Dutch law did not need a so-called small solution, as did the German law, because, in the Netherlands, the first name does not have to be unambiguously male or female. There is no fixed age limit in the law, and foreign citizens who have legally lived in the country for at least a year may also make use of the law.

Rather surprisingly, *Turkey,* in 1988, issued a very vague law to allow legal sex change. It neither regulates name change nor lists specific prerequisites apart from the very general rule that a legal sex change has to be performed when, after birth, a change of sex has taken place and has been confirmed by a health commission. As this solution was obviously too vague and unsatisfactory, Turkey has recently revised this law.

Remedy by the European Court of Human Rights

Complaints against national jurisdiction in cases of transsexual applicants for legal sex change had been brought to the European Court of Human Rights since 1974, first from Germany and then later from Belgium, Italy, the United Kingdom, and France. For Italy and Germany, these complaints clearly promoted the passing of the respective laws. In March 1979, the European Commission of Human Rights had acknowledged sexual identity as a fundamental human right and had reprimanded Belgium for not acknowledging this right in the case *Van Oosterwijck*.

The rights and freedoms guaranteed in Section 1 of the European Convention of Human Rights include the right of respect for private life (including gender identity), under article 8, and the right to marry and found a family, under article 12.

In the United Kingdom, where a legal name change is rather easy to obtain, and is sufficient for most practical purposes of everyday life except marriage, the courts denied the rectification of the birth certificate and thus the right to marry in the new gender role. The European Court of Human Rights dealt with a number of applications from the United Kingdom (*Rees*, *Cossey*, *Sheffield,* and *Horsham*), and it seemed that it would be just a matter of time until the United Kingdom would adopt a freer stance (Cole-Wilson, 1998; European Court of Human Rights, Strasbourg, 2002). In 1992, the European Court of Human Rights had already sentenced France and awarded damages of 100,000 and costs of 35,000 francs for having refused the legal sex change B. had applied for. The situation in France has since much improved even though it may still not be satisfactory from the perspective of patients (Gromb, Chanseau, & Lazarini, 1997; Meningaud, Descamps, & Herve, 2000).

These examples demonstrate that we seemed still far from a conclusive and consistent European legislation and jurisdiction in matters of the legal acknowledgement of SRS (Council of Europe, 1995), let alone from an international consensus. However, on July 11, 2002, the European court of Human Rights (2002) decided unanimously in the case of Christine Goodwin v. the United Kingdom that denying legal recognition to the change of a post-operative transsexual was no longer sustainable; it modified established case law on articles 8 and 12 of the European convention of human rights with respect for private life and the right to marry. This right is now established in all 41 countries belonging to the jurisdiction of the European court of human rights. It would be taking things too far in this context to expand on all other national legislations and jurisdictions. It may be briefly stated that legal discussions in Australia and in African, Asian, and American countries regularly include all the different elements that were or are still discussed in the examples mentioned. The most important results of the examples given here are: (1) SRS is an accepted treatment in most countries; (2) most countries grant legal sex change after SRS using various legal or administrative procedures; and (3) legal sex change implies the full range of rights of the newly acquired sex/gender in some countries, whereas in some other countries there are still restrictions.

Additional Legal Issues

In the context of SR and as a consequence of legal sex change there are a number of additional legal problems that have to be solved (Green, 1994) and that have found varied solutions in different countries. First of all, who pays for SRS and other aspects of SR treatment (e.g., psychotherapy, hormone treatment, depilation, and speech training)? Does the National Health Service cover such expenses, and/or are health insurance companies obliged to reimburse expenses? Is there employment discrimination, and how can the patient be protected against it? How can transsexuals keep their privacy if they wish so and stay anonymous as regards their former history? Where should they be placed in a prison setting—in the wing for male or in the wing for female prisoners? Should post-op transsexuals be allowed to serve in the military? In which gender league should they compete in Olympic games? All these and many more similar questions were brought to courts, and they found different solutions in different countries. It is important, however, to emphasize that there are also numerous cases in which such conflicts were solved without appealing to a court, just by good will, by commonsense negotiations, and by having an eye for the individual needs and resources of the conflicting partners involved.

LEGAL ISSUES OF GENDER IDENTITY DISORDER IN CHILDHOOD AND ADOLESCENCE

Rare Events

Practically nothing is known about the prevalence of GID in children and adolescents (see Chapter 4). The *DSM-IV* (American Psychiatric Association, 1994) gives no data as to this subgroup of GID. It only provides older figures from European countries about the prevalence of GID in adults. There are very few specialized treatment centers for GID in children and adolescents, which are mainly in the United States, Canada (Blanchard & Steiner, 1990; Zucker & Bradley, 1995), the United Kingdom (Di Ceglie & Freedman, 1998), and the Netherlands (Cohen-Kettenis, 1994). In those countries, the specialized centers usually draw patients from all over the country. Zucker and Bradley (1995, p. 31), for example, report the referrals to their institution in Toronto, Canada, of children and adolescents who were assessed for GID: With the exception of the year 1991, when they had 27 referrals, they had 4–18 per year in the period 1977-1994. The Gender Identity Development Clinic, founded by Di Ceglie in 1989 in the Department of Child Psychiatry at St. George's Hospital in London and transferred to the Tavistock and Portman NHS Trust in 1996, has seen 150 children and adolescents with GID in 9 years

(Di Ceglie & Freedman, 1998, pp. 305-306). At our institutions in Utrecht, the Netherlands, and Hamburg and Ulm, Germany, about 350 children and adolescents with GID have been seen since 1987. In other countries, if those disorders are at all recognized, they may be handled either by the general practitioner or by the pediatrician, who often just advises the families involved to wait for future development of their child. Sometimes such children and adolescents may be referred to Gender Identity Clinics for adults or respective specialists, who are, however, often not familiar with the specific developmental problems of children and adolescents and therefore may offer only very dilated counseling with low effectiveness. Additionally, one has to keep in mind that even special treatment centers for adults with GID are scarce and often long distances have to be traveled, which makes regular treatment sessions difficult.

From February to July 2001, the *Maine Gender Resource and Support Service* (MeGReSS; 2002) conducted an anonymous survey via the Internet, additionally making printed copies available at a variety of transgender conferences. The purpose of the survey was to gather data for the production of a day-long workshop about transgendered youth in schools to be offered to mental health providers, school administrators, school counselors, and other associated professionals who work with youths. The results of the poll are available via e-mail (megress@tds.net) or the Internet (http://personalpages.tds.net/-megress). It is interesting to see that only 72 persons responded, 52 (72.2%) females, 18 (25%) males, and 1 (1.4%) intersexed individual. Their ages ranged from 16 to 27, with an average age of 20 and a median age of 19.5 years. Asked about their lives as a "trans person" (the term that is used in the survey), where multiple responses were possible, 75% said they lived openly as a trans person, 68% did so online, 56.9% at school, 55.5% at home, 38.9% at work, and only 6.9% nowhere. Of the sample, 83.3% had at least once considered taking hormones and/or having SRS, and 22% were already on hormones. All those taking hormones were older than 18 years. Those who did not fully live their trans identity hesitated to do so because of fear of either not being socially accepted (54.2%) or possible violence or harassment directed against them (45.8%). In free answers many of the respondents gave detailed reports of the early onset of their feeling different as well as of legal problems they had anticipated or actually experienced when wanting to change their names and fully live in the desired gender role. Of course, this study is not representative, and it includes a large number of younger adults and only a very small proportion of youngsters and adolescents below the age of legal maturity. Yet it does give an impression of how much suffering there is on the part of the children and adolescents, and how much misunderstanding on the part of the adults they have to deal with.

It is obvious that such small numbers do not call for special legal regulations such as exist for adult transsexuals. Instead, when treating children and adolescents with GID, one has to explore general legal restrictions and regulations. Before doing so, it is worthwhile considering the recommendations for their treatment as formulated by medical boards.

Guidelines for Clinical Management of Gender Identity Disorder in Children and Adolescents

The Royal College of Psychiatrists (Di Ceglie et al., 1998) was the first medical board to issue guidelines for the management of GID in children and adolescents that went beyond what individual treatment teams or clinics may have considered their locally valid guiding principles. Meanwhile, these guidelines of The Royal College of Psychiatrists were incorporated into the 6th version of the Harry Benjamin International Gender Dysphoria Association's *Standards of Care for Gender Identity Disorders* (Meyer et al., 2001) and thus have gained international distribution and recognition.

For good reasons their emphasis lies on psychological and social interventions, including a full assessment not only of the children and adolescents themselves but also of their families and social surroundings. Most prominent is the recognition and acceptance of the gender identity problem and the removal of secrecy, which can already bring great relief. Counseling and psychotherapy should not focus solely on the GID but include comorbidity and social functioning inside and outside of the family context (see also Chapters 6 and 7). These parts of the treatment are usually not controversial.

Physical interventions such as cross-sex hormone treatment and SRS, however, give rise to controversy. Nobody advocates them for children, but for adolescents they may be, as some clinicians think, feasible and should even be recommended, while other clinicians are strongly opposed to starting such physical treatment before the legal maturity of the patients. According to the guidelines of The Royal College of Psychiatrists they "should be delayed as long as it is clinically appropriate" (Di Ceglie, 1998, p. 5). The clinical appropriateness is, however, what is contentious.

Opponents refer to the yet-unfinished gender identity development of adolescents. They emphasize the irreversibility of such interventions and doubt if it is responsible to start physical treatment at such an early developmental phase. The treatment is judged as risky if not as malpractice as there is a lack of long-term follow-up data, and role reversals might occur at a later time in life. Psychodynamically oriented psychotherapists argue that the adolescent patient may be deprived of developing a gender identity in accordance with his or her somatic outfit when the therapist considers SR as a possible choice. A number of case studies seem to support this view (Barlow, Reynolds, & Agras, 1973; Davenport & Harrison, 1977; Kronberg, Tyano, Apter, & Wijsebeck, 1981; Meyenburg, 1994, 1999; Philippopoulos, 1964). The number of such reports is, however, small and all these authors were clearly opposed to physical interventions in adolescence and by no means neutral. One of these authors, who used to call the initiation of cross-sex hormone treatment before the age of 18 a "serious therapeutic mistake" (Meyenburg, 1994) if not malpractice, conceded, however, that most of his patients did not give up the desire for sex change. One might ask, therefore, if those youngsters giving up their wish for SR really suffered from GID or if they were only gender confused and thus benefited from psychotherapy in a way, which, as a rule, cannot be expected from adolescents with the full picture of GID.

Those clinicians favoring an early onset of physical treatment mainly refer to the potential developmental arrest and the suffering of their patients (see also Chapter 7). They expect that early hormone treatment reduces suffering immediately. In addition, it is apt to prevent later physical treatment, for instance, surgical removal of the breasts in FMs, and painful and expensive electrolysis of facial hair and shaving of the Adam's apple in MFs. Additionally, MFs will pass more easily as females (Cohen-Kettenis, 1994; Cohen-Kettenis & van Goozen, 1998; Wren, 2000). Successful adaptation after surgery is associated with an early rather than a late start to physical treatment (Eicher, 1984/1992; Ross & Need, 1989). Finally, Wren (2000) contests the claim of "psychiatric orthodoxy that treats gender dysphoria as caused by a combination of social factors such as early separations, inadequate sex-typing by parents, possibly secondary to parental psychopathology (Coates et al., 1991; Green, 1974; Zucker & Bradley, 1995)," and she continues: "There is little evidence, however, that any psychological treatments have much effect in changing gender identity although some treatment centers continue to promote this as an aim" (Wren, 2000, p. 222). According to Zucker and Bradley's (1995) findings in Toronto, about every second adolescent seen in their service goes on to have SRS as an adult. It made no difference if they had had psychotherapy as adolescents or not. According to Wren's (2000) unpublished data from her service in London, about a third of children and adolescents move on to services for adults to get SRS there. One has to keep in mind, however, that Wren's follow-up times are very short and the proportion of those adolescents who will have SRS as adults may well turn out to be much bigger in the long run. Wren's (2000, p. 222) conclusion sounds plausible: "What does seem to be clear from the research and from clinical descriptions is that, regardless of the numbers who do and who do not successfully obtain surgery, gender-identity disordered adolescents (unlike gender dysphoric prepubertal children) almost invariably become gender-identity disordered adults."

Which Age Limits for Physical Treatment Are Adequate and Legally Acceptable?

The guidelines of The Royal College of Psychiatrists (Di Ceglie et al., 1998) as well as the Harry Benjamin International Gender Dysphoria Association's *Standards of Care for Gender Identity Disorders* (Meyer et al., 2001) distinguish between three types of physical interventions: wholly reversible (puberty-delaying hormones), partly reversible (feminizing or masculinizing hormones), and irreversible (surgery) (see Chapter 7). One might see these three groups of interventions as stages. "Moving from one stage to another should not occur until there has been adequate time for the young person fully to assimilate the effects of intervention to date" (Di Ceglie et al., 1998, p. 5). The guidelines refrain from giving defined ages at which such physical interventions may be indicated, except for the surgical interventions. Here they state: "Interventions which are irreversible (surgical procedures) should not be carried out prior to adulthood at age 18" (Di Ceglie et al., 1998, pp. 5-6). They warn against an automatism of procedure, once the first stage has been accomplished: "The threshold of 18 should be seen as an eligibility criterion and not an indicator in itself for more active intervention as the needs of many adults may also be best met by a cautious, evolving approach" (Di Ceglie et al., 1998, p. 6).

What is the rationale for an age limit for SRS of 18 years? Obviously it is above all a legal argument to keep medical doctors and psychologists on the safe side when the issue of malpractice is at stake. This conclusion inevitably results from looking at the history of SRS. As long as individual states still had a higher age limit for legal maturity, for example, 21 years, no medical team dared to operate on a transsexual below this age. When Germany passed its Law for Transsexuals in 1980, the age limits for both the small solution (change of first name) and the big solution (change of legal sex status) were set even higher, to 25 years, referring to the argument that a person younger than 25 years would not be mature enough to decide on such important issues. When contested at the Federal Constitutional Court by a 21-year-old post-op transsexual this high age limit did not stand up and had to be removed from the Law for Transsexuals. The constitutional principle of legal equality before the law did not allow discrimination against transsexuals by establishing such an additional and high age hurdle. Since the early 1980s all 15 states within the European Community have harmonized their age limits for legal maturity, which is now being fixed at 18 years. A person who has come of age clearly is endowed to take the decision for SRS. There may be a loophole in Turkish law. In Turkey, getting married simultaneously grants legal maturity, even at the age of 15. Getting married in the original sex role is, however, not what adolescents with GID would usually want. It is rather unlikely that they would make use of this loophole.

In countries outside of the European Community and the United States the age limits for legal maturity vary. Some countries do not even have a fixed age (e.g., Saudi Arabia and Oman). There, legal maturity is reached with sexual maturity. In Nepal and Iceland the age limit is set at 16, in Sudan at 18 lunar years, which is approximately 17½ years. In many Latin American (e.g., Argentina, Bolivia, Brazil, and El Salvador) and African (e.g., Burundi, Ivory Coast, Cameroon, and Chad) countries legal maturity is reached only at the age of 21 years. Some countries have other limits, for example, 19 years in Algeria and 20 years in Japan. Taking legal maturity as a limit for the legal performance of SRS, one would expect that SRS might be performed either earlier or later. The arbitrary fixation of legal maturity in different countries leads to the question if it is reasonable to take the age of legal maturity as the threshold for the legitimacy of SRS. Even if one decided in favor of such a limit, one would have to allow other forms of SR (e.g., change of first name, enrolling at school as a member of the opposite sex, and puberty-delaying hormone treatment and cross-sex hormone treatment) at earlier ages to prepare the patient for SRS.

Apart from legal maturity there are a number of additional legal age limits, differing from state to state, for example, for criminal responsibility, for the choice of becoming a member of a specific religion, to agree to an adoption, to swear an oath before court, to get a license for driving a car or flying a plane, to carry a weapon, to be drafted into the army, to become a civil servant, and to run for election for parliament or for presidency of the state. Some of these rights are granted before the age of legal maturity, whereas others are granted much later in life. If they are granted earlier, it is expected from the juvenile that he or she will fulfill his or her respective responsibilities.

When a child or adolescent needs a risky medical treatment normally the parents have to consent, but from a defined age (differing in different states) onward, the child and adolescent may decide on his or her own behalf. It seems clear that no medical team would perform SRS on a non-consenting adolescent whose parents asked for it. This absurd example demonstrates that the adolescent would be granted the right to take care of his or her integrity. Exchanging the roles makes the situation much more controversial: The adolescent asks for SRS, but the parents are opposed. Should the adolescent go to court and fight for his or her right? Would he or she be successful? In most countries, probably not. That is true for now. But the situation may change, and adolescents may fight for their right. If SR is the best way for some gender-dysphoric young people to establish an identity, what, then, is the rationale for refusing it? (Wren, 2000).

VIGNETTE: George, 14 years

George, a very feminine boy of non-Dutch origin, came to our clinic at the age of 14. He lived in an institution because of a physical handicap. His parents, who were divorced, had been declared unable to have full parental responsibility. The mother rarely attended appointments with his caretakers at the institution. When George told his parents that he wanted to be a girl and wanted to visit a gender clinic, they were both heavily opposed. The mother did not want to accompany him to the clinic. The father came the first time only to explain that he would resist the treatment, as SR would never be accepted within their culture. After that he either canceled appointments or did not show up for almost a year. George became more and more depressed. At some point he was so angry with his parents, because of the delay in the procedure they caused, that he no longer wanted to see them.

George's caretakers repeatedly tried to get his parents' cooperation in finding solutions for daily GID-related problems, but they never wanted to discuss the subject. The caretakers were convinced for years that he had a gender identity disorder. For a long time they did not want to permit him to cross-dress or to pursue other cross-gendered interests against his parents' will. However, they noticed how he suffered. When they occasionally allowed him to cross-dress he cheered up.

After George had passed the first part of the diagnostic procedure, he was considered eligible for puberty-delaying hormones despite his parents' resistance. The Dutch law criteria for allowing him to start this part of the procedure included the following: (1) it was his explicit wish to have treatment, (2) the steps that were to be taken were in his best interests, (3) he fully understood the positive and negative consequences of his decision, and (4) he knew what the alternatives were. George was even entitled to request that his doctors not inform his parents about his treatment and to deny them access to his medical files.

An analogous, yet slightly different, situation would be when it has to be decided if an abortion is legal in an underage pregnant girl. Should a 16-year-old girl, for instance, be endowed to decide on her own behalf whether to have an abortion? Unlike SRS this decision certainly would not allow much delay. Whatever the result of the conflict, nobody can really foretell if she will suffer more from giving birth to a child or from having an abortion. Again, it is obvious that parents could not push through their wish to have the abortion against the declared will of their daughter. But courts are still reluctant to grant the girl her own will if she wants to have the abortion and the parents do not consent.

Although Holloway (1974, p. 33) stated the following more than 25 years ago: "An examination of case law in the United States leads to the conclusion that a physician or surgeon may, without fear of criminal liability, perform a sex reassignment operation upon a consenting adult or upon a consenting minor where permitted by statute," we are not aware of such SRS being done on minors so far. Within the European context we know of not a single such court decision. In the United Kingdom children's rights to consent to and to refuse treatment are framed by the Children Act of 1989, giving considerable autonomy to children and establishing the principle of parental responsibilities rather than parental rights (Wren, 2000). It ruled that it is artificial to impose fixed age limits to determine competence to make decisions when the well-being of children and adolescents is at stake. Taking this into account one is inclined to agree with Downs and Whittle (1998), who argue forcefully that doctors must clarify their refusal to provide physical treatment for adolescents with GID. Those authors argue mainly in favor of an early onset of pubertal postponement treatment, the first stage of the recommendation of The Royal College of Psychiatrists, but their arguments are also applicable to the second and third stages as long as the individual development of the adolescent and his or her specific state of maturity are taken into account.

Herein lies the core of the legal problem. The law is based on rules for everybody and everything. It has to define limits so that every citizen knows what he or she is in for when starting an action. This holds true for the adolescent patient with GID as well as for his or her parents and the persons treating him or her psychologically and medically. In accordance with the Children Act of 1989 we hold that it is artificial to impose fixed age limits to determine the clinical appropriateness of starting physical treatment in adolescent patients with GID. The age of psychological and somatic maturity varies largely interindividually. It would be as arbitrary to fix the legitimate age to start that treatment at 18 as at 17 or 16. What counts is the thorough evaluation of the individual case.

We expect adolescents to be better protected when all those involved in their treatment closely observe the guidelines of the royal College of Psychiatrists and the Harry Benjamin Gender Dysphoria Association than if there is a fixed age limit which invites fast routine decisions. In-depth discussions of individual cases, involving the parents and, if controversial, involving also the family court, have proved to be very helpful and effective in those cases of individual patients where we recommended wholly reversible physical treatment for pubertal delay or partly reversible physical treatments for feminizing or masculinizing purposes and finally the very exceptional cases where patients were recommended SRS even before the age of 18.

In any case, such steps are normally rather late steps in the treatment that have to be taken after many more practical matters have already been solved during the preceding treatment. Some of them also have legal impacts, for example, cross-gender living, including enrolment in school as a girl (in the case of MF) or as a boy (in the case of FM). Such issues are tricky in themselves. Most gender-dysphoric adolescents do not want others to know about their biological sex. Suppose an FM youngster begins a sexual relationship with a female classmate who later discovers that her "boyfriend" is a biological female and ends up traumatized. The school could be liable for supporting deception. The example was shared by a North American colleague and seems rather fantastic in our European eyes. It is, absurd as it may sound, however, apt to demonstrate that it is impossible to settle all possible problems by legal regulations. What is needed is an open-minded approach that takes into account the individual resources and needs of the adolescents involved, including the persons in his or her social surroundings. With parents living in divorce and still fighting each other, the adolescent patient with GID is often the battleground for continuing the ongoing fights. In such cases it may be helpful to address the family court. According to our observations, experienced judges would rather avoid passing a judgment allowing or prohibiting, for example, hormone treatment to delay puberty or induce feminization or masculinization. Instead, they would prefer to include all parties in finding a solution acceptable for all. Sometimes judges negotiate more successfully than therapists without having to pass a sentence.

As mentioned above, quite a few national legislations on legal sex change do not explicitly mention age limits for such procedures. One may suppose that they implicitly take it for granted that no minor may make use of them. Alternatively, one may just as well suppose that the respective legislators were open enough to allow individual solutions for legal minors.

SUMMARY

Children who were born with ambiguous genitals have been treated very differently throughout history. In some periods they were murdered, in other times they were declared a boy or a girl until they were old enough to decide for themselves how they wanted to live, while in yet other times they were always assigned to the male sex. Scientifically there was not much interest in these patients. Only in the 20th century, after the discovery of chromosomes and hormones, did the phenomenon of (pseudo-)hermaphroditism became a major research field. The French *Code Civil* of 1804, which influenced most of the legislation of continental Europe and beyond, left the decision of the sex of a person mainly to medical judgment. Doctors focused on the appearance of the external genitals only. For the law, this appearance was the decisive criterion for legal sex determination. In case of errors of sex assignment, they were easily rectified without the involvement of courts. This may explain why many are so interested in biological determinants of transsexualism. If transsexualism were a condition comparable with intersexuality, the legal situation would be much more simple in many countries.

The first sex reassignment operations in adults were performed in the early 20th century. They took place in a society where a sexual relationship between same-sex partners was still a felony. It was therefore deemed necessary to invent the term and create the category transvestism. Many of these persons would now be considered transsexual or transgendered. In Europe, sex reassignment surgery was discussed extensively and performed on a modest scale for many years, long before the topic was discussed internationally. Even legal sex changes had been allowed. However, this treatment drew wide attention only in 1951, when the surgery of a former GI, Christine Jorgenson, was published. While in the United States there was much resistance against SR, the tradition of treating transsexuals developed continuously and steadily in Europe. Some European countries took the lead in solving legal problems related to SR. Sweden was the first country to pass a specific law in 1972.

Though there was virtually no interest in the legal implications of cross-sex hormone treatment, surgical interventions in somatically healthy persons did pose legal challenges. If a doctor were to chop off the patient's hand on the demand of a patient, he or she would be brought to court for grievous bodily harm. It would offend common decency and morals to thus injure a healthy person. In the same way removal of genitals could be judged as an attack on the integrity of the person (a "crime of mayhem"). To justify SRS doctors first pointed out the suffering of the patients. They classified their acts as taking the last resort (*ultima ratio*). Later, gender identity clinics were started that researched and published the results of SRS. Also standards of care for the treatment of transsexuals were issued to protect surgeons from lawsuits of malpractice. The question of whether cross-sex hormone treatment and SRS were legitimate procedures found a short answer: Practice was faster and stronger than any doubts as to their legitimacy. They were accepted before any court or legislator could effectively stop them.

In many countries that derive their law from Napoleon's *Code Civil* of 1804, the birth certificate is the source for all other personal documents. Therefore it is essential to change the sex in this document to endow a person with the full rights of his or her new gender. In Anglo-American countries it is easier to adopt a new first name. However, registration of official documents is not centralized. As a result, a person can be male according to one and female according to another document. Following Sweden's lead, many other countries either had specific laws or administrative solutions, implying that SRS has become a fairly well-accepted treatment for adults.

The Royal College of Psychiatrists was the first medical board that issued guidelines for the management of GID in children and adolescents, now incorporated in the Standards of Care of the Harry Benjamin International Gender Dysphoria Association. The physical interventions mentioned in these documents, such as cross-sex hormone treatment and SRS, give rise to controversy. They may be feasible for adolescents according to some clinicians, whereas other clinicians are strongly opposed to such physical treatment before the legal maturity of the patients.

The current guidelines for the treatment of adolescents with GID distinguish between three types of physical interventions: wholly reversible, partly reversible, and irreversible. The guidelines give no defined ages for the physical interventions, but an exception is surgery, which should not be performed before legal adulthood (age 18). The rationale of the arbitrary age of 18 years is probably based more on a fear of malpractice suits (it is the age of legal maturity in both the European Community and the United States) than on something intrinsically good for SR applicants. Outside Europe and the United States the ages of legal maturity vary between 16 in Iceland and Nepal and 21 in many African and Latin American countries, while some countries do not even have a fixed age. Though the fixed age limits are an attempt to protect children from maltreatment, in the case of adolescents with GID they often seem to work against them. The age of psychological and somatic maturity varies largely interindividually. Adhering to such limits would severely hamper the development of a mature adolescent and might even facilitate fast routine decision making when a still immature 18-year-old wanted to start SR. We expect adolescents are well protected when all those involved in their treatment closely observe the guidelines of the Royal College of Psychiatrists and the Harry Benjamin Gender Dysphoria Association and extensively discuss and weigh the pros and cons of SR for an individual patient.

REFERENCES

Abraham, F. (1931). Genitalumwandlung an zwei männlichen Transvestiten. *Zeitschrift für Sexualwissenschaft und Sexualpolitik*, *18*, 223-226.

Abraham, F. (1998). Genital reassignment on two male transvestites [On-line]. Available: http://www.symposion.com/ijt/ijtc0302.htm

Abramowitz, S. I. (1986). Psychosocial outcomes of sex reassignment surgery. *Journal of Consulting and Clinical Psychology, 54,* 183-189.

Abramovitch, R., Corter, C., Pepler, D. J., & Stanhope, L. (1986). Sibling and peer interactions: A final follow-up and a comparison. *Child Development, 57*, 217-229.

Achenbach, T. M., & Edelbrock, C. S. (1981). Behavioral problems and competencies reported by parents of normal and disturbed children aged four through sixteen. *Monographs of the Society for Research in Child Development, 46,* 1-82.

Achenbach, T. M., & Edelbrock, C. S. (1983). *Manual for the Child Behavior Checklist and revised Profile.* Burlington, VT: University of Vermont Department of Psychiatry.

Achenbach, T. M., & Edelbrock, C. S. (1986). *Manual for the Teacher's Report Form and Teacher Version of the Child Behavior Profile*. Burlington, VT: University of Vermont Department of Psychiatry.

Achenbach, T. M., & Edelbrock C. S. (1987). *Manual for the Youth Self Report and Profile*. Burlington, VT: University of Vermont Department of Psychiatry.

Ako, T. (2001). Beginnings of sex reassignment in Japan [On-line]. Available: http://www.symposion.com/ijt/ijtvo05no01_02.htm

Alanko, A., & Achté, K. (1971). Transsexualism. *Psychiatrica Fennica,* 343-358.

Al-Attia, H. M. (1996). Gender identity and role in a pedigree of Arabs with intersex due to 5 alpha reductase-2 deficiency. *Psychoneuroendocrinology, 8*, 651-657.

Alizai, N. K., Thomas, D. F. M., Lilford, R. J., Batchelor, G. G., & Johnson, F. (1999). Feminizing genitoplasty for adrenal hyperplasia: What happens at puberty. *Journal of Urology, 161*, 1588-1591.

Althof, S., & Keller, A. (1980). Group therapy with gender identity patients. *International Journal of Group Psychotherapy*, *30,* 481-489.

American Psychiatric Association. (1980). *Diagnostic and statistical manual of mental disorders (DSM-III).* Washington, DC: Author.

American Psychiatric Association. (1994). *Diagnostic and statistical manual of mental disorders (DSM-IV)*. Washington, DC: Author.

Annett, M. (1985). *Left, right, hand and brain: The right shift theory*. Hillsdale: Lawrence Erlbaum.

Arnold, A. P. & Breedlove, S. M. (1985). Organizational and activational effects of sex steroids on brain and behavior: A reanalysis. *Hormones and Behavior, 19,* 469-498.

Bailey, J. M., & Zucker, K. J. (1995). Childhood sex-types behavior and sexual orientation: A conceptual analysis and quantitative review. *Developmental Psychology, 31*, 43-55.

Baker, F., Telfer, M., Richardson, C. E., & Clark, G. R. (1970). Chromosome errors in men with antisocial behavior: Comparison of men with Klinefelter's and XYY chromosome pattern. *Journal of the American Medical Association, 214*, 869-878.

Bakker, A., van Kesteren, P., Gooren, L. J. G., & Bezemer, P. D. (1993). The prevalence of transsexualism in the Netherlands. *Acta Psychiatrica Scandinavica, 87,* 237-238.

Bamrah, J. S., & Mackay, M. E. (1989). Chronic psychosis in Turner's syndrome: Case report and a review. *British Journal of Psychiatry, 155*, 857-859.

Bancroft, J., Axworthy, D., & Ratcliffe, S. (1982). The personality and psychosexual development of boys with 47XXY chromosome constitution. *Journal of Child Psychology and Psychiatry, 23,* 169-180.

Bandura, A. (1977). *Social learning theory*. Englewood Cliffs, NJ: Prentice Hall.

Bandura, A. (1986). *Social foundations of thought and action: A social cognitive theory.* Englewood Cliffs, NJ: Prentice Hall.

Bangsboll, S., Qvist, I., Lebech, P. E., & Lewinsky, M. (1992). Testicular feminization syndrome and associated gonadal tumors in Denmark. *Acta Obstretica et Gynecologica Scandinavica, 71,* 63-66.

Barlow, D. H., Abel, G., & Blanchard, G. (1979). Gender identity change in transsexuals. *Archives of General Psychiatry, 36*, 1001-1007.

Barlow, D. H., Reynolds, E. J., & Agras, W. S. (1973). Gender identity change in a transsexual. *Archives of General Psychiatry, 28*, 569-576.

Bartlett, N. H., Vasey, P. L., & Bukowski, W. M. (2000). Is gender identity disorder in children a mental disorder? *Sex Roles, 43*, 753-785.

Bates, J. E., & Bentler, P. M. (1973). Play activities of normal and effeminate boys. *Developmental Psychology, 9,* 20-27.

Bates, J. E., Bentler, P. M., & Thompson, S. K. (1973). Measurement of deviant gender behavior in boys. *Child Development, 44*, 591-598.

Bates, J. E., Bentler, P. M., & Thompson, S. K. (1979). Gender-deviant boys compared with normal and clinical control boys. *Journal of Abnormal Child Psychology, 7,* 243-259.

Beatrice, J. (1985). A psychological comparison of heterosexuals, transvestites, preoperative transsexuals and postoperative transsexuals. *Journal of Nervous and Mental Disease, 173,* 358-365.

Bell, A. P., Weinberg, M. S., & Hammersmith, S. K. (1981). *Sexual preference: Its development in men and women.* Bloomington: Indiana University Press.

Bem, S. L. (1981). Gender schema theory: A cognitive account of sex typing. *Psychological Review, 88,* 354-364.

Bem, S. L. (1989). Genital knowledge and gender constancy in preschool children. *Child Development, 60,* 649-662.

Bender, B. G., Harmon, R. J., Linden, M. G., & Robinson, A. (1995). Psychosocial adaptation of 39 adolescents with sex chromosome abnormalities. *Pediatrics, 96,* 302-308.

Bender, B. G., Linden, M. G., & Robinson, A. (1987). Environment and developmental risk in children with sex chromosome abnormalities. *Journal of the American Academy of Child and Adolescent Psychiatry, 26*, 499-503.

Benjamin, H. (1953). Transvestism and transsexualism. *International Journal of Sexology, 7*, 12-14.

Benjamin, H. (1964). Nature and management of transsexualism. With a report on thirty-one operated cases. *Western Journal of Surgery, Obstetrics and Gynecology, 72*, 105-111.

Benjamin H. (1966). *The transsexual phenomenon: A scientific report on transsexualism and sex conversion in the human male and female.* New York: Julian Press.

Bentler, P. M. (1976). A typology of transsexualism: Gender identity theory and data. *Archives of Sexual Behavior, 5,* 567-584.

Berenbaum, S. A. (1999). Effects of early androgens on sex-typed activities and interests in adolescents with congenital adrenal hyperplasia. *Hormones and Behavior, 35*, 102-110.

Berenbaum, S. A. (2000). Psychological outcome in congenital hyperplasia. In B. Stabler & B. B. Bercu (Eds.), *Therapeutic outcome of endocrine disorders: Efficacy, innovation, and quality of life* (pp. 186-199). New York: Springer-Verlag.

Berenbaum, S. A., Duck, S. C., & Bryk, K. (2000). Behavioral effects of prenatal versus post-natal androgen excess in children with 21-hydroxylase-deficient congenital adrenal hyperplasia. *Journal of Clinical Endocrinology and Metabolism, 85*, 727-733.

Berenbaum, S. A, & Resnick, S. M. (1997). Early androgen effects on aggression in children and adults with congenital adrenal hyperplasia. *Psychoneuroendocrinology, 22*, 505-515.

Besnier, N. (1994). Polynesian gender liminality through time and space. In G. Herdt (Ed.), *Third sex, third gender: Beyond the dimorphism in culture and history* (pp. 285-328). New York: Zone Books.

Birnbacher, R., Marberger, M., Weissenbacher, G., Schober, E., & Frisch, H. (1999). Gender identity reversal in an adolescent with mixed gonadal dysgenesis. *Journal of Pediatric Endocrinology and Metabolism, 12,* 687-690.

Blackless, M., Charuvastra, A., Derryck, A., Fausto-Sterling, A., Lauzanne, K., & Lee, E. (2000). How sexually dimorphic are we? Review and synthesis. *American Journal of Human Biology, 12*, 151-166.

Blair, S. L. (1992). The sex-typing of children's household labor: Parental influences on daughters' and sons' housework. *Youth and Society, 24,* 178-203.

Blanchard, R. (1985). Typology of male-to-female transsexualism. *Archives of Sexual Behavior, 14,* 247-261.

Blanchard, R. (1988). Nonhomosexual gender dysphoria. *Journal of Sex Research, 24,* 188-193.

Blanchard, R. (1989). The classification and labeling of nonhomosexual gender dysphoria. *Archives of Sexual Behavior, 18,* 315-334.

Blanchard, R. (1997). Birth order and sibling sex ratio in homosexual versus heterosexual males and females. *Annual Review of Sex Research, 8*, 27-67.

Blanchard, R. (2001). Fraternal birth order and the maternal immune hypothesis of male homosexuality. *Hormones and Behavior, 40*, 105-114.

Blanchard, R., Dickey, R., & Jones, C. L. (1995). Comparison of height and weight in homosexual versus nonhomosexual male gender dysphorics. *Archives of Sexual Behavior, 24,* 543-554.

Blanchard, R., & Steiner B. W. (1990). *Clinical management of gender identity disorders in children and adults*. Washington, DC: American Psychiatric Press.

Blanchard, R., Steiner, B. W., Clemmensen, L. H., & Dickey, R. (1989). Prediction of regrets in postoperative transsexuals. *Canadian Journal of Psychiatry, 34,* 43-45.

Bodlund, O., & Armelius, K. (1994). Self-image and personality traits in gender identity disorders: An empirical study. *Journal of Sex and Marital Therapy, 20,* 303-317.

Bodlund, O., & Kullgren, G. (1996). Transsexualism – General outcome and prognostic factors: A five-year follow-up study of nineteen transsexuals in the progress of changing sex. *Archives of Sexual Behavior, 25,* 303-316.

Bodlund, O., Kullgren, G., Sundblom, E., & Höjerback, T. (1993). Personality traits and disorders among transsexuals. *Acta Psychiatrica Scandinavica, 88,* 322-327.

Bolin, A. (1994). Transcending and transgendering: Male-to-female transsexuals, dichotomy and diversity. In G. Herdt (Ed.), *Third sex, third gender: Beyond the dimorphism in culture and history* (pp. 447-486). New York: Zone Books.

Boss, M. (1950-1951). Erwiderung zum Bericht über mein Referat auf der 66. Wanderversammlung der südwestdeutschen Psychiater und Neurologen in Badenweiler. *Psyche, 4,* 394-400.

Bower, H. (2001). The gender identity disorder in the DSM-IV classification: A critical evaluation. *Australian and New Zealand Journal of Psychiatry, 35,* 1-8.

Bradley, S. J., Blanchard, R., Coates, S., Green, R., Levine, S. B., Meyer-Bahlburg, H. F. L. Pauly, I. B., & Zucker, K. J. (1991). Interim report of the DSM-IV Subcommittee on Gender Identity Disorders. *Archives of Sexual Behavior, 20,* 333-343.

Bradley, S. J., Oliver, G. D., Chernick, A. B., & Zucker, K. J. (1998). Experiment of nurture: Ablatio penis at 2 months, sex reassignment at 7 months, and a psychosexual follow-up in young adulthood [On-line]. Available: http://www.pediatrics.org/cgi/content/full/102/1/e9

Bradley, S. J., & Zucker, K. J. (1998). A reply to Menvielle. *Journal of the American Academy of Child and Adolescent Psychiatry, 37,* 244-245.

Braiterman, J. (1998). Sexual science: Whose cultural difference? *Sexualities, 1,* 313-326.

Breedlove, S. M. (1994). Sexual differentiation of the human nervous system. *Annual Review of Psychology, 45,* 389-418.

Brems, C., Adams, R., & Skillman, D. (1993). Person drawings by transsexual clients, psychiatric clients, and nonclients compared: Indicators of sex-typing and pathology. *Archives of Sexual Behavior, 22,* 253-264.

Bryden, M. P. (1988). Cerebral specialization: Clinical and experimental assessment. In F. Boller & J. Grafman (Eds.), *Handbook of neuropsychology* (pp. 143-159). Amsterdam: Elsevier Science.

Brzek, A., & Sipova, L. (1983). Transsexuelle in Prag. *Sexualmedizin, 3,* 110-112.

Buhrich, N., Barr, R., & Lam-Po-Tang, P. R. L. C. (1978). Two transsexuals with 47, XYY karyotype. *British Journal of Psychiatry, 133,* 77-81.

Buhrich, N., & McConaghy, N. (1978). Two clinically discrete syndromes of transsexualism. *British Journal of Psychiatry, 133,* 73-76.

Bullough, V. L., & Bullough, B. (1993). *Cross dressing, sex, and gender.* Philadelphia: University of Pennsylvania Press.

Bullough, B., Bullough, V. L., & Elias, J. (Eds.). (1997). *Gender blending.* Armherst, NY: Prometheus Books.

Bürger-Prinz, H., & Weigel. H. (1940). Über den Transvestitismus bei Männern. *Monatsschrift für Kriminalbiologie und Strafrechtsreform, 31,* 125-143.

Burns, A., Farrell, M., & Brown, J. C. (1990). Clinical features of patients attending a gender-identity clinic. *British Journal of Psychiatry, 157,* 265-268.

Burns, R. C., & Kaufman, S. H. (1972). *Actions, styles and symbols in Kinetic Family Drawing (K-F-D): An interpretative manual.* New York: Brunner and Mazer.

Bussey, K., & Bandura, A. (1999). Social cognitive theory of gender development and differentiation. *Psycholgical Review, 106,* 676-713.

Butler, J. (1998). Afterword. *Sexualities, 1,* 355-359.

Callender, C., & Kochems, L. (1983). The North American berdache. *Current Anthropology, 24,* 443-470.

Canter, R. J., & Ageton, S. S. (1984). The epidemiology of adolescent sex-role attitudes. *Sex Roles, 11,* 657-767.

Carter, D. B. (1987). The roles of peers in sex role socialization. In D. B. Carter (Ed.), *Current conceptions of sex roles and sex typing: Theory and research* (pp. 101-121). New York: Praeger.

Carter, D. B., & Levy, G. D. (1988). Cognitive aspects of children's early sex-role development: The influences of gender schemas on preschoolers' memories and preferences for sex-typed toys and activities. *Child Development, 59,* 782-793.

Cauldwell, D. C. (1949). Psychopathia transexualis. *Sexology, 16,* 274-280.

Chan-Cua, S., Freidenberg, G., & Jones, K. L. (1989). Occurrence of male phenotype in genotypic females with congenital virilizing adrenal hyperplasia. *American Journal of Medical Genetics, 34,* 406-412.

Charatan, F. B., & Galef, H. (1965). A case of transvestism in a six-year-old boy. *Journal of the Hillside Hospital, 14,* 160-177.

Chase, C. (1997, October 14-15). Spare the knife, study the child [Letter]. *Ob.Gyn. News, 1.* Available: http://hiv.medscape.com/IMNG/ClinPsychNews/1997/v25.n09/cpn2509.08.1.html.

Cherry, L. (1975). The preschool-teacher dyad: Sex differences in verbal interaction. *Child Development, 46*, 532-535.

Chiland, C. (1988). Enfance et transsexualisme. *Psychiatrie de l'enfant, 31,* 313-373.

Chiland, C. (2000). The psychoanalyst and the transsexual patient. *International Journal of Psychoanalysis, 81*, 24-35.

Chivers, M. L., & Bailey, J. M. (2000). Sexual orientation of female-to-male transsexuals: A comparison of homosexual and nonhomosexual types. *Archives of Sexual Behavior, 29,* 259-278.

Coates, S. (1985). Extreme boyhood femininity: Overview and new research findings. In Z. De Fries, R. C. Friedman, & R. Corn (Eds.), *Sexuality: New perspectives* (pp. 101-124). Westport, CT: Greenwood.

Coates, S. (1990). Ontogenesis of boyhood gender identity disorder. *Journal of the American Academy of Psychoanalysis, 18,* 414-438.

Coates, S., Friedman, R., & Wolfe, S. (1991). The etiology of boyhood gender identity disorder: A model for integrating temperament, development and psychodynamics. *Psychoanalytic Dialogues, 1*, 481-523.

Coates, S., & Person, E. S. (1985). Extreme boyhood femininity. Isolated behavior or pervasive disorder? *Journal of the American Academy of Child Psychiatry, 24,* 702-709.

Coates, S., & Wolfe, S. (1997). Gender identity disorders of childhood. In J. D. Noshpitz (Ed.) & S. Greenspan, S. Wieder, & J. Osofsky (Vol. Eds.), *Handbook of child and adolescent psychiatry: Vol. I. Infants and preschoolers: Development and syndromes* (pp. 453-472). New York: Wiley.

Cohen, H., & Forget, H. (1995). Auditory cerebral lateralization following cross-gender hormone therapy. *Cortex, 31,* 565-573.

Cohen, L., de Ruiter, C., Ringelberg, H., & Cohen-Kettenis, P. T. (1997). Psychological functioning of adolescent transsexuals: Personality and psychopathology. *Journal of Clinical Psychology, 53*,187-196.

Cohen, C. C. C., van Goozen, S. H. M., Cohen-Kettenis, P. T., & Buitelaar, J. K. (2001). *Effects of prenatal exposure to testosterone on cerebral lateralization: A twin study.* Poster presented at the 10th International Congress on Twin Studies, Imperial College, London.

Cohen-Kettenis, P. T. (1994). Die Behandlung von Kindern und Jugendlichen mit Geschlechtsidentitätsstörungen an der Universität Utrecht. *Zeitschrift für Sexualforschung, 7*, 231-239.

Cohen-Kettenis, P. T. (2001). Gender identity disorder in DSM? *Journal of the American Academy of Child and Adolescent Psychiatry*, 40, 391.

Cohen-Kettenis, P. T., & van Goozen, S. H. M. (1997). Sex reassignment of adolescent transsexuals: A follow-up study. *Journal of the American Academy of Child and Adolescent Psychiatry,* 36, 263-271.

Cohen-Kettenis, P. T., & van Goozen, S. H. M. (1998). Pubertal delay as an aid in diagnosis and treatment of a transsexual adolescent. *European Child and Adolescent Psychiatry, 7*, 246-252.

Cohen-Kettenis, P. T., van Goozen, S. H. M., Doorn C., & Gooren, L. J. G. (1998). Cognitive ability and cerebral lateralization in transsexuals. *Psychoneuroendocrinology, 23*, 631-641.

Cohen-Kettenis, P. T., van Goozen, S. H. M., & Snoek, H. (2000). *Internalizing disorders in prepubertal children with gender identity disorder*. Poster presented at the 26th annual meeting of the International Academy of Sex Research, Paris, France.

Cohen-Kettenis, P. T., Owen, A., Bradley, S. J., Kaijser, V. G., & Zucker, K. J. (in press). Demographic characteristics, social competence, and behavior problems in children with gender identity disorder: A cross-national, cross-clinic comparative analysis.

Cohen-Kettenis, P. T., & Sandfort, T. (1996). Seksueel gedrag van kinderen: Een kwantitatief onderzoek onder moeders. *Tijdschrift voor Seksuologie, 20*, 254-265.

Cole, C. M., O'Boyle, M., Emory, L. E., & Meyer, W. J. (1997). Comorbidity of gender dysphoria and other major psychiatric diagnoses. *Archives of Sexual Behavior, 26*, 13-26.

Cole-Harding, S., Morstad, A. L., & Wilson J. R. (1988). Spatial ability in members of opposite sex twins pairs [Abstract], *Behavior Genetics, 18*, 710.

Coleman, E., Bockting, W. O., & Gooren, L. (1993). Homosexual and bisexual identity in sex-reassigned female-to-male transsexuals. *Archives of Sexual Behavior, 22,* 37-50.

Coleman, E., & Cesnik, J. A. (1990). Skoptic Syndrome: The treatment of an obsessional gender dysphoria with lithium carbonate and psychotherapy. *American Journal of Psychotherapy, 2,* 204-217.

Coleman, E., Colgan, P., & Gooren L. J. G. (1992). Male cross-gender behavior in Myanmar (Burma). *Archives of Sexual Behavior, 21,* 313-322.

Cole-Wilson, Y. I. (1998). *Corbett v Corbett: Is it still good law*? Unpublished manuscript, presented at the Third International Congress on Sex and Gender, Exeter College, Oxford, UK, 18-20 September, 1998 [On-line abstract]. Available: http://www.symposion.com/ijt/whittle_congress.htm

Collaer, M. L., & Hines, M. (1995). Human behavioral sex differences: A role for gonadal hormones during early development? *Psychological Bulletin, 118,* 55-107.

Committee on Genetics/American Academy of Pediatrics. (1995). Health supervision for children with Turner syndrome. *Pediatrics, 96*, 1166-1172.

Cordua, G. D., McGraw, K. O., & Drabman, R. S. (1979). Doctor or nurse: Children's perception of sex typed occupations. *Child Development, 50,* 590-593.

Coren, S. (1995). Family patterns in handedness: Evidence for indirect inheritance mediated by birth stress. *Behavior Genetics, 25,* 517-524.

Council of Europe (Ed.). (1995). *Transsexualism, medicine and law*. Strasbourg: Author.

Creighton, S. M. (2001). Managing intersex: Most vaginal surgery in childhood should be deferred. *British Medical Journal, 323*, 1264-1265.

Creighton, S. M., Minto, C. L., & Steele, S. J. (2001). Objective cosmetic and anatomical outcomes at adolescence of feminizing surgery for ambiguous genitalia done in childhood. *Lancet, 358*, 124-125.

Cryan, E. M. J., & O'Donoghue, F. P. (1992). Transsexualism in a Klinefelter male: A case report. *Journal of Psychological Medicine, 9*, 45-46.

Daly, R. F. (1969). Mental illness and patterns of behavior in 10 XYY males. *Journal of Nervous and Mental Disease, 144,* 318-327.

Daaboul, J., & Frader, J. (2001). Ethics and the management of the patient with intersex: A middle way. *Journal of Pediatric Endocrinology and Metabolism, 14*, 1575-1583.

Darby, P. L., Garfinkel, P. E., Vale, J. M., Kirwan, P. J., & Brown, G. M. (1981). Anorexia nervosa and 'Turner syndrome': Cause or coincidence? *Psychological Medicine, 11,* 141-145.

Davenport, C. W., & Harrison, S. I. (1977). Gender identity change in a female adolescent transsexual. *Archives of Sexual Behavior, 6*, 327-340.

Davidson, P. W. (1966). Transsexualism in Klinefelter's Syndrome. *Psychosomatics, 7,* 94-98.

De Cuypere, G. (1995). *Transsexualiteit: Psychiatrische aspecten in het kader van de geslachtsaanpassende behandeling*. Gent, Belgium: University of Gent.

De Jong, T. P., & Boemers, T. M. (1995). Neonatal management of female intersex by clitorovaginoplasty. *Journal of Urology, 154,* 830- 832.

Deaux, K. (1993). Commentary: Sorry, wrong number: A reply to Gentile's call. Sex or gender? *Psychological Science, 4,* 125-126.

Dekker, R. M., & van de Pol, L. C. (1989). *The tradition of female transvestitism in early modern Europe*. Badingstoke, UK: Macmillan.

Derogatis, L. R., Meyer, J. K., & Boland, P. (1981). A psychological profile of the transsexual II: The female. *Journal of Nervous and Mental Disease, 169,* 157-168.

Dessens, A. B., Cohen-Kettenis, P. T., Mellenbergh, G. J., van de Poll, N. E., Koppe, J. G., & Boer, K. (1999). Prenatal exposure to anticonvulsants and psychosexual development. *Archives of Sexual Behavior, 28,* 31-44.

Diamond, M., & Sigmundson, H. K. (1997). Sex reassignment at birth: Long-term review and clinical implications. *Archives of Pediatrics and Adolescent Medicine, 151*, 298-304.

Di Ceglie, D. (1998). Management and therapeutic aims in working with children and adolescents with gender identity disorders, and their families. In D. Di Ceglie & D. Freedman (Eds.), *A stranger in my own body: Atypical gender identity development and mental health* (pp. 185-197). London: Karnac Books.

Di Ceglie, D., & Freedman, D. (Eds.) (1998). *A stranger in my own body: Atypical gender identity development and mental health*. London: Karnac Books.

Di Ceglie, D., Freedman, D., McPherson, S., & Richardson, P. (2002). Children and adolescents referred to a specialist gender identity development service: Clinical features and demographic characteristics [On-line]. Available: http://www.symposion.com/ijt/ijtvo06no0101.htm

Di Ceglie, D., Sturge, C., & Sutton, A. (1998). *Gender identity disorders in children and adolescents: Guidelines for management* (Council Report CR63). London: Royal College of Psychiatrists.

Dittmann, R. W. (1998). Ambiguous genitalia, gender identity problems, and sex reassignment. *Journal of Sex and Marital Therapy, 24*, 255-271.

Dittmann, R. W., Kappes, M. H., Kappes, M. E., Börger, D., Stegner, H., Willig, R. H., & Wallis, H. (1990). Congenital adrenal hyperplasia I: Gender-related behavior and attitudes in female patients and sisters. *Psychoneuroendocrinology, 15,* 401-420.

Dittmann, R. W., Kappes, M. E., & Kappes, M. H. (1992). Sexual behavior in adolescent and adult females with congenital adrenal hyperplasia. *Psychoneuroendocrinology, 17*, 151-170.

Dörner, G., Rohde, W., Schott, G., & Schnabl, C. (1983). On the LH response to estrogen and LHRH in transsexual men. *Experimental and Clinical Endocrinology, 82,* 257-267.

Dörner, G., Rohde, W., Seidel, K., Haas, W., & Schott, G. S. (1976). On the evocability of a positive estrogen feedback action on LH secretion in transsexual men and women. *Endokrinologie, 67,* 20-25.

Downey, J., Ehrhardt, A. A., Gruen, R., Bell, J. J., & Morishima, A. (1989). Psychopathology and social functioning in women with Turner's syndrome. *Journal of Nervous and Mental Disease, 177,* 191-201.

Downey, J., Ehrhardt, A. A., Morishima, A., Bell, J. J., & Gruen, R. (1987). Gender role development in two clinical syndromes: Turner's Syndrome versus constitutional short stature. *Journal of the American Academy of Child and Adolescent Psychiatry, 26,* 566-573.

Downs, C., & Whittle, S. (1998). *Ethical questions relating to the postponement of puberty in adolescents with gender dysphoria*. Paper presented at the Third International Congress on Sex and Gender, Exeter College, Oxford, UK [On-line]. Available: http://www.symposion.com/ijt/whittle_congress.htm

Dreger, A. D. (Ed.). (1999a). *Intersex in the age of ethics*. Hagerstown, MD: University Publishing Group.

Dreger, A. D. (1999b). A history of intersex: From the age of gonads to the age of consent. In A. D. Dreger (Ed.), *Intersex in the age of ethics*. Hagerstown, MD: University Publishing Group.

Eaton, W. O., Chipperfield, J. G., & Singbeil, C. E. (1989). Birth order and activity level in children. *Developmental Psychology, 25*, 668-672.

Egan, S. K., & Perry, D. G. (2001). Gender identity: A multidimensional analysis with implications for psychosocial adjustment. *Developmental Psychology, 37*, 451-463.

Ehrhardt, A. A., Evers, D. K., & Money, J. (1968). Influence of androgen and some aspects of sexually dimorphic behavior in women with late treated adrenogenital syndrome. *Johns Hopkins Medical Journal, 123*, 115-122.

Ehrhardt, A. A., Greenberg, N., & Money, J. (1970). Female gender identity and absence of fetal gonadal hormones: Turner syndrome. *Johns Hopkins Medical Journal, 126*, 237-248.

Eicher, W. (1984/1992). *Transsexualismus.* Stuttgart: Fisher.

Ekins, R., & King, D. (1996). *Blending genders. Social aspects of cross-dressing and sex-changing.* London/New York: Routledge.

Ekins, R., & King, D. (2001). *Transgendering, migrating and love of oneself as a woman: A contribution to a sociology of autogynephilia* [On-line]. Available: http://www.symposion.com/ijt/ijtvo05no03_01.htm

Eklund, P. L. E., Gooren, L. J. G., & Bezemer, P. D. (1988). Prevalence of transsexualism in the Netherlands. *British Journal of Psychiatry, 152*, 638-640.

El Abd, S., Turk, J., & Hill, P. (1995). Annotation: Psychological characteristics of Turner syndrome. *Journal of Clinical Psychology and Psychiatry, 36*, 1109-1125.

Elbe, L. (1932). *Ein Mensch wechselt sein Geschlecht: Eine Lebensbeichte.* Dresden: Carl Reissner.

Eldh, J., Berg, A., & Gustafsson, M. (1997). Long-term follow up after sex reassignment surgery. *Scandinavian Journal of Plastic and Reconstructive Hand Surgery, 31*, 39-45.

Elisabeth, P. H., & Green, R. (1984). Childhood sex role behaviors: Similarities and differences in twins. *Acta Geneticae Medicae et Gemellologiae, 33*, 173-179.

Elliot, C. (1998). Why can't we go on as three? *Hastings Center Report, 28*, 36-39.

Ellis, L., & Ebertz, L. (Eds.). (1997). *Sexual orientation: Toward a biological understanding.* London: Praeger.

Emmerich, W., Goldman, K. S., Kirsh, B., & Sharabany, R. (1977). Evidence for a transitional phase in the development of gender constancy. *Child Development, 48*, 930-936.

European Court of Human Rights, Strasbourg (2002). Judgement of 11 July 2002 (Grand Chamber) – Application no. 28957/95 – Christine Goodwin v. the United Kingdom. *Human Rights Law Journal, 23*(1-4), 72-85.

Fagot, B. I. (1977). Teachers' reinforcement of sex-preferred behaviors in Dutch preschools. *Psychological Reports, 41,* 1249-1250.

Fagot, B. I. (1985). Changes in thinking about early sex role development. *Developmental Review, 5,* 83-98.

Fagot, B. I. (1995). Psychosocial and cognitive determinants of early gender role development. *Annual Review of Sex Research, 6*, 1-31.

Fagot, B. I., & Leinbach, M. D. (1985). Gender identity: Some thoughts on an old concept. *Journal of the American Academy of Child Psychiatry, 24*, 684-688.

Fagot, B. I., & Leinbach, M. D. (1989). The young child's gender schema: Environmental input, internal organization. *Child Development, 60*, 663-672.

Fagot, B. I., & Leinbach, M. D. (1993). Gender-role development in young children: From discrimination to labeling. *Developmental Review, 13*, 205-224.

Fagot, B. I., Leinbach, M. D., & Hagan, R. (1986). Gender labeling and the adoption of sex-typed behaviors. *Developmental Psychology, 22*, 440-443.

Fausto-Sterling, A. (1992). *Myths of gender*. New York: Basic Books.

Feder, E. K. (1997). Disciplining the family: The case of gender identity disorder. *Philosophical Studies, 85,* 195-211.

Feitz, W. F., Van Grunsven, E. J., Froeling, F. M., & de Vries, J. D. (1994). Outcome analysis of the psychosexual and socio-economical development of adult patients born with bladder exstrophy. *Journal of Urology, 152,* 1417-1419.

Finegan, J. K, Niccols, G. A., & Sitarenios, G. (1992). Relations between prenatal testosterone levels and cognitive abilities at 4 years. *Developmental Psychology, 28*, 1075-1089.

Fishbain, D. A., & Vilaruso, A. (1980). Exclusive adult lesbianism associated with Turner's syndrome mosaicism. *Archives of Sexual Behavior, 9,* 349-353.

Fisk, N. M. (1973). Gender dysphoria syndrome (the how, what and why of a disease). In D. R. Laub & P. Gandy (Eds.), *Proceedings of the 2nd Interdisciplinary Symposium on Gender Dysphoria Syndrome*. Stanford, CA: Division of Reconstructive and Rehabilitation Surgery, Stanford University Medical Center.

Fitch, R. H , & Denenberg, V. H. (1998). A role for ovarian hormones in sexual differentiation of the brain. *Behavior and Brain Sciences, 21,* 311-327.

Fleming, M., Jones, D., & Simons, J. (1982). Preliminary results of pre- and postoperative transsexuals. *Journal of Clinical Psychology, 38,* 408-514.

Fleming, M., MacGowan, B., & Costos, D. (1985). The dyadic adjustment of female-to-male transsexuals. *Archives of Sexual Behavior, 14,* 47-55.

Fleming, M., Steinman, C., & Bocknek, G. (1980). Methodological problems in assessing sex-reassignment surgery: A reply to Meyer and Reter. *Archives of Sexual Behavior, 9,* 451-456.

Freund, K., Steiner, B. W., & Chan, S. (1982). Two types of cross-gender identity. *Archives of Sexual Behavior, 11*, 49-63.

Fridell, S. R., Zucker, K. J., Bradley, S. J., & Maing, D. M. (1996). Physical attractiveness of girls with gender identity disorder. *Archives of Sexual Behavior, 25,* 17-31.

Friedman, R. C. (1988). *Male homosexuality: A contemporary psychoanalytic perspective.* New Haven, CT: Yale University Press.

Fryns, J. P., Kleczkowska, A, Kubien, E., & Van den Berghe, H. (1995). XYY syndrome and other Y chromosome polysomies: Mental status and psychosocial functioning. *Genetic Counseling, 6,* 197-206.

Garber, M. (1992). *Vested interests: Cross-dressing and cultural anxiety.* London: Penguin.

Gay American Indians & Roscoe, W. (Eds.). (1988). *Living the Spirit: A gay American Indian anthology.* New York: St. Martin's Press.

George, F. W., & Wilson, J. D. (1988). Sex determination and differentiation. In E. Knobil and J. Neill (Eds.), *The physiology of reproduction* (pp. 3-26). New York: Raven Press.

Godlewski, G. (1988). Transsexualism and anatomic sex: Ratio reversal in Poland. *Archives of Sexual Behavior, 17,* 547-549.

Golombok, S., & Fivush, R. (1994). *Gender development.* New York: Cambridge University Press.

Golombok, S., & Rust, J. (1993). The pre-school activities inventory: A standardized assessment of gender role in children. *Psychological Assessment, 5,* 131-136.

Goodman, R. E., Anderson, D. C., Bulock, D. E., Sheffield, B., Lynch, S. S., & Butt, W. R. (1985). Study of the effect of estradiol on gonadotropin levels in untreated male-to-female transsexuals. *Archives of Sexual Behavior, 14,* 141-147.

Gooren, L. J. G. (1986). The neuroendocrine response of luteinizing hormone to estrogen administration in heterosexual, homosexual and transsexual subjects. *Journal of Clinical Endocrinology and Metabolism, 63,* 583-588.

Gooren, L. J. G. (1988). An appraisal of endocrine theories of homosexuality and gender dysphoria. In J. M. A. Sitsen (Ed.), *Handbook of sexology: Vol. 6. The pharmacology and endocrinology of sexual function* (pp. 410-424). Amsterdam: Elsevier.

Gooren, L. J. G. (1992). Gender dysphoria in Pakistan: The Khusra. A traveller's report. *Gender Dysphoria, 1,* 35-36.

Gooren, L. J. G., & Cohen-Kettenis, P. T. (1991). Development of male gender identity/role and a sexual orientation towards women in a 46,XY subject with an incomplete form of the androgen insensitivity syndrome. *Archives of Sexual Behavior, 20,* 459-470.

Gooren, L. J. G., & Delemarre-de Waal, H. (1996). The feasibility of endocrine interventions in juvenile transsexuals. *Journal of Psychology & Human Sexuality, 8,* 69-74.

Gorski, R. A. (2000). Sexual differentiation of the nervous system. In E. R. Kandel, J. H. Schwartz, & T. M. Jessell (Eds.), *Principles of neural science* (4th ed., pp. 1131-1148). New York: McGraw-Hill.

Gotz, M. J., Johnstone, E. C., & Ratcliffe, S. G. (1999). Criminality and antisocial behaviour in unselected men with sex chromosome abnormalities. *Psychological Medicine, 29,* 953-962.

Graham, J. M., Bashir, A. S., Stark, R. E., Silbert, A., & Walzer, S. (1988). Oral and written language abilities of XXY boys: Implications for anticipatory guidance. *Pediatrics, 81,* 795-806.

Green, R. (1966). Transsexualism: Mythological, historical, and cross-cultural aspects. In H. Benjamin (Ed.), *The transsexual phenomenon* (pp. 173-185). New York: Julian Press.

Green, R. (1974). *Sexual identity conflict in children and adults.* New York: Basic Books.

Green, R. (1987). *The "sissy boy syndrome" and the development of homosexuality.* New Haven, CT: Yale University Press.

Green, R. (1994). Transsexualism and the law. *Bulletin of the American Academy of Psychiatry and the Law, 22*, 511-517.

Green, R., & Fleming, D. (1990). Transsexual surgery follow-up: Status in the 1990s. *Annual Review of Sex Research, 1,* 163-174.

Green, R., & Money, J. (1969). *Transsexualism and sex reassignment.* Baltimore, MD: Johns Hopkins University Press.

Green, R., Newman, L. E., & Stoller, R. J. (1972). Treatment of boyhood "transsexualism." *Archives of General Psychiatry, 26,* 213-217.

Green, R., & Young, R. (2001). Hand preference, sexual preference, and transsexualism. *Archives of Sexual Behavior, 30*, 565-574.

Greenberg, R. P., & Laurence, L. (1981). A comparison of the MMPI results for psychiatric patients and male applicants for transsexual surgery. *Journal of Nervous and Mental Disease*, 69, 320-323.

Greens, B. (2000). Gender and culture. In A. E. Kazdin (Ed.), *Encyclopedia of psychology* (Vol. 3, pp. 430-433). Oxford, UK: Oxford University Press.

Grémaux, R. (1994). Woman becomes man in the Balkans. In G. Herdt (Ed.), *Third sex, third gender: Beyond the dimorphism in culture and history* (pp. 241-281). New York: Zone Books.

Grimshaw, G. M., Bryden, M. P., & Finegan, J. (1995). Relations between prenatal testosterone and cerebral lateralization in children. *Neuropsychology, 9,* 68-79.

Grimshaw, G. M., Sitarenios, G., & Finegan, J. (1995). Mental rotation at 7 years: Relation with prenatal testosterone levels and spatial play performance. *Brain and Cognition, 29*, 85-100.

Gromb, S., Chanseau, B., & Lazarini, H. J. (1997). Judicial problems related to transsexualism in France. *Medicine Science and the Law, 3,* 27-31.

Grumbach, M. M., & Conte, F. (1998). Disorders of sexual differentiation. In J. W. Wilson & D. W. Foster (Eds.), *Williams textbook of endocrinology* (9th ed., pp. 1400-1405). Philadelphia, PA: W. B. Saunders.

Haber, C. H. (1991). The psychoanalytic treatment of a preschool boy with a gender identity disorder. *Journal of the American Psychoanalytic Association, 39*, 107-130.

Haberman, M., Hollingsworth, F., Falek, A., & Michael, R. P. (1975). Gender identity confusion, schizophrenia and a 47 XYY karyotype: A case report. *Psychoneuroendocrinology, 1*, 207-209.

Hage, J. J., & Mulder, J. W. (Eds.). (1995). *Plastische chirurgie van het genitale gebied.* Leeuwarden: Nederlandse Vereniging voor Plastische en Reconstructieve Chirurgie.

Halpern, D. F. (1992). *Sex differences in cognitive abilities* (2nd ed.). Hillsdale, NJ: Lawrence Erlbaum.

Hamburger, C. (1953). The desire for change of sex as shown by personal letters from 465 men and women. *Acta Endocrinologica, 14*, 361-375.

Hamburger, C., Stürup, G., & Dahl-Iversen, E. (1953). Transvestism. Hormonal, psychiatric and surgical treatment. *Journal of the American Medical Association, 152*, 391-396.

Hampson, E., Rovet, J. F., & Altmann, D. (1998). Spatial reasoning in children with congenital adrenal hyperplasia due to 21-hydroxylase deficiency. *Developmental Neuropsychology, 14*, 299-320.

Haraldsen, I. R., & Dahl, A. A. (2000). Symptom profiles of gender dysphoric patients of transsexual type compared to patients with personality disorders and healthy adults. *Acta Psychiatrica Scandinavica, 102*, 276-281.

Harmon-Smith, H. (1998). A mother's 10 commandments to medical professionals: Treating intersex in the newborn. In A. D. Dreger (Ed.), *Intersex in the age of ethics* (pp. 195-196). Hagerstown, MD: University Publishing Group.

Harris, L. J. (1992). Left-handedness. In I. Rapin & S.J. Segalowitz (Eds.), *Handbook of neuropsychology* (pp. 145-208). Amsterdam: Elsevier Science.

Harry, J. (1982). *Gay children grow up: Gender culture and gender deviance.* New York: Praeger.

Haugh, S. S., Hoffman, C. D., & Cowan, G. (1980). The eye of the very young beholder: Sex typing of infants by young children. *Child Development, 51*, 598-600.

Heiman, E. M., & Lé, C. V. (1975). Transsexualism in Vietnam. *Archives of Sexual Behavior, 4,* 89-95.

Hekma, G. (1994). "A female soul in a male body": Sexual inversion as gender inversion in nineteenth-century sexology. In G. Herdt (Ed.), *Third sex, third gender: Beyond the dimorphism in culture and history* (pp. 213-239). New York: Zone Books.

Helleday, J., Bartfai, A., Ritzén, M., & Forsman, M. (1994). General intelligence and cognitive profile in women with congenital adrenal hyperplasia (CAH). *Psychoneuroendocrinology, 19,* 343-356.

Herdt, G. (1994a). *Third sex, third gender: Beyond the dimorphism in culture and history.* New York: Zone Books.

Herdt, G. (1994b). Mistaken sex: Culture, biology and third sex in New Guinea. In G. Herdt (Ed.), *Third sex, third gender: Beyond the dimorphism in culture and history* (pp. 419-445). New York: Zone Books.

Herdt, G., & Davidson J. (1988). The Sambia "Turnim-man": Sociocultural and clinical aspects of gender transformation in male pseudohermaphroditism with 5-alpha reductase deficiency in Papua Guinea. *Archives of Sexual Behavior, 17*, 33-56.

Herman, A., Grabowska, A., & Dulko, S. (1993). Transsexualism and sex related differences in hemispheric asymmetry. *Acta Neurobiologiae Experimentalis, 53*, 269-274.

Herrn, R. (1995). Vom Geschlechtsumwandlungswahn zur Geschlechtsumwandlung. *Pro Familia Magazin, 23,* 14-18.

Hertoft, P., & Sörensen, T. (1979). Transsexuality: Some remarks based on clinical experience. In *Sex, hormones and behavior* (pp.165-181). Amsterdam: Ciba Foundation Symposium 62.

Hines, M., Ahmed, S. F., & Hughes, I. A. (2000). *Psychological development in androgen insensitivity syndrome.* Poster presented at the 26th annual meeting of the International Academy of Sex Research, Paris, France.

Hirschauer, S. (1993). *Die soziale Konstruktion der Transsexualität: Über die Medizin und den Geschlechtswechsel.* Frankfurt am Main: Suhrkamp.

Hirschauer, S. (1997). The medicalization of gender migration [On-line]. Available: http://www.symposion.com/ijt/ijtc0104.htm

Hirschfeld, M. (1910). *Die Transvestiten: Eine Untersuchung über den erotischen Verkleidungstrieb mit umfangreichem casuistischem und historischem Material* (Vols. I-II). Berlin: Alfred Pulvermacher & Co.

Hirschfeld, M. (1918). *Sexuelle Zwischenstufen: Vol. 2. Sexualpathologie.* Bonn: Marcus & Webers.

Hirschfeld, M. (1923). Die intersexuelle Konstitution. *Jahrbuch für sexuelle Zwischenstufen, 23,* 3-27.

Hiscock, M., Inch, R., Jacek, C., Hiscock-Kalil, C., & Kalil, K. M. (1994). Is there a sex difference in human laterality? 1: An exhaustive survey of auditory laterality studies from six neuropsychology journals. *Journal of Clinical and Experimental Neuropsychology, 16,* 423-435.

Hoaken, P. C. S., Clarke, M., & Breslin, M. (1964). Psychopathology in Klinefelter's Syndrome. *Psychosomatic Medicine, 26,* 207-223.

Hochberg, Z., Gardos, M., & Benderly, A. (1987). Psychosexual outcome of assigned females and males with 46,XX virilizing congenital adrenal hyperplasia. *European Journal of Pediatrics, 146,* 497-499.

Hoenig, J. (1985). The origin of gender identity. In B. W. Steiner (Ed.), *Gender dysphoria: Development, research, management* (pp. 11-32). New York: Plenum Press.

Hoenig, J., Kenna, J., & Youd, A. (1971). Surgical treatment for transsexualism. *Acta Psychiatrica Scandinavica, 47*, 106-133.

Holl, R. W., Kunze, D., Etzrodt, H., Teler, W., & Heinze, E. (1994). Turner syndrome: Final height, glucose tolerance, bone density and psychosocial status in 25 adult patients. *European Journal of Pediatrics, 15,* 11-16.

Holloway, J. P. (1974). Transsexuals: Legal considerations. *Archives of Sexual Behavior, 3*, 33-50.

Hook, E. B., & Warburton, D. (1983). The distribution of chromosomal genotypes associated with Turner's syndrome: Live birth prevalence rates and evidence for diminished fetal mortality and severity in genotypes associated with structural X abnormalities or mosaicism. *Human Genetics, 64*, 24-27.

Horowitz, M., & Glassberg, K. I. (1992). Ambiguous genitalia: Diagnosis, evaluation, and treatment. *Urologic Radiology, 14,* 306-318.

Huelke, H. H. (1949). Ein Transvestit (Der Fall Hinrich B.). *Kriminalistik, 3,* 91-92.

Hunt, D. D., Carr, J. E., & Hampson, J. L. (1981). Cognitive correlates of biologic sex and gender identity in transsexualism. *Archives of Sexual Behavior, 10*, 65-77.

Hurtig, A. L. (1992). The psychosocial effects of ambiguous genitalia. *Comprehensive Therapy, 18*, 22-25.

Hurtig, A. L., & Rosenthal, I. M. (1987). Psychological findings in early treated cases of female pseudohermaphroditism caused by virilizing congenital adrenal hyperplasia. *Archives of Sexual Behavior, 16,* 209-223.

Imperato-McGinley, J., Guerrero, L., Gautier, T., & Petersen, R. E. (1974). Steroid 5alpha-reductase deficiency in man: An inherited form of male pseudohermaphroditism. *Science, 27,* 1213-1215.

Imperato-McGinley, J., Peterson, R. E., Gautier, T., & Sturla, E. (1979). Androgens and the evolution of male-gender identity among male pseudohermaphrodites with 5alpha-reductase deficiency. *New England Journal of Medicine, 300*, 1233-1237.

Imperato-McGinley, J., Peterson, R. E., Stoller, R, & Goodwin, W. E. (1979). Male pseudo-hermaphroditism secondary to 17ß-hydroxysteroid dehydrogenase deficiency: Gender role change with puberty. *Journal of Clinical Endocrinology and Metabolism, 49*, 391-395.

Intons-Peterson, M. J. (1988a). *Children's concepts of gender*. Norwood, NJ: Ablex.

Intons-Peterson, M. J. (1988b). *Gender concepts of Swedish and American youth*. Hillsdale, NJ: Lawrence Erlbaum.

Isay, R. A. (1997). Remove gender identity in DSM. *Psychiatric News, 32*, 9 and 13.

Jacklin, C. N., Maccoby, E. E., & Doering, C. H. (1983). Neonatal sex-steroid hormones and timidity in 6–18 month-old boys and girls. *Developmental Psychobiology, 16*, 163-168.

Jacklin, C. N., Thompson-Wilcox, K., & Maccoby, E. E. (1988). Neonatal sex-steroid hormones and cognitive abilities at six years. *Developmental Psychobiology, 21*, 567-574.

Jenssen Hagerman, R. (1999). *Neurodevelopmental disorders: Diagnosis and treatment.* New York/Oxford: Oxford University Press.

Kandemir, N., & Yordam, N. (1997). Congenital adrenal hyperplasia in Turkey: A review of 273 patients. *Acta Paediatrica, 86,* 22-25.

Kando, T. (1973). *Sex change: The achievement of gender identity among feminized transsexuals.* Springfield, IL: Charles C. Thomas.

Karush, R. K. (1993). Sam: A child analysis. *Journal of Clinical Psychoanalysis, 2*, 43-62.

Kavanaugh, J. G., & Volkan, V. D. (1978-1979). Transsexualism and a new type of psychosurgery. *International Journal of Psychoanalytic Psychotherapy, 7*, 366-372.

Kemp, B. D., Groveman, S. A., Tako, H. D., Irwin, K. M., Natarajan, A., & Sullivan, P. (1996). Sex, lies, and androgen insensitivity syndrome. *Canadian Medical Association Journal, 154*, 1827-1834.

Kernberg, O. (1975). *Borderline conditions and pathological narcissism.* New York: Science House.

Kessler, S. J. (1998). *Lessons from the intersexed.* New Brunswick, NJ: Rutgers University Press.

Kimball, M. M. (1986). Television and sex-role attitudes. In T. M. Williams (Ed.), *The impact of television: A natural experiment in three communities* (pp. 265-301). Orlando, FL: Academic Press.

King, D. (1986). *The transvestite and the transsexual: A case study of public categories and private identities*. Ph.D. Thesis, University of Essex.

Klein, C. H. (1998). From one 'battle' to another: The making of a *travesti* political movement in a Brazilian city. *Sexualities,* 327-342.

Kockott, G., & Fahrner, E. M . (1988). Male-to-female and female-to-male transsexuals: A comparison. *Archives of Sexual Behavior, 6,* 539-546.

Kohlberg, L. A. (1966). A cognitive-developmental analysis of children's sex role concepts and attitudes. In E. E. Maccoby (Ed.), *The development of sex differences* (pp. 82-173). Stanford, CA: Stanford University Press.

Kohn, G., Lasch, E. E., El-Shawwa, R., Elrayyes, E., Litvin, Y., & Rösler, A. (1985). Male pseudohermaphroditism due to 17ß-hydroxysteroid dehydrogenase deficiency (17ß HSD) in a large Arab kinship: Studies on the natural history of the defect. *Journal of Pediatric Endocrinology, 1*, 29-37.

Kronberg, J., Tyano, S., Apter, & Wijsenbeck, H. (1981). Treatment of transsexualism in adolescence. *Journal of Adolescence 4,* 177-185.

Kruijver, F. P., Zhou, J., Pool, C., Hofman, M. A., Gooren, L. J. G., & Swaab, D. F. (2000). Male-to-female transsexuals have female neuron numbers in a limbic nucleus. *Journal of Clinical Endocrinology and Metabolism, 85*, 2034-2041.

Kubie, L. S., & Mackie, J. B. (1968). Critical issues raised by operations for gender transmutations. *Journal of Nervous and Mental Disease, 14,* 431-444.

Kuhn, D., Nash, S. C., & Brucken, L. (1978). Sex role concepts of two- and three-year old children. *Child Development, 49*, 445-451.

Kuhnle, U., Bullinger, M., & Schwarz, H. P. (1995). The quality of life in adult female patients with congenital adrenal hyperplasia: A comprehensive study of the impact of genital malformations and chronic disease on female patients' life. *European Journal of Pediatrics, 154,* 708-716.

Kuiper, A. J. (1991). *Transseksualiteit: Evaluatie van de geslachtsaanpassende behandeling.* Utrecht: Elinkwijk.

Kuiper, A. J., & Cohen-Kettenis, P. T. (1998). *Gender role reversal among postoperative transsexuals* [On-line]. Available: http://www.symposion.com/ijt/ijtc0502.htm

Kulick, D. (1998a). Transgender in Latin America: Persons, practices and meaning, *Sexualities, 1,* 259-260.

Kulick, D. (1998b). Fe/male trouble: The unsettling place of lesbians in the self-images of Brazilian *travesti* prostitutes. *Sexualities, 1*, 299-312.

La Freniere, P., Strayer, F. F., & Gauthier, R. (1984). The emergence of same-sex affiliative preferences among preschool peers: A developmental/ethological perspective. *Child Development, 55,* 1958-1965.

Lamb, M. E., & Roopnarine, J. L. (1979). Peer influences on sex role development. *Child Development, 50,* 1219-1222.

Lancaster, R. N. (1998). Transgenderism in Latin America: Some critical introductory remarks on identities and practices. *Sexualities, 1,* 261-274.

Landèn, M., Wålinder, J., Hambert, G., & Lundström, B. (1998). Factors predictive of regret in sex reassignment. *Acta Psychiatrica Scandinavica, 97,* 284-289.

Landèn, M., Wålinder, J., & Lundström, B. (1996). Prevalence, incidence and sex ratio of transsexualism. *Acta Psychiatrica Scandinavica, 93,* 221-223.

Landèn, M., Wålinder, J., & Lundström, B. (1998). Clinical characteristics of a total cohort of female and male applicants for sex reassignment: A descriptive study. *Acta Psychiatrica Scandinavica, 97,* 189-194.

Lang, S. (1998). *Men as women, women as men. Changing gender in native American cultures.* Austin: University of Texas Press.

Laron, Z., Dickerman, Z., Zamir, R., & Galatzer, A. (1982). Paternity in Klinefelter's Syndrome. A case report. *Archives of Andrology, 8,* 149-151.

La Torre, R. A., Gossmann, I., & Piper, W. E. (1976). Cognitive style, hemispheric specialization, and tested abilities of transsexuals and nontranssexuals. *Perceptual and Motor Skills, 43*, 719-722.

Leaper, C., & Anderson, K. J. (1997). Gender development and heterosexual romantic relationships during adolescence. *New Directions in Child Development, 78*, 85-103.

Leaper, C., Anderson, K. J., & Sanders, P. (1998). Moderators of gender effects on parents' talk to their children: A meta-analysis. *Developmental Psychology, 34*, 3-27.

Leavitt, F., & Berger, J. C. (1990). Clinical patterns among male transsexual candidates with erotic interest in males. *Archives of Sexual Behavior, 19,* 491-505.

Leavitt, F., Berger, J., & Hoeppner, J. (1980). Presurgical adjustment in male transsexuals with and without hormonal treatment. *Journal of Nervous and Mental Disease, 168,* 693-697.

Leinbach, M. D., & Fagot, B. I. (1986). Acquisition of gender labeling: A test for toddlers. *Sex Roles, 15*, 655-666.

Levi, H. (1998). Lean mean fighting queens: Drag in the world of Mexican professional wrestling. *Sexualities, 1, 275-286.*

Lewis, V. G., & Money, J. (1983). Gender identity/role: G-I/R Part A: XY (androgen-insensitivity) syndrome and XX (Rokitansky) syndrome of vaginal atresia compared. In L. Dennerstein & G. Burrows (Eds.), *Handbook of psychosomatic obstetrics and gynaecology* (pp. 51-60). Amsterdam: Elsevier Biomedical.

Lim, M. H., & Bottomley, V. (1983). A combined approach to the treatment of effeminate behaviour in a boy: A case study. *Journal of Child Psychology and Psychiatry, 3,* 469-479.

Lindemalm, G., Körlin, D., & Uddenberg, N. (1986). Long-term follow-up of "sex change" in 13 male-to-female transsexuals. *Archives of Sexual Behavior, 15,* 187-210.

Lindgren, T. W., & Pauly, I. B. (1975). A body image scale for evaluating transsexuals. *Archives of Sexual Behavior, 4*, 639-656.

Linn, M. C., & Petersen, A. C. (1985). Emergence and characterization of sex differences in spatial ability: A meta-analysis. *Child Development, 56*, 1479-1498.

Loehlin, J. C., & Martin, N. G. (2000). Dimensions of psychological masculinity–femininity in adult twins from opposite-sex and same-sex pairs. *Behavior Genetics, 30*, 19-28.

Lothstein, L. M. (1982). Sex reassignment surgery: Historical, bioethical, clinical and theoretical issues. *American Journal of Psychiatry, 139,* 417-426.

Lothstein, L. M. (1984). Psychological testing with transsexuals: A 30 year review. *Journal of Personality Assessment, 48,* 500-507.

Lundström, B., Pauly, I., & Wålinder, J. (1984). Outcome of sex reassignment surgery. *Acta Psychiatrica Scandinavica, 70,* 289-294.

Lutz, S. E., & Ruble, D. N. (1995). Children and gender prejudice: Context, motivation, and the development of gender concepts. *Annals of Child Development, 10*, 131-166.

Lytton, H., & Romney, D. M. (1991). Parents' differential socialization of boys and girls: A meta-analysis. *Psychological Bulletin, 109,* 267-296.

Maccoby, E. E. (1998). *The two sexes: Growing up apart coming together*. Cambridge, MA: The Belknap Press of Harvard University Press.

Maccoby, E. E., & Jacklin, C. N. (1987). Gender segregation in childhood. In H. Reese (Ed.), *Advances in child development and behavior* (Vol. 20, pp. 239-287). New York: Academic Press.

MacDonald, P. C., Madden, J. D., Brenner, P. F., Wilson, J. D., & Siiteri, P. K. (1979). Origin of estrogen in normal men and in women with testicular feminization. *Journal of Clinical Endocrinology and Metabolism, 49,* 905-916.

Maine Gender Resource and Support Service (MeGReSS) (2002). *Transgender youth survey* [On-line]. Available at: megress@tds.net and http://personalpages.tds.net/-megress

Maltz, D. N., & Borker, R. A. (1982). A cultural approach to male-female miscommunication. In J. A. Gumperz (Ed.), *Language and social identity* (pp. 195-216). New York: Cambridge University Press.

Mandoki, M. W., & Summer, G. S. (1991). Klinefelter Syndrome: The need for early identification and treatment. *Clinical Pediatrics, 30*, 161-164.

Marantz, S., & Coates, S. (1991). Mothers of boys with gender identity disorder: A comparison of matched controls. *Journal of the American Academy of Child and Adolescent Psychiatry, 30,* 310-315.

Marks, I., Green, R., & Mataix-Cols, D. (2000). Adult gender identity disorder can remit. *Comprehensive Psychiatry, 41*, 273-275.

Martin, C. L., & Halverson, C. F. (1981). A schematic processing model of sex typing and stereotyping in children. *Child Development, 52*, 1119-1134.

Martin, C. L., & Halverson, C. F. (1983). The effects of sex typing schemas on young children's memory. *Child Development, 54,* 563-574.

Martin, C. L., Wood, C. H., & Little, J. K. (1990). The development of gender stereotype components. *Child Development, 61*, 1891-1904.

Martini, E., Geraedts, J. P., Liebaers, I., Land , J. A., Capitanio, G. L., Ramaekers, F. C., & Hopman, A. H. (1996). Constitution of semen samples from XYY and XXY males as analysed by in-situ hybridization. *Human Reproduction, 11*, 1638-1643.

Masica, D. N., Ehrhardt, A. A., & Money, J. (1971). Fetal feminization and female gender identity in the testicular feminizing syndrome of androgen insensitivity. *Archives of Sexual Behavior, 1,* 131-142.

Mate-Kole, C. (1988). Psychiatric symptoms in transsexualism. *British Journal of Psychiatry, 150,* 550-553.

Matzner, A. (in press). The politics of re-presentation: An analysis of Western academic treatments of male transgenderism in Thailand.

McCauley, E., & Ehrhardt, A. A. (1977). Role expectations and definitions: A comparison of female transsexuals and lesbians. *Journal of Homosexuality, 3,* 137-147.

McCauley, E., Feuillan, P., Kushner, H., & Ross, J. L. (2001). Psychosocial development in adolescents with Turner syndrome. *Journal of Developmental and Behavioral Pediatrics, 22*, 360-365.

McCauley, E., Ross, J. L., Kushner, H., & Cutler, G. (1995). Self-esteem and behavior in girls with Turner syndrome. *Journal of Developmental and Behavioral Pediatrics, 16,* 82-88.

McDermid, S. A., Zucker, K. J., Bradley, S. J., & Maing, D. M. (1998). Effects of physical appearance on masculine trait ratings of boys and girls with gender identity disorder. *Archives of Sexual Behavior, 27,* 253-267.

McEwen, B. S. (1992). Steroid hormones: Effects on brain development and function. *Hormone Research, 37*(Suppl. 3), 1-10.

McKain, T. L. (1996) Acknowledging mixed-sex people. *Journal of Sex and Marital Therapy, 22*, 265-274.

Mead, M. (1928). *Coming of age in Samoa*. New York: William Morrow & Co.

Mead, M. (1930). *Growing up in New Guinea*. New York: William Morrow & Co.

Mead, M. (1935). *Sex and temperament*. New York: William Morrow & Co.

Mendez, J. P., Ulloa-Aguirre, A., Imperato-McGinley, J., Brugmann, A., Delfin, M., Chavez, B., Shackleton, C., Kofman-Alfaro, S., & Perez-Palacios, G. (1995). Male pseudohermaphroditism due to primary 5a-reductase deficiency: Variation in gender identity reversal in seven Mexican patients from five different pedigrees. *Journal of Endocrinological Investigation, 18*, 205-213.

Mendonca, B. B., Inacio, M., Costa, E. M., Arnhold, I. J., Silva, F. A., Nicolau, W., Bloise, W., Russell, D. W., & Wilson, J. D. (1996). Male pseudohermaphroditism due to steroid 5alpha-reductase 2 deficiency: Diagnosis, psychological evaluation, and management. *Medicine (Baltimore), 7,* 64-76.

Meningaud, J. P., Descamps, M. A., & Herve, C. (2000). Sex reassignment surgery in France: Analysis of the legal framework and current procedures and its consequences for transsexuals. *Medicine and Law, 19,* 827-837.

Menvielle, E. M. (1998). Gender identity disorder. *Journal of the American Academy of Child and Adolescent Psychiatry, 37*, 243-244.

Meyenburg, B. (1994). Kritik der hormonellen Behandlung Jugendlicher mit Geschlechtsidentitätsstörungen. *Zeitschrift für Sexualforschung,* 7, 343-349.

Meyenburg, B. (1999). Gender identity disorder in adolescence: Outcomes of psychotherapy. *Adolescence, 34,* 305-313.

Meyer, J. (1982). The theory of gender identity disorders. *Journal of the American Psychoanalytic Association, 30*, 381-418.

Meyer, J. K., & Reter, D. (1979). Sex reassignment: Follow-up. *Archives of General Psychiatry, 36,* 1010-1015.

Meyer, W., Bockting, W. O., Cohen-Kettenis, P. T., Coleman, E., Di Ceglie, D., Devor, H., Gooren, L. J. G., Hage, J. J., Kirk, S., Kuiper, A. J., Laub, D., Lawrence, A., Menard, Y., Patton, J., Schaefer, L., Webb, A., & Wheeler, C. C. (2001). *Standards of care for Gender Identity Disorders of the Harry Benjamin International Gender Dysphoria Association (6th ed.)* [On-line]. Available: http://www.symposion.com/ijt/soc2001/index/htm.

Meyer-Bahlburg, H. F. L. (1985). Gender identity disorder of childhood: Introduction. *Journal of the American Academy of Child Psychiatry, 24*, 681-683.

Meyer-Bahlburg, H. F. L. (1993). Gender identity development in intersex patients. *Child and Adolescent Psychiatric Clinics of North America, 2,* 501-512.

Meyer-Bahlburg, H. F. L. (1994). Intersexuality and the diagnosis of gender identity disorder. *Archives of Sexual Behavior, 23*, 21-40.

Meyer-Bahlburg, H. F. L. (1998). Gender assignment in intersexuality. *Journal of Psychology and Human Sexuality, 10*, 1-21.

Meyer-Bahlburg, H. F. L. (1999). What causes low rates of child-bearing in congenital adrenal hyperplasia? *Journal of Clinical Endocrinology and Metabolism, 84,* 1844-1847.

Meyer-Bahlburg, H. F. L. (2002). Gender identity disorder in young boys: A parent- and peer based treatment protocol. *Clinical Child Psychology and Psychiatry, 7*, 360-376.

Meyer-Bahlburg, H. F. L., Gruen, R. S., New, M. I., Bell, J. J., Morishima, A., Shimshi, M., Bueno, Y., Vagas, I., & Baker, S. W. (1996). Gender change from female to male in classical congenital adrenal hyperplasia. *Hormones and Behavior, 40,* 319-332.

Meyer-Bahlburg, H. F. L., Sandberg, D. E., Yager, T. J., Dolezal, C. L., & Ehrhardt, A. A. (1994). Questionnaire scales for the assessment of atypical gender development in girls and boys. *Journal of Psychology and Human Sexuality, 6,* 19-39.

Meyer-Bahlburg, H. F. L., Sandberg, D. E., Dolezal, C. L., & Yager, T. J. (1994). Gender-related assessment of childood play. *Journal of Abnormal Child Psychology, 22*, 643-660.

Miach, P. P., Berah, E. F., Butcher, J. N., & Rouse, S. (2000). Utility of the MMPI-2 in assessing gender dysphoric patients. *Journal of Personality Assessment, 75*, 268-279.

Miller, H. J. (1972). A case of transsexualism exhibiting intersexuality, having a possible XXY-sex determining mechanism. *Journal of the American Society of Psychosomatic Dentistry and Medicine, 20*, 58-60.

Miller, W. L. (1999). Dexamethasone treatment of congenital adrenal hyperplasia in utero: An experimental therapy of unproven safety. *Journal of Urology, 162*, 537-540.

Miller, A., & Caplan, J. (1965). Sex role reversal following castration of a homosexual transvestite with Klinefelter's Syndrome. *Canadian Psychiatric Association Journal, 10*, 223-227.

Miller, E. M., & Martin, N. (1995). Analysis of the effect of hormones on opposite-sex twin attitudes. *Acta Geneticae Medicae et Gemellologiae, 44*, 41-52.

Miller, C. L., Younger, B. A., & Morse, P. A. (1982). Categorization of male and female voices in infancy. *Infant Behavior and Development, 5*, 143-159.

Mischel, W. (1966). A social-learning view of sex differences in behavior. In E. E. Maccoby (Ed.), *The development of sex differences* (pp. 57-81). Stanford, CA: Stanford University Press.

Mischel, W. (1979). On the interface of cognition and personality: Beyond the person-situation debate. *American Psychologist, 34*, 740-754.

Mitscherlich, A. (1950-1951). 66. Wanderversammlung der Südwestdeutschen Psychiater und Neurologen, Badenweiler, 2./3. Juni 1950. I. Erstes Leitthema: Daseinsanalyse. *Psyche, 4*, 226-234.

Mitscherlich, A., Bally, G., Binder, H., Binswanger, L., Bleuler, M., Brun, R., Dührssen, A., Gollner, W. E., Jores, A., Jung, C. G., Kranz, H., Kemper, W., Meng, H., Mohr, F., Müller, M., Schultz-Hencke, H., Seitz, W., Staehelin, J. E., Steck, H., & Weizsäcker. V. V. (1950-1951a). Rundfrage über ein Referat auf der 66. Wanderversammlung der Südwestdeutschen Psychiater und Neurologen in Badenweiler. *Psyche, 4*, 448-477.

Mitscherlich, A., Georgi, F., Göppert, H., Gundert, H., Mauz, F., Zutt, J., & Boss. M. (1950-1951b). Rundfrage über ein Referat auf der 66. Wanderversammlung der Südwestdeutschen Psychiater und Neurologen in Badenweiler. *Psyche, 4,* 626-640.

Money, J. (1968). *Sex errors of the body.* Baltimore: Johns Hopkins.

Money, J. (1975a). Ablatio penis: Normal male infant sex-reassigned as a girl. *Archives of Sexual Behavior, 4*, 65-71.

Money, J. (1975b). Human behavior cytogenetics: Review of psychopathology of 3 syndromes 47 XXY, 47XYY and 45X. *Journal of Sex Research, 2*, 181-200.

Money, J. (1993). *The Adam principle: Genes, genitals, hormones & gender: Selected readings in sexology*. Buffalo, NY: Prometheus Books.

Money, J. (1994). Concept of gender identity disorder in childhood and adolescence after 39 years. *Journal of Sex & Marital Therapy, 20,* 163-177.

Money, J., & Daléry, J. (1976). Iatrogenic homosexuality: Gender identity in seven 46XX chromosomal females with hyperadrenocortical hermaphroditism with a penis: Three reared as boys, four reared as girls. *Journal of Homosexuality, 1,* 357-371.

Money, J., & Ehrhardt, A. A. (1970). Transsexuelle nach dem Geschlechtswechsel. In G. Schmidt, V. Sigusch, & E. Schorsch (Eds.), *Tendenzen der Sexualforschung* (pp. 70-87). Stuttgart: Enke.

Money, J., & Ehrhardt, A. A. (1972). *Man and woman, boy and girl: Differentiation and dimorphism of gender identity from conception to maturity.* Baltimore, MD: Johns Hopkins University Press.

Money, J., Ehrhardt, A. A., & Masica, D. N. (1968). Fetal feminization by androgen insensitivity in the testicular feminizing syndrome: Effect on marriage and maternalism. *Johns Hopkins Medical Journal, 123*, 105-114.

Money, J., & Epstein, R. (1967). Verbal aptitude and eonism and prepubertal effeminacy: A feminine trait. *Transactions of the New York Academy of Sciences, 29*, 448-454.

Money, J., & Gaskin, R. (1970-1971). Sex reassignment. *International Journal of Psychiatry, 9,* 249-269.

Money, J., Gaskin, R., & Hull, H. (1970). Impulse, aggression and sexuality in the XYY syndrome. *St. John's Law Review, 44*, 220-235.

Money, J., Hampson, J. G., & Hampson, J. L. (1955). An examination of some basic sexual concepts: The evidence of human hermaphroditism. *Bulletin of the Johns Hopkins Hospital, 97*, 301-319.

Money, J., Hampson, J. G., & Hampson, J. L. (1957). Imprinting and the establishment of gender role. *Archives of Neurology and Psychiatry, 77*, 333-336.

Money, J., & Mittenthal, S. (1970). Lack of personality pathology in Turner's syndrome: Relation to cytogenetics, hormones and physique. *Behavior Genetics, 1,* 43-56.

Money, J., & Ogunro, C. (1974). Behavioral sexology: Ten cases of genetic male intersexuality with impaired prenatal and pubertal androgenization. *Archives of Sexual Behavior, 3,* 181-205.

Money, J., & Russo, A. J. (1979). Homosexual outcome of discordant gender identity/role: Longitudinal follow-up. *Journal of Pediatric Psychology, 4,* 29-41.

Money, J., & Schwartz, M. (1977). Dating, romantic and non-romantic friendships and sexuality in 17 early-treated adrenogenital females, aged 16-25. In P. A. Lee, L. P. Plotnick, A. A. Kowarski, & C. J. Migeon (Eds.), *Congenital adrenal hyperplasia*. Baltimore, MD: University Park Press.

Money, J., Schwartz, M., & Lewis, V. G. (1984). Adult erotosexual status and fetal hormonal masculinization and demasculinization: 46,XX congenital virilizing adrenal hyperplasia and 46,XY androgen insensitivity compared. *Psychoneuroendocrinology, 9,* 405-414.

Mühsam, R. (1926). Chirurgische Eingriffe bei Anomalien des Sexuallebens. *Therapie der Gegenwart, 6,* 451-455.

Mulaikal, R. M., Migeon, C. J., & Rock, J. A. (1987). Fertility rates in female patients with congenital adrenal hyperplasia due to 21hydroxylase deficiency. *New England Journal of Medicine, 316,* 178-182.

Mureau, M. A., Slijper, F. M., Nijman, R. J., van der Meulen, J. C., Verhulst, F. C., & Slob, A. K. (1995). Psychosexual adjustment of children and adolescents after different types of hypospadias surgery: A norm-related study. *Journal of Urology, 154*, 1902-1907.

Murray, D. A. B. (1998). Defiance or defilement? Undressing cross-dressing in Martinique's carnival. *Sexualities, 1*, 343-354.

Murray, J. F. (1985). Borderline manifestations in the Rorschachs of male transsexuals. *Journal of Personality Assessment, 49,* 454-466.

Nanda, S. (1994). Hijras: An alternative sex and gender role in India. In G. Herdt (Ed.), *Third sex, third gender: Beyond the dimorphism in culture and history* (pp. 373-417). New York: Zone Books.

Neugebauer, F. L. (1908). *Hermaphroditismus beim Menschen.* Leipzig: Dr. Werner Klinkhardt.

Nicholls, D., & Stanhope, R. (1998). Turner's syndrome, anorexia nervosa, and anabolic steroids. *Archives of Disease in Childhood, 79,* 94.

New, M. I. (1995). Steroid 21-hydroxylase deficiency (congenital adrenal hyperplasia). *American Journal of Medicine, G8*(1A), 2S-8S.

Nielsen, J., Christensen, K. R., Friedrich, U., Zeuthen, E., & Ostergaard, O. (1973). Childhood of males with XYY syndrome. *Journal of Autism and Childhood Schizophrenia, 2,* 5-26.

Nielsen, J., & Pelsen, B. (1987). Follow-up 20 years later of 34 Klinefelter males with karyotype 47XXY and 16 hypogonadal males with karyotype 46XY. *American Journal of Human Genetics, 77,* 188-192.

Nielsen, J., Pelsen, B., & Sørensen, K. (1988). Follow-up of 30 Klinefelter males treated with testosterone. *Clinical Genetics, 33*, 262-269.

Nielsen, J., Sørensen, A. M., & Sørensen, K. (1982). Follow-up until age 7 to 11 of 25 unselected children with sex chromosome abnormalities. *Birth Defects: Original Article Series, 18,* 61-97.

Nielsen, J., & Wohlert, M. (1991). Chromosome abnormalities found among 34,910 newborn children: Results from a 13-year incidence study in Arhus, Denmark. *Human Genetics, 87*, 81-83.

Orlebeke, J. F., Boomsma, D. I., Gooren, L. J. G., Verschoor, A. M., & van den Bree, M. J. M. (1992). Elevated sinistrality in transsexuals. *Neuropsychology, 6,* 351-355.

Overzier, C. (Ed.). (1961). *Die Intersexualität.* Stuttgart: Thieme.

Pauly, I. (1968). The current status of the change of sex operation. *Journal of Nervous and Mental Disease, 147,* 460-471.

Pauly, I. (1981). Outcome of sex reassignment surgery for transsexuals. *Australian and New Zealand Journal of Psychiatry, 15,* 45-51.

Pavlidis, K., McCauley, E., & Sybert, V. P. (1995). Psychosocial and sexual functioning in women with Turner syndrome. *Clinical Genetics, 47,* 85-89.

Pennington, B. F., Bender, B., Puck, M., Salbenblatt, J., & Robinson, A. (1982). Learning disabilities in children with sex chromosome anomalies. *Child Development, 53,* 1182-1192.

Person, E., & Ovesey, L. (1974a). The transsexual syndrome in males I: Primary transsexualism. *American Journal of Psychotherapy, 28,* 4-20.

Person, E., & Ovesey, L. (1974b). The transsexual syndrome in males II: Secondary transsexualism. *American Journal of Psychotherapy, 28,* 174-193.

Petersen, M. E., & Dickey, R. (1995). Surgical sex reassignment: A comparative study of international centers. *Archives of Sexual Behavior, 24,* 135-156.

Pfäfflin, F. (1981). Psychiatric and legal implications of the new law for transsexuals in the Federal Republic of Germany. *International Journal of Law and Psychiatry, 4*, 191-198.

Pfäfflin, F. (1992). Regrets after sex reassignment surgery. *Journal of Psychology and Human Sexuality, 5*, 69-85.

Pfäfflin, F. (1993). *Transsexualität: Beitrage zur Psychopathologie, Psychodynamik und zum Verlauf.* Stuttgart: Enke.

Pfäfflin, F. (1997). *Sex reassignment, Harry Benjamin, and some European roots* [On-line]. Available: http://www.symposion.com/ijt/ijtc0202.htm

Pfäfflin, F., & Junge, A. (1992). *Geschlechtsumwandlung: Abhandlungen zur Transsexualität.* Stuttgart: Schattauer.

Pfäfflin, F., & Junge, A. (1998). *Sex reassignment: Thirty years of international follow-up studies. A comprehensive review, 1961-1991* [On-line]. Available: http://www. symposion. com/ijt/books/index.htm

Phoenix, C. H., Goy, R. W., Gerall, A. A., & Young, W. C. (1959). Organizing action of prenatally administered testosterone propionate on the tissues mediating behavior in the female guinea pig. *Endocrinology, 65*, 369-382.

Philippopoulos, G. S. (1964). A case of transvestism in a 17-year-old girl. *Acta Psychotherapeutica, 12*, 29-37.

Phornphutkul, C., Fausto-Sterling, A., & Grupposo, P. A. (2000). Gender self-reassignment in an XY adolescent female born with ambiguous genitalia. *Pediatrics, 106,* 135-137.

Picariello, M. L., Greenberg, D. N., & Pillemer, D. (1990). Children's sex-related stereotyping of colors. *Child Development, 61*, 1453-1460.

Plante, E., Boliek, C., Binkiewicz, A., & Erly, W. K. (1996). Elevated androgen, brain development and language/learning disabilities in children with congenital adrenal hyperplasia. *Developmental Medicine and Child Neurology, 38,* 423-437.

Pleak, R. R. (1999). Ethical issues in diagnosing and treating gender-dysphoric children and adolescents. In M. Rottnek (Ed.), *Sissies and tomboys: Gender noncomformity and homosexual childhood* (pp. 34-51). New York: New York University Press.

Price, W. H., & Whatmore, P. B. (1967). Behavior disorders and pattern of crime among XYY males identified at a maximun security hospital. *British Medical Journal, 1*, 533-536.

Prieur, A. (1998). Bodily and symbolic constructions among homosexual men in Mexico. *Sexualities, 1,* 287-289.

Quattrin, T., Aronica, S., & Mazur, T. (1990). Management of male pseudohermaphroditism: A case report spanning twenty-one years. *Journal of Pediatric Psychology, 15*, 699-709.

Raboch, K., Kobilkova, J., Horejsi, J., Starka, L., & Raboch, J. (1987). Sexual development and life of women with gonadal dysgenesis. *Journal of Sex and Marital Therapy, 13,* 117-127.

Rakic, Z., Starcevic, V., Maric, J., & Kelin, K. (1996). The outcome of sex reassignment in Belgrade: 32 patients of both sexes. *Archives of Sexual Behavior, 25,* 515-525.

Randell, J. (1969). Preoperative and postoperative status of male and female transsexuals. In R. Green & J. Money (Eds.), *Transsexuals and sex reassignment* (pp. 355-381). Baltimore, MD: Johns Hopkins University Press.

Randell, J. B. (1959). Transvestism and transsexualism: A study of 50 cases. *British Medical Journal, 2,* 1448-1452.

Rangecroft, L., Brain, C, Creighton, S., Di Ceglie, D., Ogilvy-Stuart, A. Malone, P., & Turnock, R. (2001). *Statement of the British Association of Paediatric Surgeons' Working Party on the Surgical Management of Children Born with Ambiguous Genitalia* [On-line]. Available: http://www.baps.org.uk/documents/intersex%20statement.htm

Ratcliffe, S. G. (1999). Long term outcome in children of sex chromosome abnormalities. *Archives of Disease in Childhood, 80,* 192-195.

Ratcliffe, S. G., Bancroft, J., Axworthy, D., & McClaren, W. (1982). Klinefelter's syndrome in adolescence. *Archives of Diseases in Childhood, 57*, 6-12.

Ratcliffe, S. G. Butler, G. E., & Jones, M. (1990). Edinburgh study of growth and development of children with sex chromosome abnormalities. *Birth Defects: Original Article Series, 26,* 1-44.

Ratcliffe, S. G., Masera, N., Pan, H., & McKie, M. (1994). Head circumference and IQ of children with sex chromosome abnormalities. *Developmental Medicine and Child Neurology, 36,* 533-544.

Ratcliffe, S. G., Murray, L., & Teaque, P. (1986). Edinburgh study of growth and development of children with sex chromosome abnormalities. *Birth Defects: Original Article Series, 22,* 73-118.

Reiner, W. G. (1997). To be male or female—That is the question [Editorial]. *Archives of Pediatrics and Adolescent Medicine, 151,* 224-225.

Reiner, W. G. (2000). Developmental ramifications of aphallia: The life story perspective. *Dialogues in Pediatric Urology, 23*, 2-3.

Reinisch, J. M., Ziemba-Davis, M., & Sanders, S. A. (1992). Hormonal contributions to sexually dimorphic behavioral development in humans. *Psychoneuroendocrinology, 16*, 213-278.

Rekers, G. A. (1982). *Growing up straight: What every family should know about homosexuality.* Grand Rapids, MI: Baker Book House.

Rekers, G. A. (1995). Assessment and treatment methods for gender identity disorders and transvestism. In G. A. Rekers (Ed.), *Handbook of child and adolescent sexual problems* (pp. 272-289). New York: Lexington Books.

Rekers, G. A., & Kilgus, M. D. (1995). Differential diagnosis and rationale for treatment of gender identity disorders and transvestism. In G. A. Rekers (Ed.), *Handbook of child and adolescent sexual problems* (pp. 255-271). New York: Lexington Books.

Rekers, G. A., Kilgus, M. D., & Rosen, A. C. (1990). Long-term effects of the treatment for gender identity disorder of childhood. *Journal of Psychology and Human Sexuality, 3*, 121-153.

Rekers, G. A., Mead, S. L., Rosen, A. C., & Brigham, S. L. (1983). Family correlates of male childhood gender disturbance. *Journal of Genetic Psychology, 142*, 31-42.

Rekers, G. A., & Morey, S. M. (1989). Sex typed body movements as a function of severity on degree of gender disturbance in boys. *Journal of Psychology and Human Sexuality, 2,* 183-196.

Rekers, G. A., Rosen, A. C., & Morey, S. M. (1990). Projective test findings for boys with gender disturbance: Draw-a-Person test, IT scale, and Make-a-Picture-Story test. *Perceptual and Motor Skills, 71*, 771-779.

Rekers, G. A., & Yates, C. E. (1976). Sex-typed play in feminoid boys versus normal boys and girls. *Journal of Abnormal Child Psychology, 4*, 1-8.

Resnick, S. M., Berenbaum, S. A., Gottesman, I. I., & Bouchard, T. J. (1986). Early hormonal influences on cognitive functioning in congenital adrenal hyperplasia. *Developmental Psychology, 22,* 191-198.

Resnick, S. M., Gottesman, I. I., & McGue, M. (1993). Sensation seeking in opposite-sex twins: An effect of prenatal hormones? *Behavior Genetics, 23*, 323-329.

Richardson, J. (1999). Response: Finding the disorder in gender identity disorder. *Harvard Review of Psychiatry, 7,* 43-50.

Ringrose, K. M. (1994). Living in the shadows: Eunuchs and gender in Byzantium. In G. Herdt (Ed.), *Third sex, third gender: Beyond the dimorphism in culture and history* (pp. 85-109). New York: Zone Books.

Roback, H., McKee, E., Webb, W., Abramowitz, C. V., & Abramowitz, S. I. (1976). Psychopathology in female sex change applicants and two help-seeking controls. *Journal of Abnormal Psychology, 85,* 430-432.

Roberts, C. W., Green, R., Williams, K., & Goodman, M. (1987). Boyhood gender identity development: A statistical contrast between two family groups. *Developmental Psychology, 23,* 544-557.

Robinson, A., Bender, B., & Linden, M. (1991). Summary of clinical findings in children and young adults with sex chromosome abnormalities. *Birth Defects: Original Article Series, 26,* 225-228.

Rösing, I. (1999). *Geschlechtliche Zeit: Vol. 17. Geschlechtlicher Raum. Schriften der Philosophisch-historischen Klasse der Heidelberger Akademie der Wissenschaften.* Heidelberg: Universitätsverlag C. Winter.

Rösing, I. (2001). *Religion, Ritual und Alltag in den Anden: Die zehn Geschlechter von Amarete, Bolivien.* Berlin: Dietrich Reimer.

Rösler, A. (1992). Steroid 17ß-hydroxysteroid dehydrogenase deficiency in man: An inherited form of male pseudohermaphroditism. *Journal of Steroid Biochemistry and Molecular Biology, 43,* 989-1002.

Rösler, A., & Kohn, G. (1983). Male pseudohermaphroditism due to 17ß-hydroxysteroid dehydrogenase deficiency: Studies on the natural history of the defect and effect of androgens on gender role. *Journal of Steroid Biochemistry, 19,* 663-674.

Ross, M. W., & Need, J. A. (1989). Effects of adequacy of gender reassignment surgery on psychological adjustment: A follow-up of fourteen male-to-female patients. *Archives of Sexual Behavior, 18,* 145-153.

Ross, J., Zinn, A., & McCauley, E. (2000). Neurodevelopmental and psychosocial aspects of Turner syndrome. *Mental Retardation and Developmental Disabilities Research Reviews, 6,* 135-141.

Rovet, J. F. (1993). The psychoeducational characteristics of children with Turner syndrome. *Journal of Learning Disabilities, 26,* 333-341.

Rovet, J. F. (1995). Turner syndrome. In B. P. Rourke (Ed.), *Syndrome of nonverbal learning disabilities: Neurodevelopmental manifestations* (pp. 351-371). New York: Guilford.

Rovet, J. F., Netley, C., Keenan, M., Bailey, J., & Stewart, D. (1996). The psychoeducational profile of boys with Klinefelter Syndrome. *Journal of Learning Disabilities, 29,* 180-196.

Ruble, D. N., & Martin, C.L. (1998). Gender development. In W. Damon (Editor-in-Chief) & N. Eisenberg (Vol. Ed.), *Handbook of child psychology: Social, emotional, and personality development* (5th ed., pp. 993-1016). New York: Wiley.

Saenger, P. (1996). Turner's syndrome. *New England Journal of Medicine, 335,* 1749-1754.

Salbenblatt, J. A., Meyers, D. C., Bender, B. G., Linden, M. G., & Robinson, A. (1987). Gross and fine motor development, in 47, XXY and 47, XYY males. *Pediatrics, 80,* 240-244.

Sandfort, T. G. M. (1998). Homosexual and bisexual behaviour in European countries. In M. C. Hubert, N. Bajos, & T. G. M. Sandfort (Eds.), *Sexual behaviour and HIV/AIDS in Europe* (pp. 68-105). London: UCL Press.

Schiavi, R. C., Theilgaard, A., Owen, D., & White, D. (1984). Sex chromosome anomalies, hormones, and aggressivity. *Archives of General Psychiatry, 41,* 93-99.

Schiavi, R. C., Theilgaard, A., Owen, D., & White, D. (1988). Sex chromosome anomalies, hormones, and sexuality. *Archives of General Psychiatry, 45,* 19-24.

Schober, J. M. (1998). A surgeon's response to the intersex controversy. *Journal of Clinical Ethics, 9,* 393 –397.

Schober, J. M. (1999). Quality-of-life studies in patients with ambiguous genitalia. *World Journal of Urology, 17,* 249-252.

Seifert, D., & Windgassen, K. (1995). Transsexual development of a patient with Klinefelter's Syndrome. *Psychopathology, 28*, 312-316.

Serbin, L. A., Powlishta, K. K., & Gulko, J. (1993). The development of sex-typing in middle childhood. *Monographs of the Society for Research in Child Development, 58* (Serial No. 232).

Serbin, L. A., Tonick, I. J., & Sternglanz, S. H. (1977). Shaping cooperative cross-sex play. *Child Development, 48*, 924-929.

Seyler, L. E., Jr., Canalis, E., Spare, S., & Reichlin, S. (1978). Abnormal gonadotropin secretory responses to LRH in transsexual women after diethylstilbestrol priming. *Journal of Clinical Endocrinology and Metabolism, 47,* 176-183.

Shane, M., & Shane, E. (1995). Clinical perspectives on gender role/identity disorder. *Psychoanalytic Inquiry, 15*, 39-59.

Shell, R., & Eisenberg, N. (1990). The role of peers' gender in children's naturally occurring interest in toys. *International Journal of Behavioral Development, 13*, 373-388.

Shields, S. A. (1995). The role of emotion beliefs and values in gender development. In N. Eisenberg (Ed.), *Social development: Review of personality and social psychology* (Vol. 15, pp. 212-232). London: Sage.

Siegal, M. (1987). Are sons and daughters treated more differently by fathers than by mothers? *Developmental Review*, 7, 183-209.

Siegel, P. T., Clopper, R., & Stabler, B. (1998). The psychological consequences of Turner syndrome and review of the National Cooperative Growth Study psychological substudy. *Pediatrics, 102,* 488-491.

Signorella, M. L., Bigler, R. S., & Liben, L. S. (1993). Developmental differences in children's gender schemata about others: A meta-analytic review. *Developmental Review, 13,* 147-183.

Signorella, M. L., & Liben, L. S. (1984). Recall and reconstruction of gender-related pictures: Effects of attitude, task difficulty and age. *Child Development, 55,* 393-405.

Silverman, M. A. (1990). The prehomosexual boy in treatment. In C. W. Socarides & V. D. Volkan (Eds.), *The homosexualities: Reality fantasy and the arts* (pp. 177-197). Madison, CT: International Universities Press.

Simpson, A. W., & Erikson, M. T. (1983). Teachers' verbal and non-verbal communication patterns as a function of teachers race, student gender, and student race. *American Educational Research Journal, 20*, 183-198.

Siomopoulos, V. (1974). Transsexualism: Disorder of gender identity, thought disorder, or both? *Journal of the American Academy of Psychoanalysis, 2*, 201-213.

Skuse, D., Elgar, K., & Morris, E. (1999). Quality of life in Turner syndrome is related to chromosomal constitution: Implications for genetic counselling and management. *Acta Paediatrica, 88*(Suppl), 110-113.

Skuse, D., Percy, E. L., & Stevenson, J. (1994). Psychosocial functioning in the Turner syndrome. In B. Stabler & L. E. Underwood (Eds.), *Growth, stature, and adaptation: Behavioral, social, and cognitive aspects of growth delay* (pp. 151-164). Chapel Hill: North Carolina Press.

Slabbekoorn, D., van Goozen, S. H. M., Sanders, G., Gooren, L. J. G., & Cohen-Kettenis, P. T. (2000). The dermatoglyphic characteristics of transsexuals: Is there evidence for an organizing effect of sex hormones. *Psychoneuroendocrinology, 25*, 365-375.

Slabbekoorn, D., van Goozen, S. H. M., Gooren, L. J. G., & Cohen-Kettenis, P. T. (2001). *Effects of cross-sex hormone treatment on emotionality in transsexuals* [On-line]. Available: http://www.symposion.com/ijt/ijtvo05no03_02.htm

Slaby, R. G., & Frey, K. S. (1975). Development of gender constancy and selective attention to same-sex models. *Child Development, 52*, 849-856.

Slijper, F. M.E. (1984). Androgens and gender role behavior in girls with congenital adrenal hyperplasia (CAH). *Progress in Brain Research, 61,* 417-422.

Slijper, F. M. E., Drop, S. L. S., Molenaar, J. C., & de Muinck Keizer Schrama, S. M. P. F. (1998). Long-term psychological evaluation of intersex children. *Archives of Sexual Behavior, 27*, 125-144.

Slijper, F. M. E., Drop, S. L. S., Molenaar, J. C., & Scholtmeijer, R. J. (1994). Neonates with abnormal genital development assigned the female sex: Parent counseling. *Journal of Sex Education and Therapy, 20*, 9-17.

Slijper, F. M. E., Frets, P. G., Boehmer, A. L. M., & Drop, S. L. S. (2000). Androgen insensitivity syndrome (AIS): Emotional reactions of parents and adult patients to the clinical diagnosis of AIS and its confirmation by androgen receptor gene mutation analysis. *Hormone Research, 53*, 9-15.

Slijper, F. M. E., van der Kamp, H. J., Brandenbrug, H., de Muinck Keizer-Schrama, S. M. P. F., Drop, S. L. S., & Molenaar, J. C. (1992). Evaluation of psychosexual development of young women with congenital adrenal hyperplasia: A pilot study. *Journal of Sex Education and Therapy, 18*, 200-207.

Smith, Y. L. S. (2002). *Sex reassignment: Predictors and outcomes of treatment for transsexuals*. Doctoral thesis, University of Utrecht.

Smith, Y. L. S., Cohen, L., & Cohen-Kettenis, P. T. (2002). Postoperative psychological functioning of adolescent transsexuals: A Rorschach study. *Archives of Sexual Behavior, 31*, 255-261.

Smith, Y. L. S., van Goozen, S. H. M., & Cohen-Kettenis, P. T. (2001). Adolescents with gender identity disorder who were accepted or rejected for sex reassignment surgery: A prospective follow-up study. *Journal of the American Academy of Child and Adolescent Psychiatry, 40*, 472-481.

Snaith, R. P., Penhale, S., & Horsfield, P. (1991). Male-to-female transsexual with XYY karyotype. *Lancet, 337*, 557-558.

Socarides, C. W. (1970). A psychoanalytic study of the desire for sexual transformation ("transsexualism"): The plaster-of-Paris man. *International Journal of Psychoanalysis, 51*, 341-349.

Sørensen, K. (1992). Physical and mental development of adolescent males with Klinefelter syndrome. *Hormone Research, 37*, 55-61.

Sotiropoulos, A., Morishima, A., Homsy, Y., & Lattimer, J. K. (1976). Long-term assessment of genital reconstruction in female pseudohermaphrodites. *Journal of Urology, 115*, 599-601.

Spijkstra, J. J., Spinder, T., & Gooren, L. J. G. (1988). Short-term patterns of pulsatile luteinizing hormone secretion do not differ between male-to-female transsexuals and heterosexual men. *Psychoneuroendocrinology, 13,* 279-283.

Spinder, T., Spijkstra, J. J., Gooren, L. J. G., & Burger, C. W. (1989). Pulsatile luteinizing hormone release and ovarian steroid levels in female-to-male transsexuals compared to heterosexual women. *Psychoneuroendocrinology, 14,* 97-102.

Stein, R., Stockle, M., Fisch, M., Nakai, H., Muller, S. C., & Hohenfellner, R. (1994). The fate of the adult exstrophy patient. *Journal of Urology, 152*, 1413-1416.

Steiner, B. W., & Bernstein, S. M. (1981). Female-to-male transsexuals and their partners. *Canadian Journal of Psychiatry, 26,* 178-182.

Steinkühler, M. (1992). Geschlechtswechsel in nichtklinischer Zeit: Der Chevalier d'Eon. In F. Pfäfflin & A. Junge (Eds.), *Geschlechtsumwandlung: Abhandlungen zur Transsexualität* (pp. 45-54). Stuttgart/New York: Schattauer.

Stermac, L. (1990). Clinical management of nontranssexual patients. In R. Blanchard & B. W. Steiner (Eds.), *Clinical management of gender identity disorders in children and adults* (pp. 107-117). Washington, DC: American Psychological Association Press.

Stern, M., & Karraker, K. H. (1989). Sex stereotyping of infants: A review of gender labeling studies. *Sex Roles, 20,* 501-522.

Stewart, D. A., Bailey, J. D., Netley, C. T., & Park, E. (1990). Growth, development, and behavioral outcome from mid-adolescence to adulthood in subjects with chromosome aneuploidy: The Toronto Study. *Birth Defects: Original Articles Series, 26,* 131-188.

Stewart, D. A., Bailey, J. D., Netley, C. T., Rovet, J., Park, E., Cripps, M., & Curtis, J. A. (1982). Growth and development of children with X and Y chromosome aneuploidy from infancy to pubertal age: The Toronto study. *Birth Defecs: Original Article Series, 18,* 99-154.

Stockard, J. (1980). Sex inequities in the experience of students. In J. Stockard, P. A Schmuck, K. Kempner, P. Williams, S. K. Edson, & M. A. Smith (Eds.), *Sex inequities in education* (pp. 49-77). New York: Academic Press.

Stoller, R. J. (1968). *Sex and gender: On the development of masculinity and femininity.* New York: Science House.

Stoller, R. J. (1970). Psychotherapy of extremely feminine boys. *International Journal of Psychiatry, 9,* 278-281.

Stoller, R. J. (1975). *Sex and gender: Vol. 2. The transsexual experiment.* London: Hogarth Press.

Stoller, R. J. (1985). *Presentations of gender.* New Haven, CT: Yale University Press.

Strassberg, D., Roback, H., Cunningham, J., McKee, E., & Larson, P. (1979). Psychopathology in self-identified female-to-male transsexuals, homosexuals, and heterosexuals. *Archives of Sexual Behavior, 8,* 491-496.

Sundblom, E., Bodlund, O., & Höjerback, T. (1995). Object relations and defense operations in transsexuals and borderline patients as measured by the Defense Mechanism Test. *Nordic Journal of Psychiatry, 49,* 379-388.

Taneja, N., Ammini, A. C., Mohapatra, I., Saxena, S., & Kucheria, K. (1992). A transsexual male with 47, XYY karyotype. *British Journal of Psychiatry, 161,* 698-699.

Teh, Y. K. (2001). *Mak nyahs (male transsexuals) in Malaysia: The influence of culture and religion on their identity* [On-line]. Available: http://www.symposion.com/ijt/ijtvo05no03_04.htm

Theilgaard, A. (1983). Aggression and the XYY personality. *International Journal of Law and Psychiatry, 6,* 413-421.

Theilgaard, A. (1984). A psychological study of the personalities of XYY and XXY men. *Acta Psychiatrica Scandinavica, 315,* 1-33.

Trumbach, R. (1994). London's Sapphists: From three sexes to four genders in the making of modern culture. In G. Herdt (Ed.), *Third sex, third gender: Beyond the dimorphism in culture and history* (pp. 111-136). New York: Zone Books.

Tsoi, W. F. (1988). The prevalence of transsexualism in Singapore. *Acta Psychiatrica Scandinavica, 78,* 501-504.

Tsoi, W. F., Kok, L. P., & Long, F. Y. (1977). Male transsexualism in Singapore: A description of 56 cases. *British Journal of Psychiatry, 131,* 405-409.

Turner, P. J., & Gervai, J. (1995). A multidimensional study of gender typing in preschool children and their parents: Personality, attitudes, preferences, behavior, and cultural differences. *Developmental Psychology, 31*, 759-772.

Udry, J. R. (1994). The nature of gender. *Demography 31*, 561-573.

van der Meer, T. (1994). Sodomy and the pursuit of a third sex in the early modern period. In G. Herdt (Ed.), *Third sex, third gender: Beyond the dimorphism in culture and history* (pp. 137-212). New York: Zone Books.

van Goozen, S. H. M., Cohen-Kettenis, P. T., Gooren, L. J. G., Frijda, N. H., & van de Poll, N. E. (1995). Gender differences in behavior: Activating effects of cross-gender hormones. *Psychoneuroendocrinology, 20*, 343-363.

Verhulst, F. C., Van der Ende, J., & Koot, H. (1996). *Handleiding voor de CBCL/4-18.* Rotterdam: Afdeling Kinder- en Jeugdpsychiatrie, AZ/Erasmus Universiteit.

Verhulst, F. C., Van der Ende, J., & Koot, H. (1997). *Handleiding voor de Teacher Report Form (TRF).* Rotterdam: Afdeling Kinder- en Jeugdpsychiatrie, AZ/Erasmus Universiteit.

Veerman, J. W., Straathof, M. A. E., Treffers, P. D. A., Van den Bergh, B. R. H., & ten Brink, L. T. (1997). *De Competentiebelevingsschaal voor kinderen, CBSK: Handleiding.* Lisse: Swetz & Zeitlinger.

Vockrodt, L., & Williams, J. K. (1994). A reproductive option for women with Turner's syndrome. *Journal of Pediatric Nursing, 9,* 321-325.

Volkan, V. D., & Berent, S. (1976). Psychiatric aspects of surgical treatment for problems of sexual identification (transsexualism). In J.G. Howells (Ed.), *Modern perspectives in the psychiatric aspects of surgery* (pp. 447-467). New York: Bruner/Mazel.

Wacke, A. (1989). Vom Hermaphroditismus zum Transsexuellen – Zur Stellung von Zwittern in der Rechtsgeschichte. In H. Eyrich, W. Odersky, & F. Säcker (Eds.), *Festschrift für Kurt Rebmann zum 65 Geburtstag* (pp. 861-903). München: Beck.

Wagner, B. (1974). Ein Transsexueler mit XYY Syndrom. *Nervenarzt, 45*, 548-551.

Wålinder, J. (1967). *Transsexualism: A study of forty-three cases.* Göteborg, Sweden: Scandinavian University Books.

Wålinder, J. (1968). Transsexualism: Definition, prevalence and sex distribution. *Acta Psychiatrica Scandinavica, 44*(Suppl. 203), 255-258.

Wålinder, J., Lundström, B., & Thuwe, I. (1978). Prognostic factors in the assessment of male transsexuals for sex reassignment. *British Journal of Psychiatry, 132,* 16-20.

Walzer, S., Bashir, A. S., & Silbert, A. R. (1991). Cognitive and behavioral factors in the learning disabilities of 47XXY and 47 XYY boys. *Birth Defects: Original Article Series, 26,* 45-58.

Watson, D. B., & Coren, S. (1992). Left-handedness in male-to-female transsexualism [Letter to the editor]. *Journal of the American Medical Association, 267*, 1342.

Weitze, C., & Osburg, S. (1998). *Empirical data on epidemiology and application of the German transsexuals' act during its first ten years* [On-line]. Available: http://www.symposion.com/ijt/ijtc0303.htm

Wiesen, M., & Futterweit, W. (1983). Normal plasma gonadotropin response to gonadotropin-releasing hormone after diethylstilbestrol priming in transsexual women. *Journal of Clinical Endocrinology and Metabolism, 57,* 197-199.

Will, M. R. (1992). . . .ein Leiden mit dem Recht. Zur Namens- und Geschlechtsänderung bei transsexuellen Menschen in Europa. In F. Pfäfflin & A. Junge (Eds.), *Geschlechtsumwandlung: Abhandlungen zur Transsexualität* (pp. 113-147). Stuttgart/New York: Schattauer.

Will, M. R. (1995). Legal conditions of sex reassignment by medical intervention – situation in comparative law. In Council of Europe (Ed.), *Transsexualism, medicine and law* (pp.75-101). Strasbourg: Council of Europe.

Williams, W. L. (1986). *The spirit and the flesh: Sexual diversity in American Indian culture.* Boston: Beacon Press.

Wilson, J. D., Griffin, J. E., & Russell, D. W. (1993). Steroid 5 alpha-reductase 2 deficiency. *Endocrine Reviews, 14*, 577-593.

Wilson, B. E., & Reiner, W. G. (1999). Management of intersex: A shifting paradigm. In A. D. Dreger (Ed.), *Intersex in the age of ethics* (pp.119-135). Hagerstown, MD: University Publishing Group.

Wilson, P., Sharp, C., & Carr, S. (1999). The prevalence of gender dysphoria in Scotland: A primary care study. *British Journal of General Practice, 49*, 991-992.

Wolfe, S. M. (1990). *Psychopathology and psychodynamics of parents of boys with a gender identity disorder.* Unpublished doctoral dissertation, City University of New York, New York.

World Health Organization. (1992). *Multi axial version of ICD 10: Clinical descriptions and diagnostic guidelines*. Geneva: World Health Organization.

Wren, B. (2000). Early physical intervention for young people with atypical gender identity development. *Clinical Child Psychology and Psychiatry, 5,* 220-231.

Yee, M., & Brown, R. (1994). The development of gender differentiation in young children. *British Journal of Social Psychology, 33,* 183-196.

Yüksel, S., Kulaksizoglu, I. B., Türksoy, N., & Sahin, D. (2000). Group psychotherapy with female-to-male transsexuals in Turkey. *Archives of Sexual Behavior, 29*, 279-290.

Zeuthen, E., Hansen, M., Christensen, A. L., & Nielsen, J. (1975). A psychiatric-psychological study of XYY males found in the general male population. *Acta Psychiatrica Scandinavica, 51*, 3-18.

Zhou, J., Hofman, M. A., Gooren, L. J. G., & Swaab, D. F. (1995). A sex difference in the human brain and its relation to transsexuality. *Nature, 378,* 68-70.

Zucker, K. J. (1999). Intersexuality and gender identity differentiation. *Annual Review of Sex Research, 10,* 1-69.

Zucker, K. J., Beaulieu, N., Bradley, S. J. Grimshaw, G. M., & Wilcox, A. (2001). Handedness in boys with gender identity disorder. *Journal of Clinical Child Psychology and Psychiatry, 42,* 767-776.

Zucker, K. J., & Bradley, S. J. (1995). *Gender identity disorder and psychosexual problems in children and adolescents.* New York/London: Guilford Press.

Zucker, K. J., Bradley, S. J., & Lowry Sullivan, C. B. (1992). Gender identity disorder in children. *Annual Review of Sex Research, 3,* 73-120.

Zucker, K. J., Bradley, S. J., Doering, R. W., & Lozinsky, J. A. (1985). Sex-typed behavior in cross-gender identified children: Stability and change at a one-year follow-up. *Journal of the American Academy of Child Psychiatry, 24*, 710-719.

Zucker, K. J., Bradley, S. J., Kuksis, M., Pecore, K., Birkenfeld-Adams, A., Doering, R. W., Mitchell, J. N., & Wild, J. (1999). Gender constancy judgments in children with gender identity disorder: Evidence for a developmental lag. *Archives of Sexual Behavior, 28,* 475-502.

Zucker, K. J., Bradley, S. J., Lowry Sullivan, C. B., Kuksis, M., Birkenfeld-Adams, A., & Mitchell, J. N. (1993). A gender identity interview for children. *Journal of Personality Assessment, 61,* 443-456.

Zucker, K. J., Bradley, S. J., Oliver, G., Blake, J., Fleming, S., & Hood, J. (1996). Psychosexual development of woman with congenital adrenal hyperplasia. *Hormones and Behavior, 30*, 300-318.

Zucker, K. J., Finegan, J. K., Doering, R. W., & Bradley, S. J. (1984). Two subgroups of gender problem children. *Archives of Sexual Behavior, 13*, 27-39.

Zucker, K. J., & Green, R.(1992). Psychosexual disorders in children and adolescents. *Journal of Child Psychology and Psychiatry, 33*, 107-151.

Zucker, K. J., Green, R., Garofano, C., Bradley, S. J., Williams, K., Rebach, H. M., & Lowry Sullivan, C. B. (1994). Prenatal gender preference of mothers of feminine and masculine boys: Relation to sibling sex composition and birth order. *Journal of Abnormal Child Psychology, 22,* 1-13.

Zucker, K. J., Lightbody, S., Pecore, K., Bradley, S. J., & Blanchard, R. (1998). Birth order in girls with gender identity disorder. *European Child and Adolescent Psychiatry, 7*, 30-35.

Zucker, K. J., Wild, J., Bradley, S. J., & Lowry, C. B. (1993). Physical attractiveness of boys with gender identity disorder. *Archives of Sexual Behavior, 22,* 23-36.

Zuger, B. (1984). Early effeminate behavior in boys: Outcome and significance for homosexuality. *Journal of Nervous and Mental Disease, 172,* 90-97.

NAME INDEX

Abel, G., 138
Abraham, F., 158
Abramovitch, R., 82
Abramowitz, C. V., 139
Abramowitz, S. I., 139, 160
Achenbach, T. M., 56, 65, 76, 113 (tab), 115, 133 (tab)
Achté, K., 162
Adams, R., 139
Ageton, S. S., 8
Agras, W. S., 171
Ahmed, S. F., 45
Ako, T., 20
Al-Attia, H. M., 47
Alanko, A., 162
Alizai, N. K., 100
Althof, S., 141
American Psychiatric Association, ix, 52, 53 (tab), 168
Ammini, A. C., 33
Anderson, D. C., 78
Anderson, K. J., 10, 11
Annett, M., 81
Armelius, K., 139
Arnhold, I. J., 47
Arnold, A. P., 12
Aronica, S., 44
Axworthy, D., 29, 30

Bailey, J., 26
Bailey, J. D., 26, 28
Bailey, J. M., 63, 64, 68
Baker, F., 33
Baker, S. W., 12, 41, 77, 96
Bakker, A., 65
Bally, G., 160
Bamrah, J. S., 38
Bancroft, J., 29, 30
Bandura, A., 7, 9, 11
Bangsboll, S., 44
Barlow, D. H., 138, 171
Barr, R., 33
Bartfai, A., 41
Bartlett, N. H., 105, 106, 120
Bashir, A. S., 26, 28, 32
Batchelor, G. G., 100
Bates, J. E., 75, 113 (tab), 114, 115
Beaulieu, N., 81
Bell, A. P., 63, 64
Bell, J. J., 12, 38, 41, 77, 96
Bem, S. L., 7, 8
Bender, B., 26, 28, 32
Bender, B. G., 26, 28, 29, 32, 38
Benderly, A., 41
Benjamin, H., 18, 19, 158, 159, 162, 163
Bentler, P. M., 67, 75, 113 (tab), 114, 115
Berah, E. F., 139, 140
Berenbaum, S. A., 12, 41
Berent, S., 70
Berg, A., 151
Berger, J. C., 67, 68, 139
Bernstein, S. M., 69

Besnier, N., 20
Bezemer, P. D., 65, 66
Bigler, R. S., 8
Binder, H., 160
Binkiewtcz, A., 41
Binswanger, L., 160
Birkenfeld-Adams, A., 2, 114
Birmbacher, R., 96
Blackless, M., 24
Blair, S. L., 11
Blake, J., 42
Blanchard, G., 138
Blanchard, R., 52, 67, 68, 81, 82, 150, 168
Bleuler, M., 160
Bloise, W., 47
Bocknek, G., 160
Bockting, W. O., 18, 69, 132, 143, 144, 145, 146, 151, 163, 170, 172
Bodlund, O., 69, 139, 148
Boehmer, A. L. M, 85, 90
Boemers, T. M., 100
Boer, K., 77
Boland, P., 139
Boliek, C., 41
Bolin, A., 19
Boomsma, D. I., 81
Börger, D., 41
Borker, R. A., 10
Boss, M., 160
Bottomley, V., 122–123
Bouchard, T. J., 41
Bower, H., 145
Bradley, S. J., 2, 14, 42, 52, 62, 63, 66, 71, 72, 73, 74, 75, 77, 80, 81, 82, 105, 109, 112, 113 (tab), 114, 115, 120, 127, 168, 171
Brain, C., 100
Braiterman, J., 20
Brandenbrug, H., 41, 42
Breedlove, S. M., 11, 12, 78
Brems, C., 139
Brenner, P. F., 44
Breslin, M., 29
Brigham, S. L., 74
Brown, G. M., 38
Brown, R., 9
Brucken, L., 8
Brugmann, A., 47
Brun, R., 160
Bryden, M. P., 14, 79
Bryk, K., 41
Brzek, A., 66
Bubrich, N., 67
Bueno, Y., 12, 41, 77, 96
Buhrich, N., 33
Buitelaar, J. K., 14
Bukowski, W. M., 105, 106, 120
Bullinger, M., 42
Bullough, B., 19, 20
Bullough, V. L., 19, 20
Bulock, D. E., 78
Burger, C. W., 78
Bürger-Prinz, H., 160
Burns, R. C., 113 (tab)
Bussey, K., 7, 9, 11
Butcher, J. N., 139, 140
Butler, G. E., 32
Butler, J., 20
Butt, W. R., 78

Callender, C., 20
Canalis, E., 78
Canter, R. J., 8
Capitanio, G. L., 33
Caplan J., 29
Carr, J. E., 80
Carr, S., 66
Carter, D. B., 8, 11
Cauldwell, D. C., 51, 158
Cesnik, J. A., 137, 142
Chan, S., 67
Chan-Cua, S., 41
Chanseau, B., 167
Charatan, F. B., 70
Charuvastra, A., 24

Chase, C., 95, 100
Chavez, B., 47
Chernick, A. B., 14
Cherry, L., 11
Chiland, C., 70, 138
Chipperfleld, J. G., 82
Chivers, M. L., 68
Christensen, A. L., 33
Christensen, K. R., 28
Clark, G. R., 33
Clarke, M., 29
Clemmensen, L. H., 68, 150
Clopper, R., 35
Coates, S., 52, 72, 73, 75, 120, 127, 171
Cohen, C. C. C., 14
Cohen, H., 80
Cohen, L., 68, 139, 149
Cohen-Kettenis, P. T., 14, 18, 44, 63, 65, 68, 76, 77, 80–81, 96, 132, 133 (tab), 139, 143, 144, 145, 146, 147, 148, 149, 150 (tab), 151, 163, 168, 170, 171, 172
Cole, C. M., 139
Cole-Harding, S., 14
Cole-Wilson, Y. I., 167
Coleman, E., 18, 20, 69, 132, 137, 142, 143, 144, 145, 146, 151, 163, 170, 172
Colgan, P., 20
Collaer, M. L., 11, 12, 40, 77, 80
Committee on Genetics/American Academy of Pediatrics, 38
Conte, F., 25
Cordua, G. D., 8
Coren, S., 81
Corter, C., 82
Costa, E. M., 47
Costos, D., 69
Council of Europe, 167
Cowan, G., 8
Creighton, S., 100
Creighton, S. M., 100
Cripps, M., 28
Cryan, E. M. J., 29
Cunningham, J., 139
Curtis, J. A., 28
Cutler, G., 35

Daaboul, J., 101
Dahl, A. A., 139
Dahl-Iversen, E., 159
Daléry, J., 41
Daly, R. F., 33
Darby, P. L., 38
Davenport, C. W., 171
Davidson J., 13
Davidson, P. W., 29
De Cuypere, G., 148
De Jong, T. P., 100
de Mumck Keizer-Schrama, S. M. P. F., 41, 42, 44, 87, 96
de Ruiter, C., 139
de Vries, J. D., 96
Deaux, K., 1
Dekker, R. M., 19
Delemarre-de Waal, H., 147
Delfin, M., 47
Denenberg, V. H., 4, 11
Derogatis, L. R., 139
Derryck, A., 24
Descamps, M. A., 167
Dessens, A. B., 77
Devor, H., 18, 132, 143, 144, 145, 146, 151, 163, 170, 172
Di Ceglie, D., 18, 66, 100, 122, 123, 132, 142, 143, 144, 145, 146, 151, 163, 168, 170, 172
Diamond, M., 13, 96, 97
Dickerman, Z., 30
Dickey, R., 68, 133, 150
Dittmann, R. W., 41, 42, 96
Doering, C. H., 14
Doering, R. W., 105, 113 (tab), 114
Dolezal, C. L., 113 (tab), 115
Doorn C., 80–81

Dörner, G., 78
Downey, J., 38
Downs, C., 175
Drabman, R. S., 8
Dreger, A. D., 95, 98, 101
Drop, S. L. S., 41, 42, 44, 85, 87, 88, 90, 96
Duck, S. C., 41
Dührssen, A., 160
Dulko, S., 81

Eaton, W. O., 82
Ebertz, L., 77
Edelbrock, C. S., 56, 65, 76, 113 (tab), 115, 133 (tab)
Egan, S. K., 2
Ehrhardt, A. A., 17, 38, 41, 42, 45, 100, 115, 139, 149
Eicher, W., 171
Eisenberg, N., 11
Ekins, R., 19, 20
Eklund, P. L. E., 66
El Abd, S., 38
El-Shawwa, R., 96
Elbe, L., 158
Eldh, J., 151
Elgar, K., 35
Elias, J., 19, 20
Elisabeth, P. H., 113 (tab)
Elliot, C., 98, 101
Ellis, L., 77
Elrayyes, E., 96
Emmerich, W., 8
Emory, L. E., 139
Epstein, R., 80
Erikson, M. T., 11
Erly, W. K., 41
Etzrodt, H., 38
European Court of Human Rights, 167
Evers, D. K., 41, 42

Fagot, B. I., 2, 7, 9, 64, 113 (tab), 114
Fahrner, E. M., 69
Falek, A., 33
Fausto-Sterling, A., 13, 24, 96
Feder, E. K., 120
Feitz, W. F., 96
Feuillan, P., 35
Finegan, J., 14
Finegan, J. K., 14, 105
Fisch, M., 96
Fishbain, D. A., 38
Fitch, R. H., 4, 11
Fivush, R., 2
Fleming, D., 149
Fleming, M., 69, 139
Fleming, S., 42
Forget, H., 80
Forsman, M., 41
Frader, J., 101
Freedman, D., 66, 142, 168
Freidenberg, G., 41
Frets, P. G., 85, 90
Freund, K., 67, 160
Frey, K. S., 8, 113 (tab), 114
Fridell, S. R., 71
Friedman, R., 73, 171
Friedman, R. C., 110
Friedrich, U., 28
Frijda, N. H., 147, 148
Frisch, H., 96
Froeling, F. M., 96
Fryns, J. P., 31
Futterweit, W., 78

Galatzer, A., 30
Galef, H., 70
Garber, M., 20
Gardos, M., 41
Garfinkel, P. E., 38
Garofano, C., 71
Gaskin, R., 33, 67
Gauthier, R., 9
Gautier, T., 13, 46, 96
Gay American Indians, 20
Georgi, F., 160

Geraedts, J. P., 33
Gerall, A. A., 96
Gervai, J., 11
Glassberg, K. I., 97
Godlewski, G., 66
Goldman, K. S., 8
Gollner, W. E., 160
Golombok, S., 2, 113 (tab), 115
Goodman, M., 71
Goodman, R. E., 78
Goodwin, W. E., 46, 47
Gooren, L., 69
Gooren, L. J., 78
Gooren, L. J. G., 18, 20, 44, 65, 66, 77, 78, 80–81, 96, 132, 143, 144, 145, 146, 147, 148, 151, 163, 170, 172
Göppert, H., 160
Gorski, R. A., 4, 78, 79 (tab)
Gossmann, I., 80
Gottesman, I. I., 14, 41
Gotz, M. J., 32
Goy, R. W., 96
Grabowska, A., 81
Graham, J. M., 28
Green, R., 18, 19, 52, 62, 71, 81, 113 (tab), 122, 138, 139, 149, 167, 171
Green, R. S., 12, 41, 77, 96
Greenberg, D. N., 8
Greenberg, N., 38
Greenberg, R. P., 139
Greens, B., 19
Griffin, J. E., 96
Grimshaw, G. M., 14, 81
Gromb, S., 167
Groveman, S. A., 93, 99
Grémaux, R., 19
Gruen, R., 38
Grumbach, M. M., 25
Grupposo, P. A., 96
Guerrero, L., 96
Gulko, J., 8, 9
Gundert, H., 160
Gustafsson, M., 151

Haas, W., 78
Haber, C. H., 120, 122
Haberman, M., 33
Hagan, R., 9
Hage, J. J., 18, 132, 143, 144, 145, 146, 148, 151, 163, 170, 172
Halpern, D. F., 79
Halverson, C. F., 7, 8
Hambert, G., 150
Hamburger, C., 67, 159
Hammersmith, S. K., 63, 64
Hampson, E., 41
Hampson, J. G., 12–13, 95
Hampson, J. L., 12–13, 80, 95
Hansen, M., 33
Haraldsen, I. R., 139
Harmon, R. I., 29, 38
Harmon-Smith, H., 87
Harris, L. J., 79
Harrison, S. I., 171
Haugh, S. S., 8
Heiman, E. M., 20
Heinze, E., 38
Hekma, G., 19
Helleday, J., 41
Herdt, G., 13, 19, 20
Herman, A., 81
Herrn, R., 158
Hertoft, P., 159
Herve, C., 167
Hill, P., 38
Hines, M., 11, 12, 40, 45, 77, 80
Hirschauer, S., 19, 20, 155, 159, 160
Hirschfeld, M., 157, 158
Hiscock, M., 79
Hiscock-Kalil, C., 79
Hoaken, P. C. S., 29
Hochberg, Z., 41
Hoenig, J., 2, 162
Hoeppner, J., 139

Hoffman, C. D., 8
Hofman, M. A., 78
Hohenfellner, R., 96
Höjerback, T., 69, 139
Holl, R. W., 38
Hollingsworth, F., 33
Holloway, J. P., 161, 162, 163, 175
Homsy, Y., 100
Hood, J., 42
Hook, E. B., 35
Hopman, A. H., 33
Horejsi, J., 38
Horowitz, M., 97
Horsfield, P., 33
Huelke, H. H., 160
Hughes, I. A., 45
Hull, H., 33
Hunt, D. D., 80
Hurtig, A. L., 41, 96

Imperato-McGinley, J., 13, 46, 47, 96
Inacio, M., 47
Inch, R., 79
Intons-Peterson, M. J., 7, 9
Irwin, K. M., 93, 99
Isay, R. A., 106

Jacek, C., 79
Jacklin, C. N., 10, 14
Jelfer, M., 33
Jenssen Hagerman, R., 28, 32, 35
Johnson, F., 100
Johnstone, E. C., 32
Jones, C. L., 68
Jones, D., 139
Jones, K. L., 41
Jones, M., 32
Jores, A., 160
Jung, C. G., 160
Junge, A., 69, 148, 149, 150, 160

Kalil, K. M., 79
Kandemir, N., 41
Kando, T., 160
Kappes, M. E., 41, 42
Kappes, M. H., 41, 42
Karraker, K. H., 11
Karush, R. K., 120
Kaufman, S. H., 113 (tab)
Kavanaugh, J. G., 138
Keenan, M., 26
Kelin, K., 148–149
Keller, A., 141
Kemp, B. D., 93, 99
Kemper, W., 160
Kenna, J., 162
Kernberg, O., 139
Kessler, S. J., 95, 101
Kilgus, M. D., 120, 121
Kimball, M. M., 11
King, D., 19, 20, 159
Kirk, S., 18, 132, 143, 144, 145, 146, 151, 163, 170, 172
Kirsh, B., 8
Kirwan, P. J., 38
Kleczkowska, A., 31
Klein, C. H., 20
Kobilkova, I., 38
Kochems, L., 20
Kockott, G., 69
Kofman-Alfaro, S., 47
Kohlberg, L. A., 2, 4–5, 8
Kohn, G., 46, 47, 96
Kok, L. P., 66
Koot, H., 56, 57, 65, 76
Koppe, J. G., 77
Körlin, D., 150
Kranz, H., 160
Kruijver, F. P., 78
Kubie, L. S., 138, 160
Kubien, E., 31
Kucheria, K., 33
Kuhn, D., 8
Kuhnle, U., 42
Kuiper, A. J., 18, 69, 132, 139, 143, 144, 145, 146, 149, 150 (tab), 151, 163, 170, 172
Kuksis, M., 2, 114

Kulaksizoglu, I. B., 17, 141
Kulick, D., 20
Kullgren, G., 69, 148
Kunze, D., 38
Kushner, H., 35

La Freniere, P., 9
La Torre, R. A., 80
Lam-Po-Tang, P. R. L. C., 33
Lamb, M. E., 9
Lancaster, R. N., 20
Land, J. A., 33
Landèn, M., 150
Lang, S., 19–20
Laron, Z., 30
Larson, P., 139
Lasch, E. E., 96
Lattimer, J. K., 100
Laub, D., 18, 132, 143, 144, 145, 146, 151, 163, 170, 172
Laurence L., 139
Lauzanne, K., 24
Lawrence, A., 18, 132, 143, 144, 145, 146, 151, 163, 170, 172
Lazarini H. J., 167
Lé, C. V., 20
Leaper, C., 10, 11
Leavitt, F., 67, 68, 139
Lebech, P. E., 44
Lee, E., 24
Leinbach, M. D., 2, 7, 9, 113 (tab), 114
Levi, H., 20
Levine, S. B., 52
Levy, G. D., 8
Lewinsky, M., 44
Lewis, V. G., 42, 45
Liben, L. S., 8
Liebaers, I., 33
Lightbody, S., 82
Lilford, R. J., 100
Lim, M. H., 122–123
Lindemalm, G., 150
Linden, M., 26, 32
Linden, M. G., 26, 28, 29, 32, 38
Lindgren, T. W., 133 (tab)
Linn, M. C., 79
Little, J. K., 8
Litvin, Y., 96
Loehlin, J. C., 15
Long, F. Y., 66
Lothstein, L. M., 138, 139, 160
Lowry Sullivan, C. B., 2, 71, 105
Lowry, C. B., 71
Lozinsky, J. A., 113 (tab), 114
Lundström, B., 149, 150, 151
Lutz, S. E., 8, 9
Lynch, S. S., 78
Lytton, H., 11

Maccoby, E. E., 10, 14
MacDonald, P. C., 44
MacGowan, B., 69
Mackay, M. E., 38
Mackie, J. B., 138, 160
Madden, J. D., 44
Maine Gender Resource/Support Service, 169
Maing, D. M., 71
Malone, P., 100
Maltz, D. N., 10
Mandoki, M. W., 28
Marantz, S., 75
Marberger, M., 96
Maric, J., 148–149
Marks, I., 138
Martin, C. L., 2, 5, 7, 8
Martin, N., 15
Martin, N. G., 15
Martini, E., 33
Masera, N., 26
Masica, D. N., 45
Mataix-Cols, D., 138
Mate-Kole, C., 139
Matzner, A., 20
Mauz, F., 160
Mazur, T., 44

McCauley, E., 35, 38, 39, 139
McClaren, W., 30
McConaghy, N., 67
McDermid, S. A., 71
McEwen, B. S., 11
McGraw, K. O., 8
McGue, M., 14
McKain, T. L., 98
McKee, E., 139
McKie, M., 26
McPherson, S., 66, 142
Mead, M., 21
Mead, S. L., 74
Mellenbergh, G. J., 77
Menard, Y., 18, 132, 143, 144, 145, 146, 151, 163, 170, 172
Mendez, J. P., 47
Mendonca, B. B., 47
Meng, H., 160
Meningaud, J. P., 167
Menvielle, E. M., 120, 121
Meyenburg, B., 171
Meyer, J., 138
Meyer, J. K., 139, 160
Meyer, W., 18, 132, 143, 144, 145, 146, 151, 163, 170, 172
Meyer, W. J., 139
Meyer-Bahlburg, H. F., 52
Meyer-Bahlburg, H. F. L., 12, 41, 42, 43, 77, 96, 109, 113 (tab), 115, 120, 123, 127
Meyers, D. C., 26, 28, 32
Miach, P. P., 139, 140
Michael, R. P., 33
Migeon, C. J., 42
Miller, A., 29
Miller, C. L., 7
Miller, E. M., 15
Miller, H. J., 29
Miller, W. L., 41
Minto, C. L., 100
Mischel, W., 7
Mitchell, J. N., 2, 114
Mitscherlich, A., 160
Mittenthal, S., 38
Mohapatra, I., 33
Mohr, F., 160
Molenaar, J. C., 41, 42, 44, 87, 88, 96
Money, J., 1–2, 3 (fig), 12–13, 17, 19, 32, 33, 38, 41, 42, 44, 45, 62, 67, 80, 95, 96, 100, 139, 149
Money, J., 156
Morey, S. M., 56, 113 (tab), 115, 133 (tab)
Morishima, A., 12, 38, 41, 77, 96, 100
Morris, E., 35
Morse, P. A., 7
Morstad, A. L., 14
Mulaikal, R. M., 42
Mulder, J. W., 148
Müller, M., 160
Muller, S. C., 96
Mureau, M. A., 101
Murray, D. A. B., 20
Murray, J. F., 139
Murray, L., 28

Nakai, H., 96
Nanda, S., 20
Nash, S. C., 8
Natarajan, A., 93, 99
Need, J. A., 151, 171
Netley, C., 26
Netley, C. T., 26, 28
Neugebauer, F. L., 99, 156
New, M. I., 12, 40, 41, 77, 96
Newman, L. E., 122
Niccols, G. A., 14
Nicholls, D., 38
Nicolau, W., 47
Nielsen, J., 26, 28, 29, 30, 32, 33
Njiman, R. J., 101

O'Boyle, M., 139
O'Donoghue, F. P., 29
Ogilvy-Stuart, A., 100

Ogunro, C., l, 44, 45
Oliver, G., 42
Oliver, G. D., 14
Orlebeke, J. F., 81
Osburg, S., 66, 149
Ostergaard, O., 28
Overzier, C., 156
Ovesey, L., 67, 70
Owen, D., 29, 30, 32, 33

Pan, H., 26
Park, E., 26, 28
Patton, J., 18, 132, 143, 144, 145, 146, 151, 163, 170, 172
Pauly, I., 65, 149, 151
Pauly, I. B., 52, 133 (tab)
Pavlidis, K., 38, 39
Pecore, K., 82, 114
Pelsen, B., 29, 30
Penhale, S., 33
Pennington, B. F., 28
Pepler, D. J., 82
Percy, E. L., 35, 38
Perez-Palacios, G., 47
Perry, D. G., 2
Person, E., 67, 70
Person, E. S., 75
Petersen, A. C., 79
Peterson, R. E., 13, 46, 47, 96
Pfäfflin, F., 69, 139, 148, 149, 150, 158, 160, 165
Philippopoulos, G. S., 171
Phoenix, C. H., 96
Phornphutkul C., 96
Picariello, M. L., 8
Pillemer, D., 8
Piper, W. E., 80
Plante, E., 41
Pleak, R. R., 120, 121
Pool, C., 78
Powlishta, K. K., 8, 9
Price, W. H., 32
Prieur, A., 20
Puck, M., 28

Quattrin, T., 44
Qvist, I., 44

Raboch, J., 38
Raboch, K., 38
Rakic, Z., 148–149
Ramaekers, F. C., 33
Randell, J., 162
Randell, J. B., 67
Rangecroft, L., 100
Ratcliffe, S., 29
Ratcliffe, S. G., 26, 28, 29, 30, 32
Rebach, H. M., 71
Reichlin, S., 78
Reiner, W. G., 95, 96, 100
Reinisch, J. M., 12
Rekers, G. A., 56, 74, 113 (tab), 114, 115, 120, 121, 122, 133 (tab)
Rekers, G. A., 120, 121
Resnick, S. M., 14, 41
Reter, D., 160
Reynods, E. J., 171
Richardson, C. E., 33
Richardson, J., 105, 110
Richardson, P., 66, 142
Ringelberg, H., 139
Ritzén, M., 41
Roback, H., 139
Roberts, C. W., 71
Robinson, A., 26, 28, 29, 32, 38
Rock, J. A., 42
Rohde, W., 78
Romney, D. M., 11
Roopnarine, J. L., 9
Roscoe, W., 20
Rosen, A. C., 74, 113 (tab), 120, 133 (tab)
Rosenthal, I. M., 41
Rösing, I., 20
Rösler, A., 46, 47, 96
Ross, J., 35
Ross, J. L., 35
Ross, M. W., 151, 171

Rouse, S., 139, 140
Rovet, J., 28
Rovet, J. F., 26, 35, 41
Ruble, D. N., 2, 5, 8, 9
Russell, D. W., 47, 96
Russo, A. J., 62
Rust, J., 113 (tab), 115

Saenger, P., 39
Sahin, D., 17, 141
Salbenblatt, J., 28
Salbenblatt, J. A., 26, 28, 32
Sandberg, D. E., 113 (tab), 115
Sanders, G., 81
Sanders, P., 11
Sanders, S. A., 12
Sandfort, T., 65
Sandfort, T. G. M., 64
Saxena, S., 33
Schaefer, L., 18, 132, 143, 144, 145, 146, 151, 163, 170, 172
Schiavi, R. C., 29, 30, 32, 33
Schnabl, C., 78
Schober, E., 96
Schober, J. M., 100, 101
Scholtmeijer, R. J., 88
Schott, G., 78
Schott, G. S., 78
Schultz-Hencke, H., 160
Schwartz, M., 42
Schwarz, H. P., 42
Seidel, K., 78
Seifert, D., 29
Seitz, W., 160
Serbin, L. A., 8, 9
Seyler, L. E., Jr., 78
Shackleton, C., 47
Shane, E., 120, 122
Shane, M., 120, 122
Sharabany, R., 8
Sharp, C., 66
Sheffield, B., 78
Shell, R., 11
Shields, S. A., 9
Shimshi, M., 12, 41, 77, 96
Siegel, P. T., 35
Sigmundson, H. K., 13, 96, 97
Signorella, M. L., 8
Siiteri, P. K., 44
Silbert, A., 28
Silbert, A. R., 26, 32
Silva, F. A., 47
Silverman, M. A., 120, 122
Simons, J., 139
Simpson, A. W., 11
Singbeil. C. E., 82
Siomopoulos, V., 70
Sipova, L., 66
Sitarenios, G., 14
Skillman, D., 139
Skuse, D., 35, 38
Slabbekoorn, D., 81, 148
Slaby, R. G., 8, 113 (tab), 114
Slijper, F. M., 101
Slijper, F. M. E., 41, 42, 44, 85, 87, 88, 90, 96
Slob, A. K., 101
Smith, Y. L. S., 68, 69, 140, 149, 150 (tab), 151
Snaith, R. P., 33
Snoek, H., 76
Socarides, C. W., 70, 160
Sørensen, A. M., 32
Sørensen, K., 29, 30, 32
Sörensen, T., 159
Sotiropoulos, A., 100
Spare, S., 78
Spijkstra, J. J., 78
Spinder, T., 78
Stabler, B., 35
Staehelin, J. E., 160
Stanhope, L., 82
Stanhope, R., 38
Starcevic, V., 148–149
Stark, R. E., 28
Starka, L., 38
Steck, H., 160
Steele, S. J., 100

Stegner, H., 41
Steiman, C., 160
Stein, R., 96
Steiner, B. W., 67, 68, 69, 150, 168
Steinkühler, M., 19
Stermac, L., 141
Stern, M., 11
Sternglanz, S. H., 9
Stevenson, J., 35, 38
Stewart, D., 26
Stewart, D. A., 26, 28
Stockard, J., 11
Stockle, M., 96
Stoller, R., 46, 47
Stoller, R. J., 2, 70, 71, 122
Straathof, M. A. E., 113 (tab)
Strassberg, D., 139
Strayer, F. F., 9
Sturge C., 144, 146, 170, 172
Sturla, E., 13, 46
Stürup, G., 159
Sullivan, P., 93, 99
Summer, G. S., 28
Sundblom, E., 69, 139
Sutton, A., 144, 146, 170, 172
Swaab, D. F., 78
Sybert, V. P., 38, 39

Tako, H. D., 93, 99
Taneja, N., 33
Teaque, P., 28
Teh, Y. K., 20
Teler, W., 38
ten Brink, L. T., 113 (tab)
Theilgaard, A., 29, 30, 32, 33
Thomas, D. F. M., 100
Thompson, S. K., 75, 113 (tab), 115
Thompson-Wilcox, K., 14
Thuwe, I., 150
Tonick, I. J., 9
Treffers, P. D. A., 113 (tab)
Trumbach, R., 19
Tsoi, W. F., 66
Turk, J., 38
Türksoy, N., 17, 141
Turner, P. J., 11
Turnock, R., 100

Uddenberg, N., 150
Udry, J. R., 14
Ulloa-Aguirre, A., 47

Vale, J. M., 38
van de Pol, L. C., 19
van de Poll, N. E., 77, 147, 148
Van den Bergh, B. R. H., 113 (tab)
Van den Berghe, H., 31
van den Bree, M. J. M., 81
Van der Ende, J., 56, 57, 65, 76
van der Kamp, H. J., 41, 42
van der Meer, T., 19
van der Meulen, J. C., 101
van Goozen, S. H. M., 14, 76, 80–81, 133 (tab), 146, 147, 148, 149, 150 (tab), 171
Van Grunsven, E. J., 96
van Kesteren, P., 65
Vargas, I., 12, 41, 77, 96
Vasey, P. L., 105, 106, 120
Veerman, J. W., 113 (tab)
Verhulst, F. C., 56, 57, 65, 76, 101
Verschoor, A. M., 81
Vilaruso, A., 38
Vockrodt, L., 39
Volkan, V. D., 70, 138

Wacke, A., 155
Wagner, B., 33
Wålinder, J., 67, 149, 150, 151, 160
Wallis, H., 41
Walzer, S., 26, 28, 32
Warburton, D., 35
Watson, D. B., 81
Webb, A., 18, 132, 143, 144, 145, 146, 151, 163, 170, 172
Webb, W., 139

Weigel. H., 160
Weinberg, M. S., 63, 64
Weisen, M., 78
Weissenbacher, G., 96
Weitze, C., 66, 149
Weizsäcker. V. V., 160
Whatmore, P. B., 32
Wheeler, C. C., 18, 132, 143, 144, 145, 146, 151, 163, 170, 172
White, D., 29, 30, 32, 33
Whittle, S., 175
Wilcox, A., 81
Wild, J., 71, 114
Will, M. R., 160, 164
Will, M. R., 164
Williams, J. K., 39
Williams, K., 71
Williams, W. L., 20
Willig, R. H., 41
Wilson J. R., 14
Wilson, B. E., 100
Wilson, J. D., 44, 47, 96
Wilson, P., 66
Windgassen, K., 29
Wohlert, M., 26, 32
Wolfe, S., 73, 120, 127, 171
Wolfe, S. M., 74–75
Wood, C. H., 8
World Health Organization, 52, 55 (tab)
Wren, B., 141, 171, 174, 175

Yager, T. J., 113 (tab), 115
Yates, C. E., 113 (tab), 114
Yee, M., 9
Yordam, N., 41
Youd. A., 162
Young, R., 81
Young, W. C., 96
Younger, B. A., 7
Yüksel, S., 17, 141

Zamir, R., 30
Zbou, J., 78
Zeuthen, E., 28, 33
Zhou, J., 78
Ziemba-Davis, M., 12
Zinn, A., 35
Zucker, K. J., 2, 14, 41, 42, 47, 48, 52, 54, 62, 63, 64, 66, 71, 72, 73, 74, 75, 77, 80, 81, 82, 96, 105, 109, 112, 113 (tab), 114, 115, 120, 127, 168, 171
Zuger, B., 62
Zutt, J., 160

SUBJECT INDEX

Abortion, consent for, 175
Activating effects, of hormones, 12, 16
ADHD. *See* Attention Deficit Hyperactivity Disorder
Adolescent, diagnosing gender problem, 131–132
  desirability of sex reassignment, 131, 140–141, 152
  effects of sex reassignment, 148–152, 150 (tab), 153
Adolescent, diagnosing gender problem, first phase, 152
  differential diagnosis, 134, 137
  instruments, 133 (tab)–134
  procedure, 132–133
Adolescent, diagnosing gender problem, second phase, 152, 153
  desirability of sex reassignment, 140–141
  physical intervention eligibility, 144–148
  psychotherapy *vs.* sex reassignment, 138–140
  psychological intervention, 141–143, 153
  real-life experience, 143–144
Adrenogenital syndrome. *See* Congenital adrenal hyperplasia
AIS. *See* Androgen insensitivity syndrome
Amarete culture, alternative gender roles among, 20
Ambiguous genitals, 24, 25 (fig)
Androgen insensitivity syndrome (AIS):
  gender identity/role in, 44–45
  general aspects of, 43–44
  needs for girl with, 90–91
  sexual activity/sexual orientation/fertility in, 45
  transsexualism and, 77
  vignette concerning, 45–46
Androgens, prenatal exposure to, 11–12, 14–15, 24, 40, 41, 49, 96, 97, 103
Anglo-American country, legality of sex reassignment in, 164, 178
Anti-Müllerian hormone. *See* Müller Inhibiting Substance
Attention Deficit Hyperactivity Disorder (ADHD), 43, 108
Atypical gender disorder theory, 83–84
  biopsychological, 72–76
  gender disorder subtype, 67–70
  psychological, 70–72
Atypical gender disorder theory, biological theory, 76–83
  birth order/sibling sex ratio, 81–83
  organizational effects of sex hormones, 76–81
Atypical sexual differentiation process, 23 (tab)–26
  chromosomal/gonadal conditions (*See* Chromosomal/gonadal conditions)

female pseudohermaphroditism, 40–43
male pseudohermaphroditism, 43–48
other conditions, 48
Austria, legal sex change in, 164
Autogynephilia, 67
Automonosexual, 67

Baby-X paradigm, 11
Behavior therapy, 121–122, 128
Berdache phenomenon. *See* Two-spirit/spirited phenomenon
Berdache (parent support group), 127
Biographic questionnaire, for transsexual, 134
Biological theory. *See* Atypical gender disorder theory, biological theory
Biopsychological theory, 72–76
Blissful symbiosis, 70, 122
Body image scale, 134
BSTc, 78–79

CAH. *See* Congenital adrenal hyperplasia
CAIS. *See* Complete androgen insensitivity
Canada, GID treatment center in, 168
CBCL. *See* Child Behavior Checklist; Child behavior checklist
Central nervous system:
effect of gonadal hormones on, 4, 15
structural sex differences in, 78–79 (tab)
Child, clinical management of gender problem in, criterion for, 105–106
Child, clinical management of gender problem in, diagnosing, 106–109
cross-gender profile, 106–107 (tab)
instruments for, 111–117 (fig), 113 (fig), 116 (fig), 118 (fig)–119 (fig), 128
procedure for, 110–111
types of cross-gender, 109–110
Child, clinical management of gender problem in, interventions:
behavior therapy, 121–122, 128
combined approaches, 122–125
effectiveness of, 127, 129
psychoanalytic therapy, 122, 128–129
treatment rationales/goals, 120–121
vignette concerning, 125–127
Child Behavior Checklist (CBCL), 56, 65
Children Act of 1989, 173, 175–176
Chromosomal/gonadal conditions:
47,XYY, 31–34, 49
Klinefelter Syndrome, 26–31, 27 (fig)–28 (fig), 49
Turner Syndrome, 34–40, 36 (fig)–37 (fig), 48
Clinical management, of intersex conditions:
child counseling, 86–87
neonatal approach to, 87–88
parent counseling, 85–86, 102
Clinical management, of intersex conditions, information/support:
for parents, 88–89
Clinical management, of intersex conditions, information/support, for children, 89–90, 89–91, 102–103
phenomena known from early onward, 91
phenomena occurring with certainty, 91–92
phenomena that may/may not occur, 93–94
psychological intervention, 94–95
Clinical policy, criticism of:
genital surgery, 99–102, 103, 104
information, 99, 103–104
sex assignment at birth, 95–99, 103

Code Civil of 1804 (France), 156, 163–164, 177, 178
Cognitive developmental theory, 4–5
Complete androgen insensitivity (CAIS), 43–44, 45
Congenital adrenal hyperplasia (CAH):
 gender identity/role in, 41
 general aspects of, 40–41
 needs for girl with, 91
 sex reassignment of individual with, 96
 sexual identity/sexual orientation/fertility in, 41–42
 transsexualism and, 77
 vignette concerning, 42–43
Congenital virilizing adrenal hyperplasia (CVAH). *See* Congenital adrenal hyperplasia
Core gender identity, definition of, 2
Cross-dressing, 125
 by child, 31, 54, 56, 58, 109, 110
 by homosexual, 67, 137
 by transsexual, 68–69
 transvestic fetishism and, 137
Cryptorchism, 26
CVAH. *See* Congenital adrenal hyperplasia

D'Eon, Chevalier, 19
Department of Child and Adolescent Psychiatry (Netherlands), 110–111
DES. *See* Diethylstilbestrol
Diagnostic and Statistic Manual of Mental Disorders III-Revised (*DSM-III-R*), 105
Diagnostic and Statistic Manual of Mental Disorders IV (*DSM-IV*)
 criticism of GID criteria of, 105, 128
 GID criteria of, 53 (tab)–54 (tab), 109–110, 111, 132, 137, 139, 144–145
 prevalence of GID, 168
Diethylstilbestrol (DES), 12
Dihydrotestosterone, 13, 46
Dominican Republic, intersexed individual in, 13
Draw-a-Person test:
 for adolescent, 134, 135 (fig)–136 (fig)
 for child, 115, 116 (fig)–117 (fig), 118 (fig)–119 (fig)
DSM. *See* Diagnostic and Statistic Manual
DSM-III-R. *See* Diagnostic and Statistic Manual of Mental Disorders III-Revised
DSM-IV. *See* Diagnostic and Statistic Manual of Mental Disorders IV
Dysgenetic gonads, 100

Ego-dystonic homosexual, 137
Endocrine history, abnormal prenatal, 77
Enzyme deficiency, 46–48, 49
Europe:
 alternative to legal sex change in, 164–167
 legality of sex reassignment in, 163–164
 sex reassignment surgery in, 157, 159, 160, 162
 See also European Community; individual country
European Commission on Human Rights, 166
European Community:
 age limits for physical sex change in, 173
 legal age for maturity in, 178–179
 See also Europe; individual country
European Convention of Human Rights, 166
European Court of Human Rights, 166–167
Ex nunc status, 163

Ex tunc status, 163, 165
Experiments by nature. *See* Organizing effects, of hormones
External genitalia, development of, 4, 6 (fig)

Family risk factors, in gender identity disorder, 107–108, 115, 128
Family therapy, 124
  for cross-gendered adolescent, 141–142
  vignette concerning, 125–127
Female pseudohermaphroditism, 25, 40–43, 49
Female-to-male transsexual (FM), 68, 69
  cognitive abilities of, 80, 81
  early sex reassignment surgery on, 157
  irreversible intervention for, 148, 153
  reversible intervention for, 148, 153
  sex reassignment for young, 140
  See also Male-to-female transsexual; Transsexual; Transsexualism
5α-Reductase Deficiency (5α-RD), 46–47
FM. *See* Female-to-male transsexual
47,XXY. *See* Klinefelter Syndrome
47,XYY:
  gender identity/role in, 32–33
  general aspects of, 31–32
  sexual identity/sexual orientation/fertility in, 33
  vignette concerning, 33–34
46,XX/XY child, genital surgery for, 100
France:
  law code in, 156, 163–164, 177, 178
  legal sex change in, 167
Functional cerebral asymmetry, 79, 80–81

Gay liberation movement, 158
Gender, definition of, 1
Gender consistency, 8, 114
Gender constancy, 8
Gender development:
  affective learning and, 2, 9–10
  cognitive learning and, 2, 7–9
  environment and, 10–11, 84
  external genitalia and, 4, 6 (fig)
  nature *vs.* nurture in, 13–14
  sex hormones and, 11–15, 16
  theories of, 4–5, 7
Gender dysphoria, 106
  adolescent test battery, 133 (tab)
  child test battery, 112, 113 (tab)
  definition of, 51
Gender dysphoria scale, 134 (table)
Gender dysphoria syndrome, definition of, 51
Gender identity:
  definition of, 1, 2
  See also Gender identity/role
Gender Identity Clinic, 160, 162, 169, 178
Gender Identity Development Clinic, 168
Gender identity disorder (GID), 52, 54
  adolescent with, 59–60
  adult cross-culture/history, 18–21, 22
  benefit of cross-cultural/historical data, 18
  boys with, 54, 56
  child/adolescent cross-culture/history, 21, 22
  child risk factors in, 108
  correspondence with transsexualism, 62–64
  criteria for, 105–106
  family risk factors in, 107–108, 115, 128
  gender role in, 1
  girls with, 56–57
  prevalence of, 64–66, 168–170

rarity of clinical case, 17, 21–22
sex ratio in, 64–66
subtypes of, 70 (tab)
terminology for, 51–52, 83
treatment center for, 168–169
vignettes concerning, 58–59, 61–62
Gender Identity Disorder Not Otherwise Specified (GIDNOS), 52, 137
Gender identity disorder of adolescence and adulthood nontranssexual type (GIDAANT), 139–140
Gender Identity Interview, 114
Gender Identity Program, 160
Gender identity/role:
in androgen insensitivity syndrome, 44–45
in congenital adrenal hyperplasia, 41
in 47,XYY, 32–33
in gender identity disorder, 2
in Klinefelter Syndrome, 29
in Turner Syndrome, 38
Gender irrelevant society, 98, 101
Gender labeling. *See* Gender identity
Gender role:
alternative, 19–20
definition of, 1, 2
See also Gender identity/role
Gender Role Questionnaire, 114
Gender schema theory, 5–6
Gender segregation, of children, 9–10
Gender stability, 8, 114
Gender stereotype, child knowledge of, 8, 9
Genital surgery. *See* Sex reassignment surgery
Germany:
age limits for physical sex change in, 172
legal sex change in, 164, 166
legality of sex reassignment in, 163
sex reassignment surgery in, 157–158
treatment center in, 168
GID. *See* Gender identity disorder
GIDAANT. *See* Gender identity disorder of adolescence and adulthood nontranssexual type
GIDNOS. *See* Gender Identity Disorder Not Otherwise Specified
Gonadal differentiation disorders, 25
Gonadal dysgenesis. *See* Turner Syndrome
Gonadal hormones, effect on nervous system, 4, 15
Gonads, interference in development of, 24
Guevedoces, 13
Gynecomastia, 26, 27 (fig)–28 (fig)

Handedness, 79, 80, 81
Harry Benjamin International Gender Dysphoria Association's (HBIGDA) Standards of Care, 18, 132, 144, 146, 152, 163, 170, 172, 176, 178, 179
Hermaphroditism, 12–13, 25, 49, 97
See also Pseudohermaphroditism
Homosexuality, 42, 64
as criminal behavior, 160, 161
opposition to attempts to prevent, 117, 120, 128
in transsexual, 67–68, 140
Hormone treatment, 143
to block puberty, 145–146, 147, 153, 172
eligibility of adolescent for, 146
legitimacy of, 161, 163
for male to female transsexual, 147–148
opposition to, for child, 170–171
See also Hormones
Hormones:
activating effects of, 12, 16
effect on nervous system, 4, 15

gender development and, 11–15, 16
influence on development of transsexualism, 76, 77, 78
legitimacy of cross-sex, 161, 163
luteinizing, 77–78, 147
organizing effects of, 12, 16, 76–77, 76–81
prenatal exposure to, 11–12, 13–15, 16, 24, 40, 41, 49, 77, 80, 96, 97, 103
See also Androgen insensitivity syndrome; Hormone treatment
Hypogonadism, 31
Hypospadias, 24, 26, 100, 104

ICD-10. See International Classification of Diseases-10
In-between gender. *See* Third gender
International Classification of Diseases-10 (*ICD-10*), 52, 55 (tab), 105, 132, 137
Intersex Society of North America (ISNA), 99
Interview, gender preference, 111–112 (tab)
ISNA. *See* Intersex Society of North America
Italy, legal of sex change in, 164, 165–166

Jorgensen, Christine, 159, 161, 162, 177
Juvenile unmasculinity, 110

Klinefelter Syndrome (KS) (47,XXY)
gender identity/gender role in, 29
general aspects of, 26–29, 27 (fig)–28 (fig)
sexual activity/sexual orientation/fertility in, 29–30
vignette concerning, 30–31

Law for Transsexuals, 172
Legal implications, of gender identity in youth/adolescence:
age limits on treatment, 172–177, 178–179
against intervention, 171
passing into adulthood, 171–172
vignette concerning, 174–175
Legal implications, of transsexualism in adult:
additional issues in, 167–168
alternative to legal sex change, 164–167
legality of sex reassignment, 163–164
legitimacy of cross-sex hormones, 161, 163
legitimacy of sex reassignment surgery, 161–163
role of publicity in, 159–161
surgical sex reassignment, 157–158
terminology/politics, 158
Legal maturity, age for, 172–174, 178–179
Legal sex assignment:
historical, 155–156
in recent history, 156–157
LH. *See* Luteinizing hormone
Lutein hormone-releasing hormone (LHRH), 147
Luteinizing hormone (LH), 77–78, 147

Maine Gender Resource and Support Service (MeGReSS), 169
Male pseudohermaphroditism, 25, 49
androgren insensitivity syndrome, 43–46
enzyme deficiencies, 46–48
Male-to-female transsexual (MF), 69, 78
cognitive abilities of, 80–81
early sex reassignment surgery on, 157–158

effects of partially reversible physical intervention on, 147–148
functioning of, living as woman, 139
irreversible intervention for, 148, 153
reversible intervention for, 148, 153
sex reassignment for young, 140
See also Female-to-male transsexual; Transsexual; Transsexualism
Maturity, legal, 172–174, 178–179
MeGReSS. *See* Maine Gender Resource and Support Service
Mermaid (parent support group), 127
Metaidoioplasty, 61
MF. *See* Male-to-female transsexual
Minnesota Multiphasic Personality Inventory (MMPI)
MIS. *See* Müller Inhibiting Substance
Mixed gnadal dysgenesis, sex assignment of person with, 97
Mosaicism, 24, 26, 39, 49
Müller Inhibiting Substance (MIS), 4, 24, 43
Müllerian duct, 4, 5 (fig), 24, 100

Native American, alternative gender roles among, 19–20
Nature *vs.* nurture, in gender development, 13–14
Netherlands, 166, 168
New Guinea, intersexed individual in, 13
Noncore transsexual, sex reassignment regret by, 150

Optimal-gender policy, 95–96
Organizing effects, of hormones, 12–13, 16, 76–77

Partial androgen insensitivity syndrome (PAIS), 43, 44–45, 98
Performance IQ (PIQ), 80
Pharmacotherapy, 142
PIQ. *See* Performance IQ
Play and Games Questionnaire, 114
Progesterone, 14
Provisional sex assignment, 98
Pseudohermaphroditism:
female, 25, 40–43, 49
male, 25, 43–48, 49
See also Hermaphroditism
Psychoanalytic therapy, 122, 128–129
Psychological intervention, for child, 94–95
Psychological theory, 70–72
Psychosexual neutrality at birth, 96
Psychotherapy *vs.* sex reassignment, for adolescent, 138–140
Puberty delaying hormones, 145–146, 147, 153, 172

Real-life experience (RLE), in gender role change, 143–144, 146
Redistribution operation, 162
Ring chromosome, 35
Royal College of Psychiatrists, 144, 170, 175, 176, 178, 179

Schizophrenia, 137
Scoptic Syndrome, 137, 142
17β-Hydroxysteroid Dehydrogenase Deficiency (17β-HSD), 46–47
Sex, definition of, 1
Sex assignment:
at birth, 95–99, 103
legal, 155–157
Sex reassignment (SR), 63–64, 177
conditions for female/male sex assignment, 97
definition of, 51
desirability of, by adolescent, 131, 140–141, 152

effects on adolescent, 148–152, 150 (tab), 153
of female with congenital adrenal hyperplasia, 96
legality of, 163–164, 167, 178
psychotherapy for candidate, 142–143, 152
regret of, 150
vs. psychotherapy, 138–140
Sex reassignment surgery (SRS), 143, 148
criticism of, 99–102, 103, 104
in Europe, 157–158, 159, 160, 162
first performed, 157–158
in Japan, 20
legal consequences of, 163–164
legitimacy of, 161–163
opposition to for child, 170–171
Sex-regulated cognitive ability, 79, 80
Sexual differentiation, 2–4, 3 (fig)
Sexual dimorphic brain nuclei, 78–79 (tab)
Social cognitive theory, 7
Social learning theory. *See* Social cognitive theory
SR. *See* Sex reassignment
SRS. *See* Sex reassignment surgery
State psychopathology, 72
Streak gonads, 24, 25, 35, 39
Sweden, 164, 177, 178
Switzerland, 163–164

Teacher Report Form (TRF), 115
Testicular feminization. *See* Androgen insensitivity syndrome
Third gender, 98, 103
Tourette syndrome, 108
Trait psychopathology, 72
Transsexual/transsexualism:
definition of, 19
female-to-male (*See* Female-to-male transsexual)
homosexual, 67–68
male-to-female (*See* Male-to-female transsexual)
Transsexualism:
coining of term, 158
correspondence with gender identity disorder, 62–64
gender ratio in, 66
historical, 19
prevalence of, 65–66
See also Legal implications, of transsexualism in adult; Transsexual
Transvestic fetishism, 137
Transvestitism:
coining of term, 158
historical, 19
TRF. *See* Teacher Report Form (of the CBCL)
True hermaphroditism, 25, 49, 97
Turkey, 166, 173
Turner Syndrome (45,XO), 24
gender identity/role, 38
general aspects of, 34–38, 36 (fig)–37 (fig)
sexual activity/sexual orientation/fertility, 38–39
vignette concerning, 39–40
Two-spirit/spirited phenomenon, 20

ultima ratio, 162, 178
United Kingdom:
age limits for physical sex change in, 173
GID treatment center in, 168
legality of sex reassignment in, 164, 167, 178
See also Europe; European Community
United States:
GID treatment center in, 168

legality of sex reassignment in, 164, 168
Utrecht gender dysphoria scale, 134 (tab)

Vaginal agenesis, 104
Verbal IQ (VIQ), 80

Wolffian duct, 4, 5 (fig), 24, 43–44, 100

X chromosome. *See* Sexual differentiation

Y chromosome. *See* Sexual differentiation

ABOUT THE AUTHORS

Peggy T. Cohen-Kettenis, Ph.D., is Professor of Medical Psychology at the Vrÿe Universiteit Medical Center, Amsterdam, and Head of a gender clinic for children, adolescents, and adults. She was a pre- and postgraduate student in developmental and clinical psychology at the University of Utrecht, The Netherlands. She was trained to become a registered clinical psychologist and psychotherapist at the Utrecht Institute for Multidisciplinary Psychotherapy. After completing her Ph.D. thesis Cohen-Kettenis worked at the Department of Clinical Psychology of the Utrecht University. There she conducted a study evaluating sex reassignment, which was prompted by the advice of a committee of the Health Council, the medical advisory board of the Ministry of Public Health. The outcome of this study would also be the grounds for a new law allowing transsexuals to adjust their birth certificates. In 1987 she started the first outpatient clinic for children and adolescents with gender problems and intersex conditions in Europe at the Department of Child and Adolescent Psychiatry of the University Medical Center Utrecht. Her main areas of research are gender identity problems and gender-related psychopathology.

Friedemann Pfäfflin, M.D., Ph.D., is Professor of Psychotherapy and head of the Forensic Psychotherapy Unit at Ulm University, Ulm, Germany. Trained as psychiatrist at Hamburg University, he first engaged in transgender clinical work in the mid-1970s, when he visited the Psychohormonal Research Unit and the Gender Identity Clinic at Johns Hopkins University Clinic in Baltimore, Maryland. From 1978 to1992 he worked at the Institute of Sex Research at Hamburg University, Hamburg, Germany, and continued his work with transsexuals after moving to Ulm University in 1992. His main areas of research are transsexualism, transgenderism, psychotherapy process research, forensic psychiatry and psychotherapy, and the history of psychiatry. From 1995 to1997 he was president of the Harry Benjamin International Gender Dysphoria Association, Inc. In 1997, together with Eli Coleman, he founded *The International Journal of Transgenderism.*